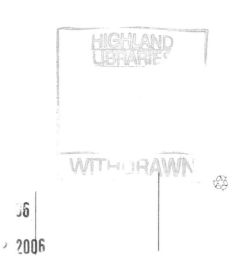

IF
DOGS
Could
Talk

Vilmos Csányi

Translated by Richard E. Quandt

IF
Dogs
Could
Talk

Exploring the Canine Mind

Vilmos Csányi

Translated by Richard E. Quandt

SUTTON PUBLISHING

First published in the United Kingdom in 2006 by
Sutton Publishing Limited · Phoenix Mill · Stroud
Gloucestershire · GL5 2BU

First published in English in the United States of America by North Point Press

Published by arrangement with Farrar, Straus and Giroux, LLC; all rights reserved.

Originally published in 2000 by Vince Kiado Kft., Hungary,
as Bukfenc és Jeromos: Hogyan gondolkodnak a kutyák?
Copyright © 2000, 2006 by Vilmos Csányi
Translation copyright © 2000 by Richard E. Guandt

British Library Cataloguing in Publication Data
A Catalogue record for this book is available from the British Library.

ISBN 0-7509-4338-6

Typeset in 10½/14pt Hoefler Text
Typesetting and origination by
Sutton Publishing Limited.
Printed and bound in England by
J.H. Haynes & Co. Ltd, Sparkford.

For Eve

Contents

Translator's Note

When I came upon Professor Vilmos Csányi's book, I was immediately enchanted, and not only because of the beguiling photographs of his own two dogs, Flip and Jerry. Here was a book that combined some first-rate science, interesting experimental results, and accounts of the discoveries of earlier scientists, with appealing anecdotes about the remarkable achievements of dogs and a genuine love of our best friends. The book can be read with enjoyment and profit by dog lovers as well as by readers who are interested in learning something about ethology, the scientific study of animal behavior. It is primarily about dogs, but because of the close social connection between dogs and humans it also devotes some attention to our own behavior as well as to that of our closest relatives, the apes.

Professor Csányi started his career as a molecular biologist and turned to ethology only later. He founded and is the chairman of the Department of Ethology at Eötvös Lóránd University in Budapest. He introduced a new approach to ethology that relies on analyzing the genetic architecture of natural components of animal behavior. He and his colleagues teach and do research in animal and human ethology, evolutionary systems, and behavioral genetics. He and his department maintain a profound interest in dog-human relationships, and this book summarizes the many findings and insights gained from his studies. I am indebted to him for allowing me to translate his book into English.

The volume begins with tracing the origins of dogs and discusses in detail their descent from wolves (as opposed to other canids that represent alternative branches of the evolutionary tree). Csányi argues that humans and wolves have formed an alliance from which both derived significant advantages. Wolves derived advantages from hanging out around early human habitations (e.g., food) and humans benefited from the presence of wolves, which performed cleanup functions and were a source of pelts. Wolves that were aggressive were killed and so tamer varieties were artificially selected by human intervention, and these eventually branched off genetically into what we call "dog." In this process, some of the attributes developed by early humans, such as the need to communicate and the ability to be constructive, have been acquired by dogs as well.

Part 2, consisting of four chapters, deals with the basic attributes of dogs. The first, and perhaps most important, of these is the fact that dogs strongly bond with humans. Dogs are always willing to undertake joint activities with humans, are eager to master rules of behavior, and on occasion, are ready to defend or serve us without regard to their own interests. Csányi laces his discussion with delightful and interesting anecdotes, being careful to note that anecdotes do not provide scientific proof, but may provide the impetus for new scientific experiments. He describes how psychological tests on children, such as the strange-situation test, have also been used in experiments with dogs. An important chapter deals with the emotions of dogs (as well as other animals). He makes it clear that certain emotions well known to us, such as pity, sorrow, and bereavement, are unknown among animals (with the possible exception of elephants and chimpanzees). It is also the case that most animals do not show their feelings; but that does not mean that they do not have feelings. He bases some of his remarks on the writings of Konrad Lorenz and Jane Goodall, who had a long struggle to get the profession to accept that chimpanzees have emotions. He goes into great detail about the emotions of dogs, and his examples will evoke a resonant chord in every dog owner. Dogs are able to identify emotionally with us and their empathy is legendary. Another chapter deals with the importance of obeying the rules. Starting out with a discussion of personal rituals and stereotypes that are important in human behavior as well, he recounts and explains the rituals of one of his own dogs, Jerry. He explains how dogs learn new rules and notes that through domestication, dogs became self-regulating, as did we. Dogs respect the rank order in the group they belong to. He next turns to cooperation and problem solving by dogs and again illustrates his discussion with many examples and descriptions of experiments.

Part 3 of the book contains excerpts from the diaries of Flip and Jerry. Being a good scientist, Csányi has kept meticulous records of the activities of his own dogs and recounts numerous examples that show their understanding and their insight into complicated situations. A whole chapter is devoted to dogs' ability to imitate behavior and he again illustrates it with anecdotes as well as accounts of carefully controlled experiments. An important chapter is devoted to animal communication. He reviews the experiments that had been done by other scientists in order to teach language to chimpanzees and notes that in spite of the fact that selected chimpanzees (and other animals) were able to learn hundreds of words ("signs") and even use them in simple sentences, these experiments were largely failures. Dogs excel in "social understanding," by which we mean that the dog behaves in such a manner that its master comes to believe that the dog has understood the situation at hand.

Part 4 of the book is devoted to the scientific study of the animal mind. This part is more demanding and introduces some basic psychological theory. Csányi first devotes a chapter to a thorough discussion of what constitutes observation, theory, and proof. He shows the errors that people are prone to when they make exaggerated claims for the talents of their animals as in cases in which people have claimed that their dog is able to read. Examples include the "clever Hans," a famous horse at the beginning of the twentieth century whose owner believed that the horse could actually carry out fairly complicated arithmetic operations. He also shows how the behavior of the experimenter can influence the course of an experiment and lead to spurious results. The gross error of George Romanes, who was a friend of Darwin, leads to a discussion of Morgan's Canon, the principle that in explaining an animal's behavior we should always look for the simplest possible explanation: to explain behavior we should not posit a higher degree of intelligence when a lower degree is sufficient. A detailed discussion of animal consciousness follows, together with a discussion of Alex, the famous parrot used in experiments by Irene Pepperberg. An analysis of mental maps and the ways in which the mind builds models, as well as the differences between the animal and human minds, are discussed in detail and the reader gets an excellent introduction into some of the fundamental principles of modern psychology. A fascinating chapter is devoted to the theory of mind: the ability of humans and of some animals to form concepts of what is in another creature's mind. It is quite amazing that some animals are able to act in a way so as to make another animal believe that something is the case; this is illustrated with an interesting example from the study of baboons and clearly shows that some animals are capable of deceit. A long section is devoted to problem solving by animals, and Csányi reports on many experiments done with chimpanzees, bonobos, and monkeys. Experiments have shown that chimpanzees are able to put themselves into another person's place much more effectively than monkeys and that they can definitely think. A chapter is devoted to the minds of children and the last chapter in this part deals with the functioning of the canine mind. In this chapter, Csányi establishes a correspondence between the human and the canine mind and shows what attributes of the human mind are also present in the minds of dogs. The final part of the book consists of a single chapter devoted to how to be a dog owner, starting from the selection of the breed, to some cogent observations about irresponsible breeding programs and some creative ideas on how smart breeding techniques might continue to further improve the intelligence and other good qualities of dogs. The book ends with a condemnation of cruelty to dogs, particularly as practiced by pharmaceutical companies and others that use dogs in experiments that inflict pain and suffering.

Csányi's style is direct and easy, and he alternates deftly between delightful examples, descriptions of interesting experiments, illustrations from the history of psychology and ethology and the evolution of our thinking about these fields, particularly in relation to animals, and the theoretical models we employ to interpret out observations. The book is easily accessible to laypeople and is both a pleasure to read and a learning experience.

I am grateful to all who were kind enough to read parts or all of the manuscript of the translation and who improved it significantly with their comments. In particular, I want to thank George Pitcher (who himself wrote a delightful book about dogs),[1] Frank Vannerson, Clare Shepley, and my wife, Midge Quandt. They all made important contributions, but none of them bears any responsibility for the final product. Finally, I am grateful to Professor Csányi, who also read the translation and made numerous important corrections and taught me a great deal in the process.

Richard E. Quandt

Preface to the British Edition

I am very pleased that this volume is now appearing under the imprint of a British publisher because the British people are known to be ardent dog lovers. In fact, I was very happy to be able to send one of my students to work at a British school for seeing-eye dogs. The present work has a long history: it originally appeared in Hungary, where it sold many copies; subsequently, it was translated into English by my good friend Richard Quandt for the US market, and a German translation is in preparation. Judging from readers' reactions to the book, it seems that I was able to show the connections between scientific research about dogs and true love for them. At the Department of Ethology of the Eötvös Lóránd University in Hungary, we have been studying dogs for some ten years, and our results have been published in professional journals of ethology and psychology. But I have always felt it important that the dog-loving general public be made aware of these results. In my view, this could be best accomplished by relating the details of my own two dogs' lives and by demonstrating in the context of their ordinary lives the ways in which science can provide answers to truly exciting questions. Readers who are not particularly interested in scientific detail may wish to skip some of the more technical material, whereas those readers who are primarily interested in science might benefit from consulting the original journal literature cited herein. Scientific researchers dealing with animal ethology are quite divided in their opinions concerning the similarities and dissimilarities between animal and human minds. There are those who believe that animals are basically biological robots that do not think but merely respond to stimuli. But there are others who belivee that every brain is capable of thinking, although there are substantial differences between the thinking that rests on human language and the thinking that employs merely images or feelings. There is much debate about these questions.

In any event, on the basis of scientific and personal observations, I think that there is a huge difference between dogs and other animals. Dogs are the creatures of humans and resemble them in various respects. That is why we love them so much.

Vilmos Csányi
2006

Part
One

The Alliance of Two Minds

Humans have coexisted for tens of thousands of years with a peculiar social predator descended from wolves, namely the dog. During this time we have accumulated much knowledge about dogs. Some of this knowledge is available in well-written and practical dog books, while some is the subject of the oral history of dogs, of anecdotes and beliefs; only a very small portion of this knowledge has found its way into the scientific literature about dogs. If we examine the practical and theoretical literature about dogs, we find much on breeding dogs, on owning and training them, and on the characteristics of particular breeds. But we will find precious little about their behavior and the functioning of their minds, and there are hardly any works that deal expressly with canine ethology.

Why Is There No Canine Ethology?[1]

Ethologists are guided by numerous motives when they select a particular species for special examination, and some of the relevant considerations may appear to be contradictory. It is useful if the animal selected for study is easily approached and observed, but it is also useful if its habitat is far away, in exotic regions, and if it is difficult to observe. It serves our purposes well if the chosen animal has a simple nervous system, but it is also appropriate for answering our scientific questions if its nervous system is among the most highly developed, and it is even better if the animal is closely related to humans. The extent to which earlier scientists have already dealt with the animal in question is also relevant: if they have studied it extensively, we no longer have to concern ourselves with observing the simplest features, but if they have hardly considered it at all, then practically every observation we make about the animal is a novel contribution to science.

These contradictory considerations are particularly valid in the case of dogs: they are simultaneously extremely desirable as well as unsuitable subjects for ethological observations. Dogs live among us and their natural environment is human society. Consequently they are readily available for observation; but at the same time, they are very difficult to observe, because to do so requires us to penetrate a wild jungle, namely the family home. Being mammals, their nervous system is quite well developed, but does not reach the level attained by the apes. These contradictions are undoubtedly the reason that except for a dozen or so learned articles there are no books on canine ethology. The reluctance of ethologists to deal with dogs is further reinforced by the fact that there is much more variation in canine behavior than within particular species that live in the wild. There are two exceptions to the uniform rule of invariant behavior within species: humans and dogs. The reason for the variability of behavior among dogs is not only that there are many hundreds of genetically different breeds among dogs, but also that their individual development can be influenced by learning, teaching, discipline, and the development of habits.[2]

Ethology offers the scientific researcher two principal opportunities for observation. The first one is the observation of the animal's behavior in its natural habitat. If a dog is a family dog, it clearly lives in the human environment. But it will also have close human contacts if it is a working dog or if its job is only to guard the house. Hence the domain of observations can be highly variable. Anyone who wants to pursue canine ethology has to have some familiarity with human ethology, as well as with psychology, because any evaluation of canine behavior must be coupled with an understanding of human behavior. It follows that we must adopt a new methodology, which is to require in our experiments that dogs and their owners both participate in them.

An alternative approach would be to examine the animal in an entirely artificial, laboratory setting. We did not seriously contemplate keeping dogs in a kennel and periodically selecting one for an experiment or for observation. Isolated dogs sooner or later become psychologically disturbed and become unsuitable as experimental subjects for behavioral observation. On the other hand, dogs kept in groups avidly observe the course of events and this again impedes objective study. For example, we examined bonding among dogs kept by an animal protective organization, which employed a common run for dogs. We soon learned that dogs vied for the honor of being selected for an experiment, and dogs that were picked more frequently were soon punished by the others' aggressive behavior. Dogs do not like exceptions.

The reader will discover many facts and data in this volume: among them the results of tests and experiments of ethological significance performed with my collaborators, as well as those of other experiments that may not be directly related to ethology but are undoubtedly of scientific importance. We shall also discuss observations that I made over a ten-year period on my own dogs. These are, of course, individual observations, but their scientific value derives from the fact that they helped us to carefully design and control experiments. Finally, I shall also provide some first-hand anecdotes that enrich my story. The reader should consider my views on the canine mind as the hypotheses of a scientific theory, the proof of which remains the task of future research. But absent more research, these are my views here and now and I shall try to support them the best way I can. Those readers with a particular bent for science will find a long chapter near the end of the book about scientific investigations into the animal mind and what the stumbling blocks are. These stumbling blocks are obviously relevant for my theories as well. For this reason the reader must resist the temptation to believe that dogs are exactly the way I see them.

Let us begin. How did the wolf turn into the dog?

Chapter 1

The Wolf

The Evolution of Canids

I shall provide convincing evidence in chapter 3 that the ancestor of the dog is the wolf and only the wolf. Until then, let us devote some detailed attention to it.[1] The scientific name for the wolf is *Canis lupus*, gray wolf (the American black wolf is also known as the timber wolf), and it is a predator. Predators can be classified into several families: the bears (*Ursidae*), the cats (*Felidae*), the hyenas (*Hyaenidae*), the civets (*Viverridae*), the weasels (*Mustelidae*), the raccoons (*Procyonidae*), and the dogs (*Canidae*) (see figure 1). These families can be traced back to an ancestral predator, the *creodont*, which lived more than a hundred million years ago in the Northern Hemisphere. Its descendant was the *miacis* (see figure 2), which lived forty million to fifty million years ago. Some of the predator families living today descended from this animal. The miacis was a tree-dwelling animal of weasel size, with short legs and a long tail. The canids' lineage descends from this to the *cynodictus*, which appeared in the pliocene era about twenty million years ago (see figure 3). This latter spent most of its time on the ground and its limbs were better suited for running than those of the miacis. It was after the miacis that the cat family separated from the canids, which descended from

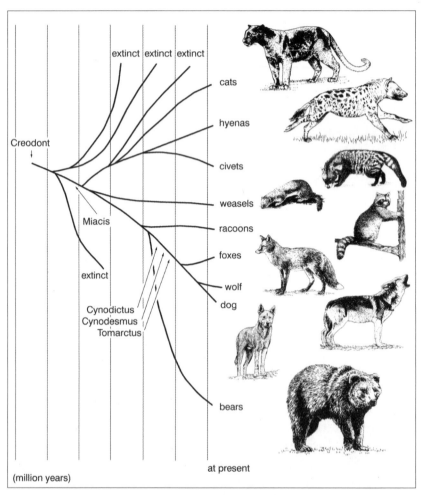

extinct extinct extinct

Creodont

cats

hyenas

civets

Miacis

weasels

racoons

foxes

extinct

wolf

Cynodictus
Cynodesmus
Tomarctus

dog

bears

at present

(million years)

Figure 1. The Evolutionary Tree of Doglike Animals

Figure 2. Miacis

Figure 3. Cynodictus

Figure 4. Tomarctus

the *tomarctus* (see figure 4). The tomarctus rather resembled our contemporary dogs, although it was much inferior in intelligence. Today, the canids comprise some ten or so different genera and approximately thirty-nine species. The genus *Canis* comprises, beside the dog (*Canis familiaris*) and the wolf (*Canis lupus*), the prairie wolf (*Canis latrans*), the golden jackal (*Canis aureus*), the silverbacked jackal (*Canis mesomelas*), the sidestriped jackal (*Canis adustus*), as well as various fox species. Additional caniform predators belong to various other genera; among these the best known may be the African wild dog (*Lyacaon pictus*).

Scientists recognize some thirty to forty subspecies of wolf, the precise number depending on which taxonomy is accepted as valid. The members of various subspecies differ among themselves in their body weight, fur, and the average size of certain bones.

The Wolf

Among the canids, the wolf is the largest, weighing 40 to 50 kilograms (88 to 120 pounds), although individuals weighing more than 60 kilograms (144 pounds) have been found. The wolf hunts in cooperative packs for prey larger than itself. Its habitat extends throughout the Northern Hemisphere, with the exception of tropical forests and arid deserts, and includes the tundra, taiga, steppe, savanna, and forests, unless it is displaced by human activity. It is superbly adapted for sustained running, and over short distances its speed can reach 60 to 70 kilometers per hour (37 to 43 miles per hour). According to some observers, when chased it is capable of jumping 4 to 5 meters (13 to 16 feet). At a moderate speed it is able to pursue prey for 15 to 20 minutes. After such an exertion it needs to rest for a comparable period of time. Its ability to swim is outstanding and wolves have been observed to tread water while killing their prey. In contrast to other canids, wolves eat only meat and bones. They have an exquisite sense of smell and hearing. Pack members can detect the smell of elk from a distance of 2 to 2.5 kilometers (1.25 to 1.55 miles) and tame wolves have been known to reply to the imitation of a howl by a familiar human from a distance of 6 kilometers (3.75 miles). This means that they can probably also hear a genuine wolf howl from this distance. Wolves' vision is particularly good in perceiving motion.

It is no exaggeration that wolves are the most intelligent predators. The volume of their brains is between 150 and 170 cubic centimeters (9.2 to 10.4 cubic inches). They acquired their extraordinary mental abilities through social interaction. The size of the pack is determined by many factors; sometimes it consists of only two or three individuals, but it appears that the optimal number is seven or eight. A larger pack is rare. Packs, even small ones, often divide into two and reunite later. One frequently encounters solitary wolves, which are usually older animals or individuals that have been ejected from the pack. The formation and life of a pack are most often studied with captive wolves, because nobody has yet succeeded in following a pack in its natural habitat for years or in identifying its members precisely. But short-term observations have been carried out by several scientists, and the information gathered in this fashion has revealed much about the wolves' social system.

The wolves that constitute the breeding *pair* are the key figures of the pack, which also consists of pups and a few adults of either sex. Adulthood is reached after two years, but a high percentage of the pups perish before reaching that age. Many observers have thought that the other adults in the pack may well be the older offspring of the breeding pair. Strange wolves are rudely chased away from the pack's habitat, but around the time that the young are born, adults that are strangers may join the pack and other adults may leave the pack; the pack may in fact divide into several parts.

Packs inhabit a predominantly exclusive territory, which extends over a large area and is inhabited by the pack for many years. It may— depending on the size of the pack—amount to as much as 300 square kilometers (116 square miles).[2] The pack moves around a great deal over this territory, but the daily movement is only 5 to 6 kilometers (3.1 to 3.7 miles). The entire area is covered in about three weeks. The pack uses well-trod paths, customary meeting places, and dens for the time of birthing. During the daily excursions the dominant individuals industriously mark the territory with urine, stool, and scratching. Wolves have scent glands on the balls of their feet and their secretions leave traces on the ground. Observations show that such a marker appears on the average every 250 meters (1,134 feet) and these marks are mostly found along frequently used paths, near branches of the paths and close to the boundaries. If the wolves encounter the scent mark of a strange wolf, they densely mark it themselves. According to observers, it is certain that they work from a cognitive map,[3] because if they are heading for a particular objective, they frequently avail themselves of shortcuts. Their image of the map is built up of scent markers and the characteristics of the terrain. It appears that wolves build their mental map out of the same elements as humans: places, roads, and boundaries. They adjust the direction of their movement according to the habitual location of their prey, the location of a carcass abandoned after a successful hunt, a meeting ground, or a den. The pack's territory is surrounded by a no-man's-land with a width of one kilometer; this is used jointly with the neighboring pack, but never at the same time. Solitary individuals also move on the periphery of the territory. An examination of the territorial behavior of neighboring packs reveals that every pack has a precisely defined territory, but there is no systematic border control as exercised by other social animals such as the hyenas, because the property rights pertaining to territory are recognized by the neighbors as well. It does occur, but infrequently, that they invade the neighboring territory, but after its cursory examination they rapidly withdraw. The new packs formed out of the dissolution of an old pack are friendly toward one another and may even reunite temporarily.

The wolf pack is a self-supporting and reproducing unit in which the individuals jointly and cooperatively procure food and jointly rear the new generation. The parents are not the only ones to participate in these endeavors, but are joined by almost every member of the pack, particularly the younger ones. The basis for the pack's cooperation is the ranking of the members established by their battles for advantage and the bonding among them. Cooperation demands a well-developed social intelligence, good problem-solving abilities, and flexible behavior that can easily adapt to circumstances. The wolf possesses all these characteristics, and until it lost out in the competition with humans, it was the dominant predator of its habitat.

Bonding

The most important behavioral precondition for the survival of the pack is that its members bond with one another. There is no widely accepted definition of bonding. In general, it is understood to mean the attraction toward members of the same species, and this can manifest itself in a number of different behaviors. The emotional state in bonding is formed in youth, during a brief period of socialization. Pups no more than three weeks old are already powerfully and solidly attracted to their parents and to other older individuals in the pack. If they are prevented from bonding, they develop symptoms of stress and they relax only if they are reunited with their group. Captive wolves can bond with dogs or even humans. Pups bond with humans most strongly when they are taken from their mothers before their eyes are open and are cared for exclusively by humans. Under ordinary, natural circumstances, pups meet adult members of the pack on the twentieth day of their lives, when their inclination to bond is at its strongest. In general, they leave the den when they are eight to ten weeks old and after that their inclination to bond diminishes rapidly. They bond not only with adults but are also strongly attached to their litter mates, since they spend most of their times with the latter. Beginning with their seventh month they accompany the pack and after that time they are less able to form social bonds with unknown individuals, unless they spend a great deal of time together. Ignoring artificially created situations, this tends to occur when adult individuals are experiencing sexual attraction. This is probably the reason why the courtship period of wolves is very long, sometimes longer than a whole year. Occasionally, the time that elapses between the formation of a couple and the onset of sexual relations is even longer. The bonding of couples is durable and may last several years.

The members of the pack bond most tightly with the strongest male. Ethologists refer to this individual as the *alpha male* and to his female as the *alpha female*. Other members of the pack are also denoted by the letters of the Greek alphabet according to their rank. The alpha male bonds most strongly with his mate, and among males with the next ranked beta male. Those at the bottom of the ranking bond less with one another, but are especially friendly with the pups and may attempt to build relationships with adult strangers.

A part of bonding behavior is that the alpha male carefully nurtures its relationships with every member of the pack. The other aspect of bonding is that the alpha individual, and often the other pack members as well, immediately attack the occasionally appearing outsider. Captive wolves kept in a kennel tend to behave in a threatening manner toward strange humans. Bonding is what enables the communal movement and cooperation of the pack during the hunt.

Bonding exhibits countless easily recognizable behavioral signs. Among these are, in the first place, the various forms of bodily contact, the playfully subordinated behavior of those of lower rank. Perhaps most important is that adult wolves are always prepared to play. If they happen not to be hunting or resting, the pack members strengthen and sometimes shape their bonding through playful behavior. The adults always play with individuals close to them in rank. Lower ranked individuals play more. The invitation to play is the same as among dogs: the individual issuing the invitation lowers its forelegs to the ground. It frequently also happens that the invitation to play is initiated by aggressive pursuit. The invited wolf pulls its tail between its legs, extends its ears rearward, and attempts to escape quickly, as if it were really being attacked; but unlike the case of a real attack, its flight is not in a straight line but along a curved arc. When this individual returns to the initiator of the challenge to play, the pursued becomes pursuer and the game continues for some time with alternation between the roles. During the game, many behavioral elements can appear that are employed in the pursuit of serious objectives, such as hunting and aggression. But it is characteristic of playful behavior that the usual behavioral norms dissolve and the various elements get thoroughly mixed together and are often repeated. The mood throughout all this activity is relaxed and the final act, the kill, is omitted.

In itself, the play has no serious purpose, but can be used for the attainment of certain objectives.[4] If the pack members are inclined to go hunting, but the alpha individual for some reason does not move, the pack members may induce it to do so with play. The alpha individual does exactly the same if it wants the pack to follow it. It grabs a stick and entices the pack by running away with it, then returns and teases the pack, tries to involve all the members in the game, and at a given moment it drops the stick and starts out in a determined manner, at which point the pack follows. A pack moving at a leisurely pace also sticks together. The alpha male always leads, but it is not the only one that determines the movement of the pack. Everybody cooperates to some extent, but it can happen that the pack and the leader want to go in different directions. In that case, the alpha individual does its very best to induce the pack follow it, but it will not go off on its own.

Bonding is the basis for the cooperation in the pack and this fact manifests itself in the selection of the direction of the hunt and in the selection and the killing of the prey. When the pack surrounds the prey, every individual attempts to remain equidistant from its two neighbors. As a rule, the attack is at the alpha male's initiative, and every pack member does its job cooperatively and with intelligence. The hunt by the pack is well organized and efficient.

Countervailing the tight bonding is frequent and heated aggression and renewed outbursts of aggressiveness for the sake of attaining a more prominent position in the ranking within the pack. This is probably the reason that while the personal distance between pack members is small, it is precisely defined and is in effect even during sleep. It can be violated only through playful surrender. The pups sleep alone from their fourth week onward.

Wolves are also characterized by xenophobia, the fear of strangers. When a strange wolf approaches,[5] a pup is anxious when only three months old, and by the time it is five months old, it is definitely afraid.

Aggression

Aggression is manifested in three different ways.[6] Its most powerful form is when an attacking wolf, without any prior warning, jumps and bites, unless the victim manages to escape. A second form is represented by aggression with restrained *pursuit*, which is always directed toward an individual of lower rank. The aggressor begins to stare fixedly at the individual selected for an attack and slowly, almost crawling, approaches it; then the approach accelerates, and as a rule the attacker executes a massive leap to close the gap. When the attacker's four feet touch the ground, it emits a peculiar sound. If the attacked animal has not noticed the attacker before, it now does and usually flees. The objective of the aggressor is clearly to chase the other animal away and not to attack it, because the flight ends the whole process. The third form is the *playful attack*. Its course is exactly the same as that of the pursuit, with the exception that the aggressor shakes its head in a broad arc or bounds in a zigzag manner. Seeing this, the victim does not flee but stands firm and the action continues with violent play.

Aggression has many functions in the life of the pack. The most important is the establishment of the rank order, which determines in cases of dispute who has automatic primacy in the distribution of resources. In a wolf pack, only the alpha individuals breed, with the proviso that if the alpha male is an older wolf, the alpha female may mate with a beta male; but in any event, only individuals near the top of the rank order can become breeders. This is the reason for the arduous struggle to rise in the rank order. Individuals that lose out in this struggle have no descendants and their characteristics are erased from the gene pool. Hence the competition for position is the most important determinant of wolves' intrapack behavior.

It is not only adults that fight for position in the rank order. A hierarchy is rapidly established even among pups. Aggression is the means by which an established position is periodically affirmed. The alpha female uses aggression to hinder the sexual activities of other females. An important role is played by a peculiar form of behavior, called *simulated ceremonial aggression*, which is initiated by lower-ranked individuals. In this, a lower-ranked individual acts provocatively toward a superior one, but then quickly surrenders by exhibiting submissive behavior. This type of behavior probably reinforces bonding. Aggression also enables the free movement of individuals and their access to prey. It has often been observed that if a large prey is killed, it is likely to be consumed quite peacefully. But smaller prey is viciously defended against poaching by others. Experiments with hungry wolves have shown that if a low-ranked wolf succeeds in appropriating a small piece of meat, it will not yield it to higher-ranked individuals, and those will not even try to take it away. But larger pieces of meat are usually taken by the alpha individuals.

It has also been observed that adult wolves bring meat not only for the pups, but also for the adults that guard the pups. Thus, wolves are familiar with the most important behavioral characteristic of higher social orders, namely the *sharing of food*. The American researcher R. D. Lawrence reports from a visit to a wolf reservation that the pack members, with the exception of the alpha male, were afraid of visitors.[7] On each visit, the caretaker threw frozen chickens to the alpha male, which first passed one to the alpha female, which suddenly emerged from its hiding place, then passed others to the beta and gamma males, and would consume only the fourth chicken itself. Once I visited the white wolves of the Hungarian keeper Frigyes Fischl and I took them a large quantity of turkey bones. The loot was immediately commandeered by the alpha male, which leisurely started to eat them. The others, some five adults, made a large circle around it. For a while, they just watched it; then, one at a time, they stealthily approached, carefully removed a bone, and ran away. According to my friend Frigyes, this occurred according to their precise rank order. Most of the bones were consumed by the alpha male, but he tolerated the theft of a few pieces without aggression. This behavior resembles remarkably the tolerance that chimpanzees exhibit toward freeloaders; the one that succeeds in grabbing the jointly pursued prey does not mind if the others manage to make off with a small portion. But in general, the male chimpanzee procures food by itself and shares it only with its young; only rarely does it give anything to the female.

Among wolves we also have examples of defensive aggression, which occurs when lower-ranked individuals refuse to yield to higher-ranked ones.

The following elements have been shown to be present among various forms of aggression:

- *Immediate biting.*
- *Wrestling.*
- *Pushing.*
- *Biting of the cheeks.*
- *Threatening growls or snarls:* This is actually a form of restrained aggression; if the threat turns out to be ineffective, the restraint may vanish and the animal attacks for real.
- *Jumping on the other:* This occurs mostly with strangers.
- *Simulated biting:* Occurs among the young.
- *Intimidation:* The initial stage of aggressive pursuit and is always initiated by an individual of higher rank.
- *Turning on another, biting:* Among wolves, as among dogs, inhibited biting develops as a result of socialization. The pups learn during play how powerful a bite may be before it hurts and provokes a response. The inhibited bite regulates the boundaries of friendly behavior for a lifetime. This can be taught to a wolf or dog if it grows up in human company without other members of its species: small punishments or the flick of a hand indicate to a pup that it has crossed the permissible boundary. If this correction is not carried out, the art of inhibited biting is not learned, and the adult animal is no longer capable of learning this behavior.
- *Pursuit:* The aggressor pursues the attacked and keeps attacking until the pursued flees. Subordination by the attacked animal is a counterpart of aggression: it curls its tail between its legs and crouches or crawls before the higher-ranked individual. This is referred to as the active form of subordination: the subordinated individual pushes the dominant one with its nose, licks it rapidly or gently takes its cheeks into its mouth.[8] Frequently it may also tap on the ground with its forepaw while wagging its tail and its entire hindquarters. The function of this behavior is to assure the higher-ranked individual that the other acknowledges its relative position, but would like to stay or participate in the division of the spoils. Passive

subordination is particularly noticeable among the young: the subordinate animal will lie on its back and usually pass some urine.

After Konrad Lorenz, many have claimed that the subordinate animal offers up its throat to the dominant one; but wolf experts consider this claim to be an error, or at least nobody has yet observed such behavior.[9]

Higher-ranked individuals frequently seek the opportunity to assert their dominance. One form of this assertion is to ambush the subordinate by pouncing from a crawling position, as if it were prey. In most cases, the subordinate acknowledges the rank of the dominant by some suitable behavior.

Aggression is always accompanied by fear. The motives of the aggressor are often both attack and fear. If the fear overcomes its lust for attack, it will take flight or assume a subordinate posture; in the reverse case, a battle ensues.

Other Forms of Social Behavior

I list here only the more important forms of social behavior:

- *Wagging of tail:* This behavior indicates a state of excitement. In friendly encounters the tail moves rapidly, while in an aggressive approach the tail is rigid and moves little. The dominant animal holds its tail up.
- *Bodily contact:* Touching or pressing or pushing of bodies, sniffing the other animal's fur, licking, sniffing the cheeks, the touching of cheeks (this can happen only among animals of equal rank), the grabbing or licking of cheeks, or the licking of wounds.
- *The sniffing of genitals, of the anus, or of the scent glands under the tail:* Dominant individuals engage in these practices mutually with each other, whereas subordinates cover their scent gland with their tail and do not sniff the dominant individual.
- *Expression of dominance:* Can be accomplished in several ways, apart from the various forms of aggression. For example, the dominant animal may place a stiff leg on the subordinate's body or may stand stiff-legged over a prone subordinate.

- *The greeting ceremony:* Two members of the pack will greet each other even after a brief absence. The greeting is actually a form of active subordination. The subordinate animal will excitedly lick, nip, and sniff the mouth of the dominant animal. Greetings often take place in a group; for example, when a previously exiled animal rejoins the pack. In such a case, the returning animal will attempt to touch the leader with its nose even from a distance, lick it, and take its cheeks in its mouth. Subordinate wolves behave exactly the same way when the pack discovers new tracks of prey during a hunt. According to David Mech, the famous wolf researcher, this is the common gesture for begging for food.[10]

- *Vocalization:* The wolves' inventory of sounds is surprisingly large and consists of growling, whimpering, whining, snarling, howling, barking, and tooth clacking. Growling and snarling convey aggressive feelings, while the varied forms of whimpering and whining convey friendliness. Barking, which may be more like yips, can mean an alert for the pack and can be threatening if an intruder approaches. The clacking of teeth is a signal to synchronize the departure of the pack. Howling can last from half a second to eleven seconds and is a continuous and fairly melodic sound that has important social functions. The howling of solitary individuals is often heard when the pack has become dispersed. When the pack members howl together for a long time, they are asserting their property rights over their territory and such howling often lasts half an hour. The synchronous howling of the pack is preceded by friendly greetings. It seems that wolves like to howl.

- *The sharing of food:* We mentioned that under certain circumstances wolves share food with one another. The pups beg for food by biting the lips of other wolves, and this is how a young wolf pays its respects to the leader. Grown wolves do the same when they ask the alpha individual to go for a hunt.

- *Sexual behavior:* Sexual behavior, birthing, the caring for the young, the forms of the mother-child relationship, and the various forms of comfort behavior are all part of the wolves' characteristic behavior patterns, but these differ from the corresponding traits of dogs only slightly and I shall not describe them further.

- *More complex behavioral forms:* An example is deception, which is well known among monkeys. It occurs sometimes among adults that an individual under attack attempts to defuse the attack by an invitation to play or tries to divert its companion's attention from a tasty morsel by playful behavior.

The older ones usually see through these ruses, and in these cases the mood can be tense.

Another example might be called "picking a scapegoat," a behavior whose role we do not entirely understand. At times, four or five individuals attack a subordinate one, the scapegoat. This attack often ends with the scapegoat being ejected from the pack. The most plausible explanation is that this behavior assists in population control, since it is not the young and strong that leave the pack when they grow up, but those that are defeated and weak. Thus, the most effective combination of individuals remains in the pack.[11]

A peculiar form of the wolves' food-gathering behavior is their herding or following groups of larger animals and periodically stampeding them. When they find a weak or older or wounded individual among their prey, they set upon it and kill it.

Summarizing what is known about the ethology of wolves, we can conclude that wolves are the most differentiated among the canids, because they live socially, while most of the others live alone or in small family units. For this reason, the wolves' social intelligence is particularly well developed and the events in the pack continually affect the individuals' ranks. Conflicts about gaining in rank or keeping one's position are frequent, and it is therefore very important that individuals observe not only their immediate superiors, but the whole pack, because opportunistic interests and alliances are very important in the battle for rank. But it would be erroneous to believe that fights occur every minute, since that, too, would prevent the formation of a stable rank order. The fact is that wolves watch each other closely and do not miss an opportunity for advancement. It is possible that no conflict will arise for weeks, but if a highly ranked individual is injured or develops some weakness, the others will take immediate advantage of this condition for improving their own position. This behavior differs markedly from human behavior. Humans also like to advance in standing, but in general they do not immediately and mercilessly exploit the weakness of their superiors. If the leader of a human group sprains his ankle, the members of the group would normally help him and would not use the impairment to demote him to the bottom of the rank order.

An attacked individual is able to correctly analyze the various forms of aggression only if it correctly understands its own and the aggressor's position in the rank order and is able to evaluate what the objective of the aggressor's behavior is in the given situation; and in its reactions it has to take into account the status of the other individuals in the pack. Such understanding is greatly assisted by the wolves' rich body language, which always needs to be interpreted within the particular context.

While other animals communicate with behavioral signs, the meaning of which is genetically fixed, wolves need to interpret the signs; in other words, the meaning of the wolf's response is not unambiguous and is not conveyed exclusively by the form of the response, but by the context as well. This behavior presupposes appreciable brain activity and it is not an accident that wolf behavior exhibits a great deal of individual variation. We can actually speak of personalities in a pack, because learning also plays a significant role in the formation of individual behavior.

According to H. Frank, we can easily distinguish two different guiding principles in the behavior of wolves.[12] The first, the older and more primitive instinctual system, consists of genetically fixed behavioral templates and provides the guiding principles for the most important survival mechanisms, such as breeding, food gathering, and defense. The cognitive system, which is to some extent independent of the former, is the more recent system and depends on learning, on the problem-solving ability of the mind, and develops in the course of hunting in groups. In the conflict between the two systems, the first always triumphs, which is why it is problematic to teach wolves, although they have excellent independent problem-solving abilities. It is difficult to train wolves and to handle them, because it is hard to have an impact on their independence and to influence their wild instincts with teaching and learning. According to Frank, the two guiding principles coalesce into a single mechanism through the domestication of the wolf into the dog. The fundamental characteristic of this unified mechanism is that the animal can be taught and its behavior can be modified.

Tame Wolves

We know a fair amount about the behavior of tame captive wolves.[13] If a pup is taken from its mother before its eyes open, and is then conscientiously cared for and fed, it becomes tame fairly easily (but not always). It will learn inhibited biting, gladly follow its master, and be able to use in its relations with humans patterns of behavior familiar in the pack. For example, it may greet a person as it would its pack mates: it will jump on the person and attempt to take his nose in its mouth. It will frequently push its nose into the person's eye and kiss him with large licks. But the tame wolf is not a dog. It will pay no attention to human speech and is not interested in what people are talking about, and when it hears its name, it will not run to its master. According to the German scholar Eric Zimen as well as others, if a tame wolf runs away and becomes a stray, it will never return home, but it will react to a well-imitated wolf howl by joining in the howling.[14]

Tame wolves will occasionally follow their master but will not obey him. Pups are positively afraid of humans carrying objects[15] and even wolf-dog crossbreeds exhibit timidity and cautiousness toward humans. Only wolves of the polar region have no fear of humans, and they are gentler with one another as well.[16] There is good reason for the wolves' fear: humans have been exterminating them mercilessly. This probably has been accompanied by some natural selection: the surviving wolves are the descendants of timid, mistrustful individuals that tended to avoid humans.

It happens frequently that wolves socialized in a human environment attack their master. Eric Zimen mentions several examples.[17] One wolf, which was entirely used to humans, started to abruptly attack visitors around the time of its sexual maturation and would bite male visitors in the area of their genitals. The wolf knew the attacked persons well and used to be gentle with them. A tame wolf belonging to a couple used to be taken regularly to school demonstrations because it was so peaceable. Suddenly, at the age of four it attacked its male owner when the latter started to limp as a result of some spinal problem.[18] The wolf probably thought that this was an opportune moment for trying to become dominant. The tame wolf therefore retains its unpredictable, wild animal behavior. The fight for position in the rank order is such a fundamental characteristic of wolves that the self-control imparted through taming is unable to erase it from the wolf's behavioral mechanisms. The tame wolf that bonds with humans accepts them as a members of the pack, and for that reason they are fair game in the struggle for position.

David Mech noted that his eleven-month-old tame female wolf escaped one night with one of his dogs and spent half the night running around. When both of them returned in the middle of the night, Mech chained up the wolf, which then started to struggle wildly to get free. As Mech said:[19]

> She was still tame and gentle with me, but she had finally gotten a taste of what it was like to act as her heritage had dictated, to be wild and free. As I watched Lightning straining desperately at her chain, pacing, whining, and jumping frantically, I realized how very wrong it is to tame a wolf.

Chapter 2

Humans

According to biologists, we can most easily understand the characteristics and lifestyle of any creature if we investigate the history of its evolution. In subsequent chapters we shall sketch the story of how dogs descended from wolves; but since the stories of humans and dogs were closely linked in the process of domestication, we need to learn a few things about humans as well. In this chapter, we shall deal mainly with those human characteristics that are most important for understanding the relationship between humans and dogs.[1]

Human Groupings

A few million years before they evinced any interest in wolves, the ancestors of today's humans in Africa began to live in small, closed groups numbering some forty to fifty individuals (and a lot of interesting speculation has been devoted to the possible causes of this). Living in closed groups thoroughly changed the social characteristics of our ancestors who resembled today's apes, but had an erect posture, were bipedal, and were able to use primitive tools. Evolutionary changes occurring over millions of years shaped the *human behavioral complex*, the functional system of behavioral forms that characterize human beings. Fairly highly developed beings can live in a closed group only if they bond with each other, are able to cooperate in procuring food, and if their aggressive tendencies toward one another have become weaker. These factors are responsible for the durable nature of the bonds within the group and the persistence of aggressiveness toward outsiders. Cooperation is important because forty to fifty mammals, roaming around in a tight group, will not find enough food for survival, and will therefore have to settle down from time to time and send out smaller parties to hunt and to gather food.[2]

The Pressure to Communicate

The more complicated forms of cooperation can take shape only if the various individuals have an interest in the ideas, plans, and objectives of their comrades, since common actions can be designed only if their thoughts are taken into account. This pressure to communicate probably manifested itself first in manifold communications on an emotional level and led to the development of empathy. Our relatives the chimpanzees are not very interested in what another feels or thinks, apart from the mother-offspring relationship. And even if they were privy to the thoughts of others, it would not do them much good, because with the exception of an occasional hunt, they gather their food and sleep alone. In the trees, grown chimpanzees have no enemies against whom they might have to fight together.

In contrast, our human ancestors living in settlements would have found it very important to know the physical and emotional state of other members of the group, such as who is worth hunting with, and whom one could trust with guarding the campsite. The need to communicate led them to imitation and mimesis, and in the final analysis, to the development of language. A mime expresses thoughts with the whole body. He easily imitates humans, animals, and actions, and is thus able to tell even complicated stories; the mind is able to interpret body language as well, and the observer therefore understands the thoughts of the mime. A simple set of tasks that might be proposed, such as two people should fetch water, three should gather mushrooms, and five should go hunting, is easily explained by miming, but there exists no group of ten chimpanzees that could be made to understand this. They would fail to understand mainly because they would not be interested; the questions "Why is that one jumping around?" "What does he want?" and "What is he thinking?" are of no interest to the chimpanzees if they do not perceive a hostile intent or do not register an alarm signal. The reason that human groups are capable of being well organized and that different tasks can be assigned to the various members is that sequences of genetic changes brought about the emergence of psychological mechanisms that harmonize and synchronize behavior. This is the reason that we can engage in the same activities as others: we work together, sing together, make music or dance together, and no other animal species does this. Humans take pleasure in these joint and harmonized actions; we are willing to follow rules, and these rules are instrumental in organizing the life of the group for the common good. A rule is a behavioral pattern that is accepted by the group, and if necessary, everybody obeys it. Following rules is a fundamentally human characteristic, which is closely connected with rank order and dominance or the dominant position derived from the rank order. Even rules can be subject to a rank order and one obeys them as if they expressed the will of a dominant personality. A rule is *impersonal dominance*; various rules occupy different positions in the rank order, and we always obey the "more powerful" rule. Of course, the lives of humans living in groups and their relationship to the rank order were altered not only by the introduction of rules.

In general, we may note that the rank order among humans living in groups has softened. To be sure, motivations and behavioral mechanisms are at work in creating a rank order, but in any given group there may well exist several simultaneous and parallel ones, and the group members' procreative success does not absolutely depend on their position in the rank order, but may be related to the diminution of their aggressive instincts.

The Ability to Be Constructive

Humans who bond with one another, heed each other, and are able to coordinate their activities have one additional ability that we rarely ob serve in the animal kingdom. This is the faculty of building, creating, and being constructive, which also derives from the conditions prevailing within a closed group. The assignment of tasks, mentioned earlier, is in itself a type of construct; it is a social construct with an inner structure. In this construct, various tasks are designated and persons are assigned to them. The task itself is a part of a greater structure that organizes the group's entire existence and that contains objectives, plans, roles, and other tasks. Histories or stories created with the modalities of language are themselves constructs in which there are actors, actions, places, problems, and solutions. Objects are also constructs: the stone ax, the fireplace, the hut, or the computer. In everyday life, humans are served by a common and harmonized system of constructs of various types. For example, a sacrificial altar is not only an object, but also a complex religious construct resulting from beliefs, actions, and social organization.

The minds of adult humans, with all their knowledge, beliefs, habits, plans, imagination, and aims, are again the end result of their constructive activities. The human mind is able to construct itself.

Chapter 3

The Alliance

People tell many stories about the origins of the alliance between wolves and humans. My story is based on the striking similarity between the lifestyles and social behavior of humans and wolves. Wolves were the reigning intelligent and sociable predators of the Northern Hemisphere, when some 130,000 to 150,000 years ago there appeared in their habitat even smarter and more sociable large predators with African origins: humans. They probably both hunted the same large prey and inhabited the same territory, and thus lived cheek by jowl. Both predators have a well-developed sense of their environment,[1] and it is reasonable to assume that they were curious about each other and observed each other's activities. They might well have lived together in peace for tens of thousands of years, since humans were quite rare and there was plentiful prey for both. Early humans lived in groups of forty to fifty, at goodly distances from one another. They feared strangers, but it is possible that at the outset they did not need to fear wolves. Why and how did these two very different species begin to approach each other?[2]

Mutual Advantages

It makes sense to take our point of departure from mutual advantage. Wolves hunted not only the large herbivores, but the smaller rodents as well, and at times did not even reject carcasses. Individual animals that had been exiled from the pack were unable to kill larger prey by themselves. Because of their tools, humans had become very successful hunters and were not forced to consume every last bit of the prey they killed. They would perhaps skin it, keep the tastiest parts for themselves, and throw the rest away. As a result, the settlements of humans were surrounded by heaps of food that could be snatched by carnivorous animals if fear did not keep them away from the loudmouthed, noisy humans.

Perhaps in the beginning it was the solitary, exiled wolves that started to follow the humans. Eventually, these solitary wolves might have grown strong again from the easily obtained food and founded new packs. Their young would have learned from them that humans were not an enemy, but rather the providers of luxurious repasts. A wolf population completely used to humans started to develop, and since humans were always nearby, the forms of bonding that characterize wolves may well have appeared in their relations with humans as well. The wolves' substantial genetic diversity may also have contributed to this development.[3]

Let us look at this from the humans' point of view. They had to be able to get rid of the less valuable foodstuff, but these remnants also attracted jackals or vultures or simply rotted. For this reason it was advantageous to have a self-appointed cleaner that one did not need to fear because it was tame, practically belonged to the human group, and kept the more obnoxious table companions at a distance. Thus, the first big advantage that humans derived from wolves was having a cleanup service always at hand. But we are talking not only about bones tossed hither and yon. Dogs have the habit, regarded as disgusting today, of eating human feces and gladly licking everything, not only a frying pan or a plate, but fannies, posteriors, or even the genitals of menstruating women. In the absence of an adequate water supply, these "services" could be quite valuable. The wolf scholar Erik Zimen filmed dog behavior and his work provides examples of these cleanup activities.

And if things did not go well, and the human troop was hungry, one could always kill and eat a few of the cleanup brigade. Also, their pelts were of great use for our ancestors who were continually driving north-ward in the temperate zones. They were warmed not only by the pelts but also by the living, tame wolves. In temperate climates, naked humans at rest are cold at night. One possibility is to acquire, with considerable effort, animal pelts and to learn how to process and preserve them. In ancient societies, one method of processing animal skins was for women to chew on the skin until all tissue subject to decay was gnawed off; then, as a result of the enzymes in the saliva, the skin would stay soft even when dried. (Please do not try this: although it may be tasty for a while, the skin needs to be chewed for a long time before it becomes usable.) A tame wolf can warm us without any chewing. A whole band of naked hu-mans could sleep in warmth if they had enough wolves available.

On cool nights, Australian aborigines use dingoes as blankets even today. An anthropologist reported that some twenty dingoes made their home around the campsite of a small band of aborigines in the Western Australian desert. They often stroked the dingoes, but did not feed them or give them names, and the dingoes had no personal contact with the humans. The dingoes did their own hunting and gathered up all edibles in the camp; in other words, they stole food when they were not closely watched. When the troop set out on a hunt, they usually tried to leave the dingoes behind in the camp lest they interfere with the hunt. The principal reason that they tolerated the dingoes was because they were a source of warmth. At night in the desert, the temperature drops near the freezing point, but the aborigines were not cold when they cuddled with dingoes. The anthropologist photographed them cuddling, but the din-goes were so frightened by the flash of the camera that they ran away and did not return for several days, leaving the aborigines to shiver in the cold for several nights.[4]

To quote from a recent account of the siege of Budapest in 1945: "In the forward positions, dogs were assigned to the men to counter the cold, because the body temperature of animals is substantially higher than that of humans."[5]

In other words, it was not only in ancient times that humans were willing to sleep with dogs. One of my colleagues, Szima Naderi, interviewed a number of people who take walks with their dogs. She asked them a lot of questions, among them, whether they allowed dogs in their beds.

To our surprise, some 50 percent confessed, self-consciously or embarrassedly, that they frequently did.

Early human groups also benefited from being alerted by the wolves that shared their sleeping quarters when a large predator was stalking the camp, because the wolves' senses of smell and hearing are much more acute that those of humans. Some human bands undoubtedly also discovered that wolves were useful for discovering prey and in mounting the hunt. Much later, a few thousand years ago, humans also began to employ the herding abilities of the by-then domesticated wolves, and these abilities were probably enhanced by appropriate breeding practices by the humans in the course of developing an agrarian society. I mentioned before that wolves occasionally stampede groups of larger animals in order to pick off those that are easiest to kill. On the basis of this characteristic and appropriate selective breeding, it is not difficult to breed a real sheepherder. It is also probable that the onset of hostilities between humans and wolves began precisely with the establishment of settlements and the domestication of large herds. Wolves did not really bother human groupings that lived far from each other and relied entirely on hunting for their livelihood. For example, the North American Indian tribes were not afraid of them and did not hate them. The conflicts arose after the formation of settled agrarian societies that kept large quantities of domesticated animals: there was much to fear in these societies, because their herds became desirable prey for the wolves. By that time, of course, dogs were the companions of humans and the cruel butchery of wolves had begun.

What Do the Genes Tell Us?

We know the history of tame animals living among humans fairly well from the bones found in human settlements. Archaeologists have long believed that the dog was the first domesticated animal and there have been many debates about what circumstances make it possible to unambiguously identify bones as wolf or dog remains. The transition was so gradual that they even introduced the concept of a tame wolf, because wolf jaws have been found that are somewhat shorter than those of wild wolves, and it was believed that these are the remains of tame wolves.

The oldest bones that are indisputably dog bones are about 14,000 years old,[6] but in Siberia and China, 20,000-year-old bones have been found that are considered to be those of tame wolves.[7] Remains that cannot be distinguished from those of wolves on the basis of bones have been found from much earlier, for example in the south of France from 150,000 years ago[8] and earlier, as well as at other sites of early human habitation. These were believed to have been the prey of humans that were accidentally mingled with the remains of human habitations.

Recent data from the realm of molecular biology have been provided by the extraordinarily thorough DNA tests carried out by Professor Robert Wayne of the University of California and his eight-person research team.[9] The tests included mitochondrial DNA samples of 162 wolves from North America, Europe, Asia, and the Arabian peninsula, of 140 dogs (representing 67 known varieties and five crossbreeds), and of a few jackal varieties and prairie wolves (the latter branched off from the true wolves about one million years ago).[10] They determined the precise order of 261 nucleotide pairs in the mitochondrial DNA control region, and their conclusions were based on these data, as well as on a secondary analysis of DNA from the cell nucleus.

The basis for the tests was the fact that mitochondrial DNA is only inherited from mother to child and is therefore particularly suitable for an analysis of genetic lines resulting from mutations over long periods. If small groups or even individuals separate from a population and their descendants live in isolation from the original group, they can ultimately grow again into a sizable population. One can determine from an analysis of the nucleotide order of their DNA the extent of mutations since their separation from the parent group. From this, one can further discover the kinship connections between groups, populations, or individuals. One can even estimate the rate of mutations, and from this, one can infer when or how long ago the various groups separated from one another.

The most important result of these analyses is that only wolves could be the ancestors of dogs, because the dog and wolf DNA differ only by twelve mutations, whereas the DNA of dogs on the one hand and of jackals and prairie wolves on the other differ in twenty-two places. A few decades ago, Konrad Lorenz believed that certain dog varieties descended from golden jackals; but taxonomists convinced him, primarily on the basis of behavioral indicators, that dogs descended exclusively from wolves.[11] The vocalization of dogs and wolves is the same, but the vocalization of the golden jackal rather resembles that of the prairie wolf.

The next surprising result is that the separation of the dogs from the wolves did not begin to occur a few thousand years ago, but rather some 135,000 years ago. This is particularly interesting because our own species, *Homo sapiens*, appeared around the same time. Wayne explains the tenfold discrepancy between the 14,000-year estimate of the archaeologists and the above time span by pointing out that canine varieties differing anatomically from wolves appeared only 14,000 to 20,000 years ago and that before that time dogs differed from wolves only in their behavior, but not in their shape or skeletal structure. This is quite logical in view of the attempt by archaeologists to explain skeletal remains exhibiting only small departures from those of wolves by coining the term "tame wolf." Of course, we must note that the timings based on DNA are not absolutely certain unless they can also be confirmed by other methods. A new, large-sample DNA study of wolves and dogs estimates that the two species separated fifteen thousand to forty thousand years ago and argues plausibly that the wolf that was domesticated was the smaller sized Asian wolf.[12]

In addition to these important conclusions, a number of other interesting results were obtained. It has become indisputable that domestication took place at two distant points in time and was an exceptional event requiring expert intelligence. The canine population created by humans multiplied rapidly and reached, along with humans, every part of the world. One can also show that those particular wolf populations, from which dogs emerged, died out, but as a result of the more recent cross breeding, certain dog varieties acquired new wolf DNA. In other words, the great genetic diversity of wild wolves contributed to shaping canine varieties bred for certain purposes. It is an interesting consequence of the more recent research that the various dog varieties are not genetically homogeneous. The external and behavioral similarity of the dog varieties hides a diversified genetic background, in which dogs resemble only one other species, namely humans. Every individual dog ever examined falls into one of four DNA categories, although several categories can be present in a particular breed (see figure 5). For example, three categories can be shown to be present in the Mexican hairless and two in the German shepherd.

The results from molecular biology strongly confirm what I have

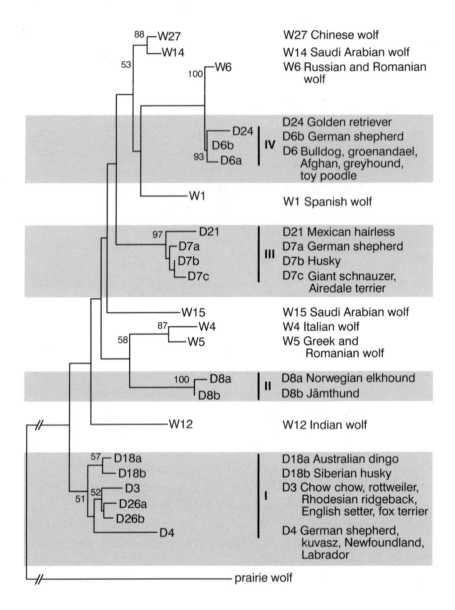

Figure 5. Dog and Wolf Kinship on the Basis of Four DNA Fragments

said so far about the probable course of domestication. I should add that while the functions of cleaning up campsites, warming humans at night, and alerting humans to intruders were satisfactorily discharged by tamed wolves for a long time, at one point—or, more accurately, on two occasions according to the results of the Wayne group—such favorable behavioral mutations occurred that our human ancestors, the groupings of *Homo sapiens* that were being formed, had a strong incentive to reinforce them by selective breeding. Dogs descended from these mutant wolves. We can only guess what these precious behavioral characteristics were, because the behavioral forms of dogs and wolves differ in many respects.

Dogs Are Artificial Animals, Very Different from Wolves

It may be worthwhile to start out not with the differences but with the manifest similarities that permitted wolves to remain among humans even before the above-mentioned mutations occurred. Humans and wolves are both highly developed social creatures, and their genetic makeup enables them to accept rank orders and dominance. The majority of free wolves live their lives in a subordinate position, and those that joined humans were forced to accept their perpetual dominance. This was not an excessively severe condition, since it was attenuated by the humans' handouts of food. The only material difference between human and lupine rank orders is that wolves fight for advancement frequently and very aggressively, whereas the corresponding activity among humans is much gentler. It follows, therefore, that in the early period of domestication individuals that rebelled from time to time against human dominance had to be selected out. Wolves or early dogs that attacked humans were killed, and hence the selection was quickly accomplished; the result was a complaisant, trustworthy dog, capable of being disciplined. Various bonding mechanisms develop in social species of animals that strengthen the attraction among members of the species. These mechanisms were present in both humans and wolves. The difference is merely that the earliest brief period of the wolves' lives plays a role in their socialization, with determining effects on the rest of their lives. A domesticated dog can have a sequence of masters, and a new master expects the dog to bond with him, too, even if it became his companion as an adult or at an advanced age. If the human treats the dog appropriately, this bonding does take place. Thus, the alteration of the genetic makeup inherited from wolves consisted of an appreciable lengthening of the period of socialization and of the ability of the dog to form lasting bonds throughout its lifetime.

Cooperation is a classic characteristic of both species. Wolves observe acutely the activities of their companions, and eagerly cooperate if they perceive opportunities for joint action. Hunting, defense, and internal group struggles provide plenty of opportunities for collaboration. In its transformation into dog, the wolf has to learn—and this requires genetic changes as well—that anything that humans are interested in can become a trigger for joint action. Dogs will help enthusiastically, but they can also be taught to hold back and to consciously regulate, stop, and restart their activities, and in particular, in accordance with the desires of humans.

The last characteristic that I consider definitive belongs in the realm of communication and is the ability to interpret. We have already seen that the wolves' signs for communication differ appreciably from those of other animal species. Their true meaning can be deciphered only in the context of events, and it follows that a process of interpretation is part of successful communication. In this respect, human communication is much more advanced and has risen to a new evolutionary level with the aid of spoken language. Wolves, as they started to become domesticated, must have had continual problems of interpretation. Humans have no tail, cannot move their ears, and their body odors are unfamiliar. On the other hand, they have hands with which they gesture about incomprehensible matters. For this reason, using and interpreting *learned* signs have a much greater role in the communication between humans and dogs. The descendants of wolves were able to remain in human company only if their minds were able to grasp the course of human actions, to interpret those small, ancillary signs that preceded the actions, and if they were able to forecast and understand from these what role they would play in the activities. The interpretation was further hampered by the fact that vocalization or speech has a prominent role in communication among humans. Dogs face a veritable maelstrom of human words from which they have to make out those that carry meaning for them. This might have been the most challenging task faced by the wolves that were entering an alliance with humans, yet this is the one that they solved most successfully.

Even a mere recitation of the differences between dogs and wolves is difficult, mainly because we barely know the minds of dogs and, in spite of the long friendship between dogs and humans, there are precious few acceptable scientific studies. And we know even less about wolves. As studies have made clear, it makes a lot of difference whether we compare only adult individuals or whether we include the young as well. Numerous characteristics that manifest themselves among wolves only as cubs are present in adult dogs. This difference also manifests itself in body language or in behavior such as barking. Wolf cubs bark a great deal, but adults only rarely. But the adult dogs' readiness to bark is a characteristic of the species. Evolutionary biologists consider this to be a classic case of neoteny. Neoteny is an evolutionary process in which a species changes so that traits characteristic of the early development of an individual, which would have normally disappeared in its normal development, remain present in the adult animal. Neoteny also explains the formation of many human traits. Chimpanzee babies resemble humans much more than they do as adults. In general, wolf cubs also resemble dogs more than adult wolves do. It makes for tremendous complications that the many hundreds of dog breeds differ among themselves in countless traits.[13] If we undertook a one-by-one comparison of canine breeds with wolves, we would conclude that numerous traits characteristic of wolves are missing from dogs. But if we considered the sum total of all dogs as a single group, as biologists do, then every lupine trait can be found in some dog variety. Of course, we would not be able to conclude generally that, say, dogs have shorter cheekbones than wolves,[14] because this holds for pugs and bulldogs, but not for many other breeds. Equally, we could not say that unlike wolves, dogs gladly fuss with objects, because this is a characteristic of retrievers but not of malamutes.

We find remarkably small differences if we examine the deepest levels of behavioral structures or compare behavioral patterns. The classic work on canine behavior and genetics by Professors Scott and Fuller[15] provides detailed comparisons of the behavioral patterns of several breeds, but they do not find many that are not shared by wolves. Cases in point are the various types of hygenic behavior.

More differences are found at the higher levels of behavioral structures.

We have already noted that among dogs the intrapack extent of aggression is considerably reduced, as it is among humans. It is also clear that the genetic selection carried out by humans has virtually stopped the wolf's ceaseless attempts to become the pack leader. Dogs in a human environment compete very gently, which is the reason that groups of several hundred may be confined in a closed and limited space. Animal shelters are excellent examples of this. If even a smaller number of wolves were locked up under such circumstances, they would frantically be at each other's throats. It is also characteristic of dogs that they treat humans as if they were the same species and are expressly attracted by the presence and touch of humans. Dog owners know well that food is not an essential component of rewards and that praise and a caress may suffice, although delicious tidbits are regarded as part of the *social reward* structure.

Substantial differences exist between wolves and dogs in hunting and herding behavior, in social characteristics, and in vocalization. Dogs can be taught to pursue and catch prey, but the average family raised dog will not know what to do with the prey once it is caught, although wolf cubs are solidly endowed with the ability to kill it quickly. Certain herding varieties such as border collies use wolflike maneuvers to stalk their "prey," but do not know how to execute the final charge and kill. If they did, they could obviously not be used for herding. There are other breeds, to wit the kuvasz and the komondor in Transylvania, that protect sheep and engage predators in fights, but do not herd.

It is characteristic of dogs that they can be called off, that they can hold back and patiently await the human's permission, which is important for sheepherders and characterizes humans as well. At the Department of Ethology of the Eötvös Lóránd University (ELTE)[16] we raised a fox. We obtained it when it was only a few weeks old and it became a very gentle animal that one could hold on one's lap and caress. There was one exception to this, namely feeding time. When the tiny fox was given a plateful of beef liver, it would hurl itself at the food and gorge. One of my colleagues wanted to adjust the position of the plate, whereupon the tame fox frantically attacked him and bit his finger. We later learned from a few similar incidents that at feeding time it was not advisable to approach nearer than about seven feet, or it would attack. A well-trained dog is easily taught to sit salivating next to its full dog dish until it is given permission to eat.

My dogs live in a home crammed full of small objects and their daily routine is fairly lively, but they have never knocked something over or broken anything, even though they never received any special training. I have noticed that if I command them to fetch some object from an end table, say a ball or a wooden object, they grab it with exquisite care, and if in the process anything else is accidentally moved, they immediately stop and ask for help by looking at me or barking. I have never taught them to respect the numerous objects that hold no special interest for them, but they nevertheless do. This behavior is probably the consequence of a new trait, obedience to the rules, to which I shall soon return.

The vocalization of dogs has also changed. Howling still exists and can be heard at times, but adult dogs bark in the manner of wolf cubs, although in a more composed manner. One behavioral genetics research group under the direction of Professor Belyaev in Russia is investigating, among other things, the domestication of silver foxes.[17] Silver foxes are bred in large numbers, and the fact that they have kept their wild, unsociable, aggressive nature creates a lot of problems for the keepers. Belyaev's group has been breeding foxes selectively for several generations on the basis of gentleness and attraction to humans, and by the eighth or ninth generation they were reasonably tamable and attracted to humans. And one other interesting characteristic emerged: these tame foxes *bark* a lot, just like dogs.[18] I have seen these animals myself and suggested as an explanation that the foxes' ability to recognize animals as being of their own species has become weakened as a result of the selective breeding, and for that reason they consider humans as if they were of their species, which makes them tame and makes them imitate the humans in their own way. The Russian researchers did not object to the suggestion that the tame foxes' bark could be regarded as their rough imitation of articulated human speech.

We should mention one additional difference between dogs and wolves: the dog's cerebral cortex is about 30 percent smaller than that of the wolf. For this reason, many think that wolves are a lot smarter; but there is no proof of this at all. First, the differences in size measurements affect primarily the brain areas controlling the senses; hence dogs are probably inferior to their ancestors in eyesight, hearing, and smell, since there was no steady pressure through natural selection for these often lifesaving senses to be maximally developed. Second, because the genuine differences are in mental agility, dogs are much easier to teach[19] and they are able to restrain themselves if that is what the successful completion of a task demands. In other words, the functioning of wolves' minds is more powerfully affected by genetic determinants, whereas dogs' minds can be developed better through environmental influences and learning, and have been shaped into a mechanism resembling the human mind in many respects. The success of this transformation is not just a function of the mass of the dog's brain.

This is easy to understand if we reflect on the purposes for which humans employ dogs. We have already mentioned the functions of cleanup, giving alarms, and providing heat, as well as hunting and herding. Of course, these have various specialized subfunctions, such as those performed by shepherds, retrievers, and setters, and there are reports of dogs specialized in capturing live tigers. In World War II, army dogs were widely used to carry messages.[20] Nowadays, apart from watchdogs, the most common dog is the family dog, treated as a member of the family and kept for our pleasure and emotional satisfaction. We use them for protection, as Seeing Eye dogs, to assist the physically challenged; and these latter are able to pick up coins from the floor, pick up and re-place a telephone receiver, turn the light on or off, and fetch objects at the command of the master. Many dogs are taught to search for and find desirable or, on the contrary, undesirable objects or to find people. Rescue dogs, bomb- and drug-sniffing dogs, and dogs that locate persons who hide or are wounded or dead are of great help to police and emergency workers. Brazilian Indians also employ dogs to warn them of the pres-ence of poisonous snakes in their path. Dogs employ their sense of smell to warn of the imminent birthing of calves or to alert foresters to the presence of harmful insects. They perform even more complicated tasks by warning their masters of an impending epileptic attack or in identify-ing certain types of skin cancer. Dogs are called to service in many ways in medical practice, and here I am not thinking of experimental animals used for testing new drugs or new surgical procedures—I think of those dogs most unwillingly—but rather of dogs used in therapeutic settings. These dogs are trained to suffer gladly the caresses and hugs of strangers and refrain from nipping even if a careless hand inflicts pain on them. They are regularly taken to retirement homes and orphanages, because it has been scientifically proven that caressing and hugging animals improves the mental states of their residents. Humans need caresses and hugs throughout their lives, and these gestures promote the production of endorphins, those compounds that have such profound effects on our complicated social regulatory systems. The endorphins released in the brain have an important role in shaping a sense of well-being. Older people exposed to therapy dogs are less prone to depression, their blood circulation improves, and their life span demonstrably lengthens.[21]

I have not mentioned yet the various sporting dogs. Recently, sled dogs have been classified in this category, but in many cases they are important helpers in everyday life situations. And let us not forget about the dogs that perform in films or in circuses. Many people indulge in the exciting and competitive hobby of breeding dogs according to the requirements prescribed for the sundry varieties. Personally, I am not in favor of competitive dog breeding because, regrettably, the behavioral characteristics are not taken into account in judging breeds, or at least not very much, which leads to the deterioration of the breed in many instances—but more about this later. No matter how many jokes are cracked about lap dogs, they are just as useful as therapy dogs. Dogs are also employed for purposes prohibited or despised in our culture. Unfortunately, there still exist bloody dogfights, and in the Far East, dogs are eaten even today. The varieties bred for this latter purpose are allegedly dull-witted or stupid, but this is small consolation, particularly for an ethologist.

The list is not complete, nor did I aspire to completeness, but I did want to show what utility humans derive from their "alliance" with dogs. There is no other domesticated animal with as many uses.

Of course, the alliance has two parties to it. The dog also receives benefits: shelter, food, and on occasion, real friendship and love. It is peculiar how humans, visibly estranged from nature, introduce dogs into their artificial environment, their homes crammed with man-made objects. It is certain that the dog is not just like one of many other animals, but rather a creature of humans, an artificial animal, which has been shaped in its behavior and appearance according to human desires. It is not unimaginable—and I hope that someday we shall be able to prove this—that the parallel evolution of humans and dogs changed not only the latter. It is noteworthy that the beginnings of the domestication of dogs and the appearance of *Homo sapiens* occurred roughly at the same time. It is not too much of a leap for a biologist to imagine that in the early phases of domestication, human groups that accepted wolves in their midst gained competitive advantages with respect to others, and if this is true, humans' genetic makeup also had to change through domestication. It is possible that the issue here is one of joint development or co-evolution, and it would be an exciting task to look for proof of this, if indeed such proof exists. It is possible that we are the descendants of early humans who had a liking for dogs or a penchant for maintaining emotional ties with dogs, and that our behavioral framework was so modified that we have an innate need to have contact with dogs. Such changes would explain the human passion for owning dogs, as a result of which we regard dogs as real companions, emotional partners, and often as child surrogates. Of course, the mores of any given culture can totally reverse such attitudes.

My theory is that humans and dogs were able to establish such tight links because, through domestication and not even conscious selective breeding, dogs acquired mental traits that *resembled those of humans in many respects*.[22] In other words, it is an artificial animal on the one hand and resembles us on the other. The similarities, if they truly exist, are important because they permit a peek into the early period of our own evolution. We began our investigations of dogs at the Department of Ethology of Eötvös Lóránd University because we hypothesized that the traits that distinguish humans from animals, the so-called *human behavioral complex* that we already discussed in the preceding chapters, have certain important elements that must be present in simpler forms in dogs as well, because without them they could not have survived this long in the human community. The natural environment of dogs is the human community. Through the process of domestication, we have continued to breed the descendants of animals that were attracted to us, understood our forms of communication best, and were most easily adapted to our social circumstances. But behind the innumerable practical objectives of selective breeding, there is a certain common denominator. For whatever purpose a dog is to be used, it is important that it be obedient, that it understand what is demanded of it, and that it be able to evaluate the situation in which it has to accomplish a task. Humans continually talk to dogs, give them commands, praise them, and if necessary, scold them as well.[23] Only those dogs that understand all such communications and are able to adapt their behavior accordingly can perform well. Selective breeding in domestication favors such individuals, because their offspring are kept in preference to those of others. Only modest selective preferences are required for genetic changes to occur in evolution if these preferences persist over many generations. The average dog living in a human environment understands at least forty to fifty expressions to some extent, obeys commands, and is able to act appropriately even in complicated situations. It is willing to collaborate with its master and is even eager to do so, it reflects the changes in the master's emotional states, and even tries to imitate the master.

If this hypothesis is not completely off base, dogs could be models of early human evolution as well. If our research were to confirm that dogs have acquired a behavioral complex similar to ours, its individual components would not be present by accident, but would rest on the underpinnings of some important mechanism of behavioral evolution. Thus, observing dogs may teach us important things about the early period of human behavioral evolution.

Attempts to reconstruct the behavior of early humans try to deduce the important stages of human evolution from the behavior of our close relatives, the apes, and particularly the chimpanzees and bonobos. This strand of research makes inferences on the basis of behavioral *homology*. The theory of evolutionary analogy and homology, which compares similarities and differences, has considerable significance in biology. The similarity of traits can result equally from evolutionary analogy or homology; but in the former case, the similarity results exclusively from the sameness of environmental preconditions, whereas in the latter case, two similar complexes of traits will share common structural origins. For example, the fins of dolphins and of similarly large fish rather resemble each other. The reason is that both serve the function of locomotion in water; but the fins of dolphins are much more recent and demonstrably developed out of the limbs of mammals, because their ancestors were, some thirty million years ago, terrestrial quadrupeds (see figure 6).

Thus, the similarity of the fins of fish and dolphins corresponds to analogy, while the functional relationship between dolphin fins and mammalian limbs rests on homology. The conceptual duality of analogy and

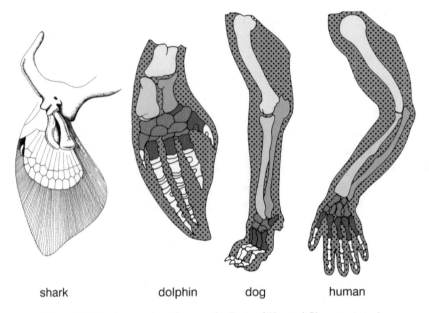

| shark | dolphin | dog | human |

Figure 6. Homology and Analogy on the Basis of Physical Characteristics*

*Bones of common origin shaded.

homology aids ethologists in making inferences from the comparisons of the behavior of various species. But homology can be misleading, because it may hide the behavioral mechanisms that appeared in response to new evolutionary pressures. Analogies reflect much more accurately the characteristics of evolutionary pressures, particularly if we study parallel developments in distant species such as humans and dogs. If we can exhibit in canine behavior the essential elements of the human behavioral complex, then—discounting or ignoring the modest mammalian homology applicable in this case—we can understand more clearly those functionally connected mechanisms that were shaped by human lifestyles through evolution.

In the next chapters I shall report on some modest results of this work.

Part
Two

Similarities between Human
and Canine Behavior

Humans and wolves are both social creatures. Their advanced social intelligence developed because they are attracted to and bond with others in their group. The alliance between wolves and humans created a brand-new situation, and its most important consequence was precisely the bonding between them.

Chapter 4

Bonding

Dogs Bond with Humans, Too

A nimals that live in groups have to solve two great problems soon after they are born. The first is to recognize others as being of the same species. Of course, solitary animals need this ability, too, because at mating time they also encounter others of the same species. It is an innate characteristic of many species that they regard animals possessing certain traits as members of their own species. Many newborn animals are helped by special learning processes to identify the animals that are of their own species, and it is useful if this learning takes place quickly. A case in point is the well-known process of imprinting, which Konrad Lorenz studied in birds.

Animals that form groups not only recognize others of the same species, but also are more or less *attracted* to each other, although in most cases this reflects their fear of losing their close contacts with others, because the group provides some protection against predators. They not only fear predators, however, but also fear each other, because of the continual competition for food, a place to sleep, and a sexual partner. Equilibrium between the fear of solitude and competition for resources brings about the so-called *agonistic* group structures; that is, those that rest on combativeness, in which adults compete with one another and do not bond a great deal, but are unable to do without the protective features of the group. While most monkeys are characterized by this type of arrangement, here and there one can find among them subgroups or alliances in which one can identify faint signs of cohesion resting on common interests.[1] According to students of primates, only three species—humans, bonobos, and chimpanzees—are characterized by a hedonistic group structure, one in which the members enjoy life. In hedonistic groups, the extent of aggressiveness is somewhat attenuated, and conciliatory behavior and appeasement make an appearance. In the case of chimpanzees, however, we do not find particularly strong bonding among adults; all that happens is that relations among them are somewhat friendlier and their mutual fear of one another is noticeably reduced.

Humans provide the most highly developed examples of hedonistic group structures. They are definitely *attracted* to other humans, and the attraction does not rest only on the fear of being alone. Humans like to undertake common actions with others, and they like to rest, play, walk, talk, and work with their fellow humans. Humans also experience exceptionally strong attraction to certain groups and persons, which is a characteristic of human *bonding*.

There is also a well-known form of bonding among animals, namely the attraction between parents and offspring, which is mostly between the mother and the young. This does not last long: usually only while the mother cares for them. The bonding among chimpanzee mothers and young lasts slightly longer, but by the time the young reach adulthood, it is much weakened and loses its significance. Among humans, bonding does not merely characterize the childhood years, but encompasses our entire lives. The bonding that arises among adult humans is one of our definitive biological characteristics.

The noted anthropologist Émile Durkheim and his students[2] found that the bonding that emerges in human groups or between two adults is characterized by four factors. The first is the undertaking of joint actions, the second, the provision of moral support, and the third, self-sacrifice. The fourth factor, the so-called transformation, is represented by behavior that makes the participants act as members of a new, higher-order unit.[3] These factors are easily identifiable in primitive religions, among the faithful in various sects, and in archaic societies, but they also appear in contemporary communities based on religion, the workplace, family, or friendship.

Anyone who has had a dog for some time and does not keep it chained up knows well that the above four factors are also present in the dog-master relationship, even if we do not habitually describe them in solemn terms like *morality* or *self-sacrifice*. Our dogs are always willing to undertake joint actions with us, to master rules of behavior, and if the circumstances demand, to defend or serve us without regard to their own interests. A dog and a master who have grown used to each other truly behave like a unit in a joint activity. But perish the thought that this type of behavior also characterizes wolves and that it can be explained as some form of pack instinct. The wolf pack, as I discussed in the preceding chapter, is a well-functioning breeding unit that is based on the alpha male and alpha female, but is cruel by our standards. All resources are devoted to serving the alphas, and it is only in times of plenty that the others get a share, which they acquire in fierce battles. Rules of behavior, in the sense of learned behavioral formats, do not exist, self-sacrifice does not take place, and every activity is motivated by immediate genetic considerations.

Apart from the scientific literature, we have known for a long time that dogs experience a special attraction toward humans. Books, newspapers, and oral tradition have recorded numerous instances of the proverbial loyalty and devotion of dogs. Many stories reveal the special relationship between the master and his dog, and how dogs are often capable of risking their lives in the defense of their human companions. Many believe that this holds only for single-master dogs reared by a human since puppyhood without other dogs in the household, but nothing could be further from the truth. Dogs are able even in old age to develop lasting and deep attachments if their love and bonding are reciprocated. Many years ago, we conducted some brief experiments with dogs in the Department of Ethology of ELTE. After we were done with the dogs, we found them permanent homes. One very sweet mutt, Balthasar, escaped from his new master three times and came back to us at the university, and so we were stuck with him. We thought that he had bonded with us so strongly that he was unable to develop new attachments. Thus, Balthasar became the watchdog at the Göd Research Station, which made everybody, including him, very happy. One day, when he was twelve years old and had to be considered a rather old dog, the research station hired an elderly person as night janitor and superintendent. One day I was looking for Balthasar in vain. My colleagues told me that recently he started to leave in the mornings with the night janitor, only to return to the "job" at night. I learned from gossip that Balthasar and the old janitor got to like each other quite a bit. "Just think," they said, "they sleep together and he even buys Balthasar hot dogs." Unfortunately, this relationship lasted only a few months, because the night janitor became ill, had to be hospitalized, and eventually died. In spite of this, Balthasar would disappear from time to time, particularly in the mornings. We tracked down what he was doing during his absences, and found that he would cross the busy highway, go to his adoptive master's old house in the village, and sit in front of it for hours.

Socialization, Species Recognition, and Bonding

Socialization is that stage of life in which a dog meets other dogs as well as humans, and in which its relationships with others, including bonding, are formed. Of course, the bonding of dogs has been the subject of psychological investigations, but frequently even the scientific literature does not distinguish between "simple" bonding and more lasting bonding with recognized and accepted members of the same species. It can be shown that recognition of a "species mate"[4] and the bonding that may follow it are different processes for dogs, but overlap in many respects.

Dogs experience a particularly delicate stage in their lives, at an age of four to twelve weeks, when the ability to recognize another animal as being of the same species is formed and when this ability is slowly transformed into the processes of personal bonding. It is sufficient for the puppy at this stage to be able to see or touch a human for just a few minutes in order to accept it as a member of its own species. If this does take place, the dog will be able to establish lasting bonds with humans in later life. Thus, personal bonding can take place not only in the period of socialization, but in adult life as well; the precondition for this, however, is appropriate early socialization.

If the puppy gets to know its subsequent and ultimate master in this early stage of life, the bonding develops particularly quickly and becomes very durable. If it gets to know several humans during the period of socialization, it will be able to bond subsequently with anyone; in other words, it will become a dog that can have multiple masters,[5] but of course only serially.[6] It has also been shown that in the period of socialization puppies fear unknown animals or objects much less than in later life. This low level of aversion is what makes it possible for them to build the required connections for recognizing species mates. These characteristics of canine bonding have been recognized by the Seeing Eye dog training schools, because it is important that these dogs consider their trainers and later the blind person equally as masters.[7]

It is possible in this period for some attraction to develop toward other animals,[8] because the processes of species recognition and bonding become intermingled. I believe that it is also possible for a personal attraction toward another animal to develop in adulthood, but I have not found scientific proof for this. However, I do have a relevant first-hand experience. Some neighbors at our country house had a dachshund-like dog, Jumpy. Its masters frequently cooked rabbit stew, and Jumpy was allowed to share these meals. One year, they got a live rabbit for Easter, and it became Jumpy's favorite playmate. Time passed and the rabbit grew up, and with the onset of winter it was no longer practical to spend a lot of time in the garden. The family decided that this rabbit would meet the fate of so many others and end its happy life as rabbit stew. This is, indeed, what happened, but Jumpy would not even eat a bite of the rabbit stew and went on a silent and dejected hunger strike for three days. Ever since, it has refused any food containing rabbit meat.

In contrast to their wolf ancestors, dogs are able to form lasting relations not only in a brief period of their lives, but also throughout their lives; moreover, they can form such relationships not only with their species mates, but also with other animals and particularly with humans.

My colleague Márta Gácsi has been studying adult-onset bonding among dogs.[9] Her research, conducted in animal shelters, shows that the process of bonding can begin quickly, within half an hour of being with a dog. It is clear that these shelter dogs want to find a master badly, and it does not take an expert to realize this.

What is peculiar from the ethological point of view is that the object of bonding here is not a species mate but a human, and one of the reasons for this is that in the period of socialization, the puppy accepts humans as conspecifics. In reality, the matter is probably more complicated than that. Animal psychologists have conducted several experiments with a view toward proving that the special and durable attraction that puppies experience toward humans is an *innate*, genetic trait.[10] With well-designed experiments we can even show that puppies are attracted more powerfully to humans than to their own species.[11] Puppies long for humans even if they experience pain or other unpleasantness in their presence; in other words, they are unable to learn that in such experimental situations they should avoid humans. This attraction is a very important characteristic of the species, and there is nothing odd in this phenomenon as far as our knowledge of behavioral genetics is concerned. If we try to tame a wolf cub, we may notice that it has an innate fear of humans and that it can be taught only with a great deal of patience and bother not to seek a safe hiding place when it is in their presence. The more timid individuals among domesticated wolves have always tried to hide or have escaped, and have not engendered feelings of caring on the part of their masters, and these individuals have only rarely, if ever, had offspring. These traits have gradually disappeared from the dog's behavioral inventory over the generations, and those individuals became predominant that sought out the proximity and the touch of humans and that felt secure with them.

The Measurement of Bonding

Durable bonding has also had an important role in human evolution. Many other human traits appeared because individuals feel secure in the proximity of others. This is particularly noticeable among small children. Psychologists have long studied the nature of the mother-child bond using a fairly complicated test, the so-called *strange-situation test*.[12] If, in a laboratory equipped with toys, a child is made to spend a few minutes with his mother, a stranger, or by himself in some particular order, we can reliably determine his bonding type from his behavioral reactions, and these results are reproducible. The bonding type is a fairly permanent trait of the personality.

My colleagues József Topál, Ádám Miklósi, Antal Dóka, and I have tried this test on dogs with a few variations.[13] Willing dog owners would

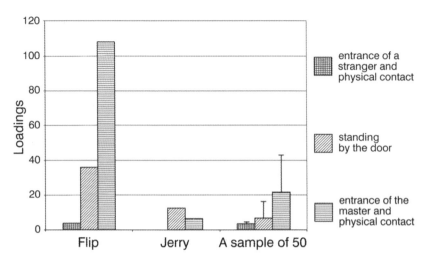

Figure 7. Average Values of Behavioral Elements Characteristic of the Several Factors
Observed in the Strange-Situation Test and Specific Values for Flip and Jerry

bring their dogs to the laboratory where we equipped a room for this purpose. Statistical computations permit the determination of the bonding
test's three factors: the extent of the *anxiety*, the *propensity to accept strangers*,
and the strength of *attraction* toward the master. These factors characterize the bonding. The statistical distributions of the measured values
of these factors have been obtained from a large sample of dogs, including the particular values attained by my own dogs, Flip and Jerry, about
whom we shall speak frequently in the coming chapters. In figure 7, we
compare some typical behavioral situations. From these we can gain
some insight into the observational basis for determining an animal's
bonding characteristics.

The tests revealed that the behavioral reactions of small children
and dogs square well with one another. A dog strongly bonded with its
master behaves in the various test phases similarly to a child strongly bonded
with his mother, and less strongly bonded dogs and children again resemble each other.

The extraordinary similarity between the bonding processes of dogs
and humans is also established by tests that have shown that the evident
depression of dogs separated from their masters can be alleviated by
precisely the same medications as that of humans. It is quite certain that
the same biochemical processes take place in both.[14]

Dogs that bond experience powerful stresses if they lose their masters, even if only temporarily. If this occurs in a familiar place, the stress is of moderate severity, but if it occurs in a strange place, it is accompanied by serious anxiety. One may often observe anxiety in dogs tied to a lamp post in front of a shop while they await their masters. Dogs that permanently lose their masters, their "family," are subject to particularly serious emotional trauma, and the symptoms of this are exactly the same as those of children suffering the same fate. A dog that has become a burden and is tossed out of a car and left to its own fate will search for its master for days, will not eat, and suffers visibly.

Anyone who rids himself of his erstwhile pet in such a fashion may delude himself by thinking that it is only an animal. Such a person does not realize that dogs are as capable of suffering as humans and are the exception among animals in that they experience rejection similarly to humans and human children. Anyone who acquires a dog assumes a substantial responsibility, and if the owner must get rid of his dog, such a person should, at a minimum, see to it that his rejected dog gets a good new master. But even euthanasia is more humane that abandoning a dog. If an abandoned dog survives this most difficult phase of its life, it will slowly accept its situation and will attempt to find a new master. If it succeeds, a durable bond may again be established.

A Human Group Instead of a Pack

Bonding is also the basis of dogs' group behavior. "Pack membership" is already well developed among wolves, and individuals bond not only with the alphas, but also to some extent with each other; they recognize their pack mates and can distinguish them from strangers. Dogs that live in human groups act the same way and know precisely who belongs to the close family group, who are welcome guests, and who are strangers. But their behavior resembles that of wolves only superficially. I have already mentioned that we do not find among dogs the merciless struggle for the number-one spot in the rank order that characterizes wolves. Their bonding is also different and they are quite a bit more attracted to humans than to their species mates. For this reason, the mixed human-dog pack does not resemble the wolf pack but is much more like a human team. Dogs readily cooperate with humans and have learned to obey the rules, which enables them to be our trustworthy, intelligent, and faithful companions.

On one occasion, at the Göd Research Station, we were able to observe the process of joining a pack. Some unknown person had tossed an ugly little mutt into the garden of the research station, perhaps in the hope that the workers at the research station would take care of it. At that time, we were working with fish, and the strange dog entered one of the aquarium buildings, where we stroked it, gave it some food, and christened it with the appropriate name of Corky. Corky then settled down in a denlike corner. Whenever the door opened and somebody as yet unknown to Corky entered, he would emerge from his hiding place and would "introduce" himself to the newcomer with vigorous tail wagging; he would sniff the newcomer, allow himself to be scratched, and then retire. "What a sweet and gentle doggie," we said. "What the hell, let it stay." Corky was truly sweet and gentle with all those he got to know on the first day, but thereafter he greeted everybody he had not seen before with bellicose barking, including one of the researchers at the aquarium. It took weeks and a lot of effort to make him accept these "latecomers." And he always attacked strangers.

Thus, dogs have a conception of the group and of its members, they observe accurately the intragroup relationships, and they behave accordingly. For example, they know precisely who the boss is, even if they themselves do not have close contact with him or her. We were much amused in the Department of Ethology by the fact that the freely roaming dogs at the department would select a master, obey him, and bond with him, but although I did not have much to do with them, they all, without exception, obeyed me, too, because I was the department chairman, and hence the top boss. In contrast, they were much less inclined to accept directives from those of my colleagues whom they did not select as their own masters and who therefore rated as being of "lower rank."

The faculty of belonging to a group also manifests itself in the relationships formed with friends outside the group. Flip and Jerry are very fond of a number of our friends and the feeling is mutual. They are very excited when one of them drops in for a visit, and the dogs express their affection toward the guest in numerous ways. But they never show signs of wanting to go home with them. They are well able to distinguish friendship from group membership. Because of a lengthy trip abroad, my friend Thomas helped us in rearing Jerry, and he treats Thomas as one of his favorites, but he does not treat him the way he treats us, his masters. At times, Thomas takes Jerry for a shorter or longer walk, but I always have to give "permission" for this. "You can go with Thomas," I say, and then he happily trots off with him. But if the permission is not forthcoming, he stays behind and does not even try to go.

Chapter 5

The Emotions of Dogs

The basic types of emotions, namely suffering, anger, and fear, exist among animals, too. The signals provided by the nervous system about these inner states are an important part of animal communication. If an animal is angry, there is a high probability that it will be aggressive, while fear may indicate that one in a pair of fighting animals expects defeat. Among animals living in groups, a signal of suffering may trigger help from animals of the same species. These signals keep animals from squandering their energies unnecessarily.

During human evolution there appeared a whole new set of expressions for the emotions. Overt manifestations of these are unknown among animals. For example, humans are quite familiar with the signs of an inner state we would call disgust, but such signs do not exist among animals. It is not difficult to explain the reason for this. Disgust is a signal that may convey important information to species mates when some inedible food is at hand. Somebody who expresses disgust derives no benefit from doing so. But a person who sees that his companion pushes a piece of food aside with disgust gains important information. In other words, this signal is unselfish and serves the well-being of the other members of the group. The signals of guilt, shame, surprise, contempt, or pride are easily recognizable from facial expressions, but these are unknown among animals, at least if we ignore the achievements of some dogs. What functions would signals for these states serve? In human society, we must continually check that the accepted cultural norms are maintained, and it follows from this that the expression of the above emotions is a mechanism that assists us in discharging our obligations to the group. Guilt is an admission that the person has violated the rules and simultaneously an indication that he will try to avoid doing so in the future. The group needs an alternative way to deal with a person who believes that he has not transgressed while violating the norms of the group. Shame is a more delicate signal, but it also communicates the violation of norms. What produces guilt or alternatively shame is culturally dependent, but their signals are the same everywhere.

In contempt, two agents are involved, and the one for whom contempt is expressed gains important information. Such a person is given to understand that he has not acted appropriately and that his social status has diminished; it is therefore a reintegrating mechanism for the maintenance of the group. Surprise is not a new emotion and occurs among animals as well, but its expression is a human trait and is an important conveyor of information in the group's internal reciprocal relations. It is easy to invent situations in which surprise can prove the honesty or innocence of a person. Hence, the signaling of surprise again serves the interests of the group.

The emotional states and the signaling of pity, sorrow, and bereavement are again unknown among animals, with the possible exception of elephants and chimpanzees. Only humans, who have highly developed behavioral forms for helping and caring for others, reveal these states. The obligation to provide help is quite universal in the many cultures.

A special role is played by sympathy and empathy. In essence, empathy is the adoption of the emotional state of another person. For example, when we see that our friend is sad, we ourselves feel sad. When we feel sympathy, we feel sadness and compassion toward a person who is in trouble, without adopting his emotional state for ourselves. Only humans are characterized by these two emotions, which have an important role in activating helping behavior.

The acceptance of moral principles and of value systems represents an important class of emotional mechanisms for the maintenance of communal life among humans. In the first stage of morality, rules are obeyed because of group pressure. The second stage is attained when the community externalizes the source of the sanctions that compel moral behavior by, say, attributing them to ancestors, vindictive spirits, or divine will. The third and most highly developed stage is a morality resting on inner conviction. Morality is an exceptionally human form of behavior that is not encountered among animals.

A substantial part of the behavioral forms that express the emotional life of humans is specific to the human species. Our complicated social life demands the increasingly precise expression of relationships and of emotional states, so that they may become *genuinely transparent*. We continually broadcast our mental states to those around us through our speech and through the expression or concealment of our emotions and we demand reciprocal behavior by others. It is of fundamental importance for group life and for the functioning of our closed, collaborative groups that members of the group have an interest in one another, which is one of the most important behavioral mechanisms for creating harmony within the group and for ensuring that its members are "on the same wavelength."

Animals Rarely Show Their Feelings

Not counting a few basic emotions discussed in the introduction to this chapter, animals would be at a disadvantage if they expressed their emotions in a clearly recognizable fashion. The reason is that their lives are devoted to endless competition, and good fortune smiles on those individuals that care about themselves and perhaps their offspring. If an adult member of a troop of monkeys were to indicate that it was in a bad mood, or that it had a headache, or that it was not interested in anything, the others would immediately use this information to their own advantage. They would not console or help it, but would mercilessly exploit its momentarily weakened condition and marginalize it in the competition.

Animals do not show their feelings, but this does not necessarily mean that they have no feelings. This is a question that deserves further study. It is a curiosity in the history of science that humans have always striven to differentiate themselves from animals, and this effort has manifested itself to this day in their denial of even the possibility of animal feelings.[1]

In the early years of the medical and biological sciences, dogs and cats were subjected to vivisection without qualms; it was thought that although they howled during the procedures, they could not have feelings or experience pain because they were not human. It was important from the ideological point of view, and not only in the Middle Ages, to prove that animals are of a lower order than humans. It was barely a decade ago that my own university instituted rules for the humane conduct of animal experiments, and I had a colleague who argued against the new regulations precisely on the basis that animals have no feelings. Until the 1980s, the medical profession thought that human neonates had no emotions and accordingly, they received no anesthetics during surgery, on the grounds that they do not experience pain and therefore their bodies should not be burdened with unnecessary chemicals.[2] The screaming of babies was simply considered vocalization, and this cruel practice was abandoned only when it was realized that babies operated on without anesthetics took twice as long to recover as those who were sedated at the time of surgery. Fortunately, surgery is not done on infants too frequently, and the passage of time has dealt a blow to the unscientific views about their feelings; but millions of unfortunate dogs, cats, and other laboratory animals have suffered senselessly in laboratories, until sober reflection and new animal protection laws have, more or less, ended these scientific forms of animal torture.

Of course, the negative views concerning the existence of animal emotions hampered their scientific study and we do not have appropriate methodologies for studying them; hence we have to rely mostly on individual observations.

For the reasons discussed above, it is not advantageous for animals to express their feelings, but every good observer who has become familiar with some particular species knows well that they do have them. Countless small signs point in this direction. Comparative evolutionary studies reveal the similarity of human and mammalian brain structures, and it is practically impossible on the basis of these studies that their identical or highly similar neurobiological and biochemical mechanisms should have brought forth different emotional states.

The writings of Konrad Lorenz on geese contain innumerable remarks characterizing their emotional states; he uses adjectives such as despondent, surrendering, victorious, uncertain, tense, nervous, joyous, alert, liberated, threatening, friendly, and so on. He explained in several writings what an important role the emotions have in regulating the animal's behavior, although their expression is different than in humans. Jane Goodall also had a long struggle to get the profession to accept the existence of chimpanzee emotions.

Apart from the fact that certain emotions are characteristic only of humans, there is one other big difference: humans are creative and constructive beings and are able to weave their emotions into a complicated behavioral matrix. In the theater, a great tragedy can give structure to, explain, and heighten the emotions. All our appreciation of theater arts is directed toward the play and the performance. But if we are talking about raw emotions, without any embellishment, evaluation, or comparison, as in situations in which we merely refer to something that hurts, or is lacking, or lost, then it is probable that the more highly developed animals often experience these, too.

J. Moussaieff Masson and S. McCarthy describe many observations about elephants, which reveal that they are capable of deep emotions. They describe an elephant calf that witnessed the killing of its mother and her companion by poachers, the cutting up of their carcasses, and the removal of the tusks. The calf, which survived this tragedy, ended up in an elephant orphanage in Kenya, and it was noted there over several years that it often had bad dreams: in its sleep it would throw itself around, convulse, and trumpet loudly. Higher order animals dream, and one can sometimes see in sleeping dogs that they are running or hunting. It seems difficult to deny the validity of emotions in creatures that can remember and dream.

I visited this Kenyan elephant orphanage, which has the mission of raising the orphans of elephants that have died and of reacclimatizing them to nature. The orphanage does not aim at raising tame elephants but wild ones, and this takes five to six years of meticulous care. The calves need a permanent caretaker, a sort of surrogate mother with whom they can bond and without whom they would perish. The management of the institution contracts with young male university graduates for six years to take charge of the raising of the calves. The contract stipulates that with the exception of a few days per year, they must be with their elephant at all times and even have to sleep with their wards in the stable. The elephant sleeps on the floor and the guardian on a shelflike bed, which is raised each year higher off the floor, lest the elephant accidentally roll over on him. During sleep, the elephant periodically touches the guardian with its trunk to make sure that he is still there, and if it does not find him, it panics and begins to search for him. They also make sure that the elephant not get used to human company in general: it has contact only with its caretaker and other humans may not go near it, may not caress it, and outside the stable the elephant is kept in as natural an environment as possible. In about six years, the elephant grows up and is then moved to the Kenyan National Park near the orphanage and it is assisted in joining an elephant herd.

A peculiar thing happened a few days before I visited there. Half a year or so earlier they released a female elephant that had been reared at the orphanage and it joined a wild herd. On the day in question, a wild elephant invaded the grounds of the orphanage amid stentorian trumpeting. The staff fled in a panic, and the elephant trotted around the various stables and other buildings and burst into one stable in which it discovered its original caretaker. Fortunately, the caretaker recognized it as the female that was released half a year earlier. He did not run but allowed the elephant to demonstrate its affection; it felt him with its trunk all over, embraced him with its trunk gently, and after half an hour departed with loud trumpeting. The story was told to me by the caretaker himself and the tears in his eyes left no doubt about his feelings and the truth of the story.

What actually happened? The elephant was finally living a natural life; it had established connections with its species mates, and suddenly it remembered a creature belonging to a different species, a person with whom the elephant had spent its youth, who cared for it, bathed it, covered it, and with whom it formed a lasting emotional bond. This memory was enough for the elephant to return six months later to that peculiar and strange place and, trumpeting nervously out of fear, to seek out the person whom it loved. I think that the simplest scientific explanation for this behavior is that it loved its caretaker.

Dogs Can Exhibit Many Kinds of Feelings

Let us get back to dogs. Almost all dog owners are convinced that dogs have a rich emotional life, and there are many easily recognizable external signs that this is the case. These signs probably appeared because dogs derived a benefit from their recognition of human emotions and from attuning their own emotions to those of humans. A cheerful dog puts a human in a good humor, and the master's sadness depresses the dog, too, and conversely. The reciprocity of emotions is advantageous for both parties, and this is another example of the behavioral similarity between humans and dogs, which developed under the impetus of evolutionary mechanisms during the many tens of thousands of years of domestication.

Of course, owners often exaggerate, and it is appropriate that we now examine the validity of the claims concerning emotions. Masson and McCarthy cleverly suggest in their book that we consider the following three different descriptions of the behavior of a particular dog: (1) Fido is irritated because we forgot his birthday; (2) Fido feels that we have forgotten about him and wants to catch our attention; (3) Fido is exhibiting the submissive behavior pattern of a low-ranked dog.

The first two are obviously anthropomorphic statements, while the third one is a dry, scientific observation understood only by ethologists. However, there is a great difference between the first two statements. If the first were true, we would be asserting that dogs are capable of keeping track of their birthdays, that they can count months and days, and are furthermore clear in their minds that it is not a nice thing to forget someone's birthday. Not even the most enthusiastic dog lovers would make this claim for their pets, because they can observe no signs of such abilities. It is possible that Fido is in a bad mood just on his birthday, but it makes no sense to couple this fact with our mania to celebrate birthdays. It is more probable that Fido is bothered by gas or a toothache or some other physical ailment. The second statement is also anthropomorphic because it deals with emotions, but we can reject this statement only if we are convinced that dogs have no emotions, that they do not notice that we have forgotten about them, and if we know that they never want to catch our attention. But most dog owners know that the latter statements are false. It follows that from the point of view of everyday usage, the second statement is the most useful one.

In the previous chapter, we discussed bonding between dog and master, but the scientific usage of the term does not refer to any kind of emotion, and especially not love. The scientific journals would have certainly rejected the paper in which we showed that the bonding between dog and master resembles that between mother and child if we had also mentioned in the paper that it follows from this that some dogs love their masters a great deal while others love them less. We could also describe bonding in scientific language without attributing an emotional content to the dog's behavior. We could say, for example: "After the master left the room, the dog was whining at the door." But we could not say that it whined *bitterly*, because that would be tantamount to sneaking human emotions into the statement. In spite of this, I will boldly assert that some dogs whine bitterly, and even that bonding is the scientific expression of a dog's love. Everything that we know about bonding in dogs corresponds precisely to what we know about it in children. If we are not forced to accept an ideology of human superiority, we can bravely identify bonding with love.

The reality of the dogs' world of emotions is established not only by bonding; it is also underscored by many other observations. The reader will find many cases discussed in detail in Masson's book,[3] but I would like to mention a few from the lives of my own dogs. Flip, the older dog, was ten years old at the time I was writing this book and Jerry was two. We live on the fifth floor of a six-story building and the corridor to our apartment is closed off by a wrought-iron door. Jerry was about one year old when the following took place. One evening after we came home, he was impatiently jumping around the iron door, waiting for me to open it. As I opened it, it hit his foot pretty hard, but fortunately nothing really bad happened and we soon forgot the incident. Not so Jerry. The next day, when I inserted the key in the lock, I noticed that Jerry was waiting for the door to be opened from a distance of some three and a half feet. *No problem*, I thought, *he is learning to respect the door*. But when the door started to open, Flip was starting to push his way through, which provoked anxious and desperate whining in Jerry, which was so convincing that Flip immediately retreated and waited for the door to be completely open. I thought it was unambiguous that Jerry was anxious for Flip because of the door.

The dogs are sometimes anxious for me, too. One winter, the weather was cold and snowy and during our walk on one of the steep hills in Budapest I slipped on a staircase and fell. The dogs had been running ahead, but when they heard my groans, they ran back, licked me, and stayed with me, visibly anxious, until I managed to get up. After this accident we did not go walking on that hill for quite some time. The following winter, again cold and snowy, I became more careful, but it appeared that the older and more deliberate Flip remembered the incident. Whenever we would traverse an icy staircase, he would run to me and slowly walk by my side, anxiously observing my steps. As soon as we would get to the bottom he would look up at me and run off. When the weather became warmer, and there was no ice on the steps, he never did that and ran ahead with Jerry as usual.4

I also know of examples of how a dog copes with his own sorrow. At the time, Flip was our only dog and could have been about three years old when the following happened. In the early evening, I was by myself when a visitor arrived and after a short while left again. I let the visitor out and returned to my study to continue my work. After about an hour, I heard a peculiar noise from the direction of the front hall, but I tried to put it out of my mind because my work required full concentration. The noise grew louder and louder and I suddenly realized that the dog was nowhere in sight. I started to call him, but he did not come and the suspicious noise became louder still. Soon it became obvious that I had accidentally locked him out, and since he did not have the habit of barking, he was asking for admittance by scratching at the door. I let him in and tried to undo my thoughtlessness with an apology, some caresses, and a good wrestle. It seemed that I had succeeded, the reproachful looks disappeared, and he resumed his favorite place by my desk. Several hours passed thus when my wife, Eve, arrived home. Instead of the customary joyous greeting, she was welcomed by Flip with a litany of complaints and with the choicest expression of canine misery. Eve rushed into my study and asked, "What have you done with this dog?"

"Let me tell you . . ."

If I analyze this story in my capacity as an ethologist, I am inclined to say that the dog suffered some unpleasantness, which was neutralized by the pleasant experience afterward. But ethology does not know what to do with the fact that some hours later the dog complained to another well-known and beloved person about the indignity suffered hours before but already atoned for. That is dog emotion at its height: sorrow, complaint, resentment.

The Basic Emotions

It will be useful to examine which of the human emotions discussed in the introduction to this chapter is matched by a corresponding canine emotion. There is no debate at all in the professional literature about the basic emotions of dogs. There is complete agreement that dogs experience pain, anger, and fear and the signs of these are easily observable. Pain is mostly signaled by vocalizations, anger by excited growls and barks, and fear by tucking their tails between their legs and trying to appear as small as possible. The signaling of these types of emotions is also important for wolves leading social lives. It is important to signal pain so that inhibited biting can develop, lest they inflict unnecessary injuries during play. The signaling of anger and fear are important for providing indications of aggression and surrender, which has been discussed before. We should add that dogs are occasionally able to disguise their feelings, which is again proof of their advanced emotional life. My dog Flip has visited a veterinarian on a number of occasions and has received injections on quite a few of these. He has always tolerated them without complaint. While the veterinarians have always treated Flip with professional expertise and kindness, they remarked on several occasions that dogs experience pain quite differently from humans; for example, needle pricks do not hurt them. Since Flip never complained, I started to believe this hypothesis until it turned out that it was a big mistake. Flip was scheduled for some minor surgery and we were in the waiting room when the veterinarian appeared and suggested that in the interest of saving some time he would administer an anesthetic injection right in the waiting room. That is what he did: unobserved by Flip, he stuck the needle in him with a practiced hand from behind, whereupon Flip leaped up and started to screech as if he were being skinned alive. In other words, the injection hurts; of course it hurts, but on the examination table the dog is counting on some unpleasantness and does not signal a minor pain, just like children who are taught to suffer such unpleasantness in heroic silence.

I also think that nobody will need to be convinced that dogs are able to experience the feelings of joy, sorrow, and excitement. Anyone who has seen a dog rejoice over the return of its master or be sad over being left at home and not being taken for a walk knows these canine feelings well. Dogs express excitement in many ways. For example, Flip trembles in his entire body, while Jerry jumps around and whimpers. I have already discussed love in connection with bonding, and anyone who has more than one dog or a dog and children will be quite familiar with jealousy.

When I caress Jerry, after a while Flip will indicate with growls that enough is enough, and the affront can be undone only by caressing him, too. If I caress a strange dog, I have to be sure to do so only briefly, because if one of my dogs notices it, I will certainly hear from him.

Dogs keep track of every morsel and every caress and want to have a part in everything. If the master ignores this, they become seriously depressed or aggressive toward the favored individual.

Contempt is a device for maintaining the rank order without aggression. Dogs are past masters at this. One summer, we spent a few days at the cottage of some friends of ours, and every morning we were visited by Betty, a young German shepherd female from the neighborhood. Flip was still a puppy and the two dogs had a great time playing together. Betty felt already so much at home in our cottage that she started to exhibit a serious interest in the dinner plates on the table that emitted some tantalizing aromas. I warned her off and thoughtlessly told Flip not to let Betty to the table. I cannot quite figure out what Flip understood from my words and gestures, but from that moment on, Betty could not approach the table closer than seven feet, because Flip would growl at her and even attack her exuberantly. Flip's hostility manifested itself only around the table, and otherwise the two dogs got along well. I am not sure whether everybody will agree with me that this story illustrates contempt, but seeing Flip strutting around the table and Betty cowering in the distance, I think that this is the most appropriate term. It is also possible that this is a case of selective aggression, since Flip exhibited hostility only around the table. But then it is also possible that when we have contempt for somebody, we are exercising selective aggression.

The basic human emotions can be classified into finely differentiated subcategories. We can love a person, or like a person, or positively adore a person. Our affection may be lasting or it may be a case of love at first sight. I believe that such refinements of feelings have come to characterize dogs, too, and I would like to support this claim with two firsthand stories. One year, we used to walk with Flip at the edge of Castle Hill where there is a large parking area and some grounds with lots of bushes. On one occasion, we met several people walking their dogs, among them a middle-aged woman with an Irish setter. I noticed that while most of the dogs fraternized with each other or approached this person or that, the Irish setter had eyes only for its mistress, played only with her, and seemed to care for her and pay attention to her exclusively. This behavior was so striking that I struck up a conversation with the woman to ask about the dog's prior history. She told me an astonishing tale. She was living by herself and discovered the Irish setter about a year earlier; the dog lived in a house on a street on which she habitually walked to go to work. Both going to and coming from work, at roughly the same time of the day, she would stop for a few minutes by the fence where the dog lived and would speak to it and reach in to caress it. This went on for a while and she was beginning to anticipate her meetings with this amiable dog. Sometimes the dog would be there, but sometimes it would not. Half a year before I struck up the conversation with her, a peculiar thing happened. She was just returning from work and the dog was there, but so was an elderly and rather well-dressed man holding a leash in his hands. The man opened the garden door and told her that he and his wife loved the dog but they really could not cope with it any longer, because the dog became restless about an hour before the woman's appearance and would go and sit in the garden to wait for her. If they locked it in the house, the dog would jump around, whine, and cry. He concluded that the dog had developed a special fondness for the woman on the other side of the fence and they decided not to torment the dog any longer but give it to her, if she was willing to take it. And then he handed her the leash. The woman was aghast at this gallant offer—the dog was an expensive purebred that she could never have afforded—and in tears she thanked the man and quickly left with a visibly happy dog. Is it not true that to behold is to love? And I particularly value the magnanimity of the original master and think that few people would be capable of such a gesture.

Perhaps the previous story is about worship, while the next one, my own, is about a sudden burst of sympathy. An important antecedent of the event is that when Flip was still a puppy, he developed a great liking for Eve's small, mouselike velvet doll (she always claimed that it was a small dog, but it is obvious by looking at it that it is a botched attempt at a mouse), which was kept on a small table and which Flip periodically borrowed. But Eve did not approve and his naughtiness was always followed by scolding. After a few weeks, Flip began to respect property rights, and for many years he did not borrow the mouse at all. In the meantime, we moved, the mouse was kept in a new place, and Flip grew up. We never noticed whether he ever removed the mouse from its new place. The years passed and at one time a weekly magazine asked me for an interview. It turned out that the reporter who interviewed me was a sympathetic, attractive, in fact positively beautiful blonde young woman. Flip greeted her with unusual joy, jumped up and down around her, licked her, and when we sat down to work, he cuddled up to her. We were chatting when suddenly Flip leaped up, left the room, and returned after a few minutes with the toy mouse in his mouth. He took it to the interviewer and gently dropped it in her lap. Does anyone need a further explanation? (To this day, Eve has smelled a rat.)

Faithfulness, Emotional Identification, and Mourning

The legendary faithfulness of dogs is easily explained by their ability to bond. A dog that bonds powerfully feels good only with its master and is capable of anything just to be with or get to its master. It is simple to assess the degree to which a dog bonds with its master. We need to observe, in a place not familiar to the dog, how it positions itself when the master remains seated for some length of time. Dogs that bond strongly will lie down in such a manner that a modicum of physical contact is maintained with the master. Dogs that bond less strongly will remain near the master but without physical contact. Touching expresses a close connection, just as among humans. Of course, there are varieties that avoid contact, such as chow-chows, but they bond just as well as contact-loving varieties.

Empathy, the ability to identify emotionally, is a characteristic human trait and is a synchronizing mechanism that was as important in early social groupings as it is now. Emotional identification helps us understand what our companions are doing, why they are doing it, and how we can help in their endeavors. Or, on the contrary, understanding their emotional motivations might help us to talk them out of something. An identical emotional state triggers in us the behavioral mechanisms with which we can help somebody. We can truly help a family member or a friend who is sick or does not feel well if we are able to feel his or her pain. In contrast to all other animals, dogs that love their masters are capable of empathy. If somebody is ill and bedridden in our family (fortunately this does not occur too often), Flip will not budge from the bedside. He even forgoes his much beloved walk and does his business right in front of the house, and then rushes back to the sick person. On one occasion, Eve suddenly felt ill; so much so that we had to call a physician, our good friend Kate. The physician pondered for quite a while what might have caused the cramp that made Eve feel ill, and she was most astonished by the fact that Flip, who would not leave the bed, exhibited the same external symptoms as the patient. He gagged, groaned, sighed, and was visibly dejected. First she thought that the dog was also sick and that both of them might have ingested some poisonous substance. Fortunately, after a few hours, the mysterious cramp disappeared. Whether this was a result of the several injections that Eve received or whether it just happened by itself was never clarified, but she suddenly began to feel better. Within two minutes, Flip also recovered, without any treatment, and accompanied our physician friend to the front door with merry leaps. As Kate was leaving, she muttered, shaking her head, "I have never seen such a thing and could not even have imagined it." I have recorded a number of similar incidents in my notes.

Emotional identification in dogs is not only the attainment of some kind of passive harmony, but enables them to carry out intelligent actions. Several cases are described by Masson.[5] A border collie called Gilly realized that the family's newborn child was not breathing. He woke the parents from their deep sleep and they were able to save the baby's life. Spurred by this success, Gilly thereafter always signaled when the unsupervised baby started to cry. In another incident, a dog trained to assist the hearing impaired noticed that the family cat, exploring on the cold kitchen stove, had accidentally turned on the gas. The dog's trainers had not thought of preparing it for such an eventuality, but the dog nevertheless called its master to the kitchen and signaled that something was wrong with the stove.

I also have a few Flip stories that illustrate the empathy of dogs and their readiness to provide intelligent help. On one occasion, after a hard day, I was tired and asked Eve to take him walking. It was already fairly late at night, when the walks tended to be short, and I soon heard the door slam when they returned. It was not the first time for this, and usually, after the walk, Flip would come in to "announce his presence," and after some caresses he would lie down in his customary sleeping place. On that evening, he came into the room, but instead of coming to me, he stopped at the door trembling and called me with his characteristic body language. I did not understand what might have happened; he had already had his dinner, water is always available to him, and they had just returned from a walk. What could he want? I got up to follow him, we walked through several rooms, and he led me to the bathroom door, where he stopped, nodded toward the door, and emitted a high-pitched "arf." I then realized that the light in the bathroom was on and I could hear the sound of running water and some tearful sniffling. It turned out that Eve had slammed the iron corridor door on her finger. It is clear that Flip recognized her emotional state, but if that was all, he might have stayed with her to console her. Instead, he came to fetch me, obviously hoping that I would provide help.

The star of another story was a dog well known to us. Flip might have been about two years old, and on our walks we often encountered Uncle George, a retired forest ranger, and his German shorthaired pointer bitch, Jacky, who was maniacally fond of balls. Jacky wanted people to throw tennis balls for her and she loved to run after them, and she could play this game for hours. When Uncle George tired of the game, Jacky would take the ball dripping with saliva and drop it in front of a stranger, just in case she could find a willing playmate. Jacky and the tennis ball were inseparable. Uncle George liked Flip a lot, and once when Jacky went into heat, he thought that Flip might be the most appropriate father of Jacky's pups. We discussed the details and settled on our apartment as the appropriate venue for the amorous encounter. At the appointed time, the bell rang and the receptive female and her master appeared to Flip's boundless joy. After a brief chase game, it seemed to us that the arranged meeting might have been a bit premature, and Jacky just lay down by her master's chair. Flip disappeared for a few moments in the depths of our apartment and soon reappeared with a tennis ball, which he placed carefully and precisely in front of Jacky's nose. Of course, Jacky grabbed it and would not let go of it until they were ready to leave. In other words, Flip recognized Jacky's infatuation with balls, was able to think about it, and was willing in the given situation to satisfy his unrequited longings out of pure love.

What is really interesting is that in the case of dogs that bond strongly, this type of caring does not manifest itself only in such overt instances. I will never forget that one summer in my country garden I was cutting the grass when it started to rain heavily. I only had a few dozen square feet left to do, and I thought I would finish the job anyway. Jerry arrived at that point and indicated with loud barks that I should stop and seek shelter. I nevertheless persisted while he waited for me, and when I finished, he accompanied me to the house with indignant barking. "Well, you sure have been dressed down," noted Eve, who witnessed the incident.

Emotional identification is an important element in cooperating with groups. Alaine Polcz describes the following case in his excellent book.[6] In 1944, during World War II, a group of a few men and women wanted to sneak through the Russian front on a cold winter night to get to a village defended by Russian troops. Earlier, two adult vizslas had joined the group. The group saw that the Russian guards were systematically patrolling back and forth in the area where they wanted to cross. After some discussion, they decided that when the patrols faced them, they would lie flat in the snow, and when the Russians turned away from them, they would jump up and run forward a short distance and lie down again before the Russians turned in their direction. They thought that they might succeed in crossing the critical area if they alternated between lying in the snow and running forward. But they did not know what to do with the two dogs. They could not chase them away, because the guards would become aware of the dogs, and they did not know what might happen if the dogs decided to run around just when it was necessary to lie down. There was no time to figure this out further and they got started anyway, alternately lying down and running, and to everybody's amazement, the two vizslas did exactly the same.

Of course, emotional identification is not a simple matter. For example, humans are able to act at cross-purposes to their given feelings. If somebody steps on our toes in the subway but mutters some apology, we are willing to suppress the feelings of aggression engendered by the act, no matter how unpleasant it felt. This is a very important element in our social relations. Dogs are also able to act contrary to their feelings. It can occur, although not very often, that during play or a walk, I inadvertently cause the dog pain by, say, stepping on his foot. In such a case, as befits a decent master, I apologize immediately, and the dogs know exactly that I did not cause the unpleasantness on purpose. At such times, Jerry would press against me and would let me know with a deep rattle in his throat that his foot hurts, for sure, but in the meantime he is cuddling with me and is licking my hand. In other words, he forgives. The story is the same in reverse if they accidentally cause me pain. As a rule, this happens if they inadvertently bite me in the course of excited play. I would then signal my pain with an audible "ouch" and they would then indicate with intensive wagging and licking that the whole thing was a mistake and they were sorry.

Conciliatory behavior is, of course, well known among the apes as well. It has also been observed among wolves that if a subordinate animal manages to gain some "illicit" advantage, for which it is punished by the dominant individuals, the subordinate will later approach the dominant ones and signal in all possible ways that it is truly a subordinate member of the group and that it had no intention whatever to consider its prank as a sign of its own superiority. If my dogs get scolded for some reason, for example, I communicate my displeasure by some shaking of skin folds or a light tap, they suffer the punishment by immediately assuming a subordinate position and try to distance themselves from me as much as possible. After a few minutes, they want to reestablish good relations and reappear, approaching with vigorous wagging and asking to be caressed. On such occasions, Flip gently takes my hand in his mouth for some minutes and holds it until he feels that I have forgiven him. Jerry also apologizes in a most expressive manner.

There are numerous, well-documented stories showing that in exceptional cases dogs are capable of experiencing the pain of grief.[7] After the death of their beloved master, they have been known to stop eating, to guard the master's tomb, and often to die. I quote from a letter by one of my readers, which illustrates behavior in connection with a death.

> My eighty-year-old father died on New Year's Day in 1990 after a minor accident, which ultimately proved fatal. He died at home. He had been bedridden for weeks and from time to time we let the dog visit him [a German shepherd called Manny] because he loved it very much. He died at 9 p.m. and the doctor came at about 11. It was cold and the dog would usually spend the evenings in the kitchen and the nights in the courtyard. I was very sad, and I was quietly caressing it and speaking to it. The doctor said that my father would not be moved until the next day and accordingly, we let the dog out in the courtyard. Nevertheless, the funeral parlor's transport arrived at 4 a.m. The dog seemed struck dumb, although at other times he would respond to the front doorbell with loud barks and jumps and was difficult to control. On this occasion he was entirely silent, even though four or five men clad in black were standing in front of the garden door. I had anticipated that he might be difficult to control, but when I called him, he silently came to me at once. I took him to the kitchen lest he interfere in some way. This was the first time that he behaved gently: he knew that something quite extraordinary had happened and that he should not bark or jump around, but should quietly go to the kitchen, lie down, and stay put. That is what he did. Next day, I let him in my father's room. The dog did not run around, did not sniff left or right, did not look for a toy, but went to the empty bed, lay down next to it, and put his head on his feet.

No matter how we might try to analyze this story, it is quite certain that dogs are capable of recognizing and identifying with the deepest feelings of humans.

Pride, Disgust, and Morality

There are many stories about dogs being able to experience pride after a job well done. Masson mentions in his book the general experience of dog trainers that as an animal progresses in mastering its task, it becomes increasingly self-confident and increasingly delighted by success and praise.[8] He even mentions a case in which a dog was proud of its own discovery. In a kennel, each dog was kept in a separate cage, and a young German shepherd bitch learned how to open the cage door. She not only opened her own cage, but before the morning exercise hour, she went from cage to cage and let all the other dogs out, and then presented herself to the upset trainers with delighted wagging of the tail. Twice they changed the locking mechanism of the cages, and both times she figured out how to open them, and signaled with increasing pride that she was able to solve this problem, too, even though nobody had praised her for it.

In the more distant past, I always reacted to these stories with skepticism, until one day in the country, Flip supplied me with eloquent proof of dogs' feelings of pride. On our afternoon walks in the country, one of his favorite occupations was to dig up the holes of field mice. After we had bought our country house, he did this for months without any results, because the field mice somehow just disappeared. One summer afternoon, persistence bore fruit. Flip was on a walk with Eve when he dug up a field mouse nest, the unfortunate inhabitants of which—a few bare babies—were unable to flee. Flip was overjoyed and took one of the by now lifeless babies in his mouth and started out for our house. After a good walk of a mile and a quarter he arrived home and haughtily placed the prey at my feet. Needless to say, I praised him for the effort, but the remains did not interest him any longer.

Many have claimed, including the famous ethologist Desmond Morris,[9] that dogs are capable of feeling ashamed when they violate some rule, for example, when they chew the master's slippers to bits and the crime is discovered. The problem with this phenomenon is that when the corpus delicti is discovered, the master usually turns to the dog with a portentous tone of voice: "What have you done?" To which the dog responds with the usual behavioral forms of the subordinate. My inclination is to attribute this more to the fact that the question always contains an element of a threat, and dogs probably recognize this and fear the reproach or the likely punishment. Shame is an emotion of very high order, and among humans, it is the expression of very complex social relations, which, I believe, dogs did not need during the course of domestication. It was much more important for them to understand the smallest signs of the master's displeasure, to which they could respond with the signals of subordination.

I am also unaware that dogs express disgust in any shape or form. They have hardly any need for that; the stomach and the constitution of predators are not much fazed by spoiled food.

Surprise is also missing from the repertoire of dogs' behavioral forms. When something unexpected happens, they get scared or aggressive, but they neither need nor exhibit the kind of surprise that is characteristic of humans in certain situations.

It is easy to see that dogs follow rules. De La Malle described a very interesting case in the nineteenth century.[10] At that time, spits in the kitchens of inns were often turned with the aid of a clever little mechanism activated by dogs walking around in a circle. In a busy kitchen, they would have several dogs assigned to this task, and according to the story, on one occasion they could not find the dog that was due to work on the next order, so they enlisted the help of another one that had been scheduled to work later. The latter put up a resistance and bared its teeth, and from under a chair threatened the staff members who were trying to make it do its job. They finally gave up and went looking for the missing dog, and when they found it, it allowed them to harness it to the mechanism without resistance, as did the previously resisting dog when its proper turn came. After all, when it is your turn, it is your turn. According to the author of the story, this provides a nice illustration of dogs' sense of justice. Masson mentions a case from more recent times: contrary to the police code of conduct, an American policeman abused a woman with his nightstick, whereupon his trained police dog attacked him and took the nightstick away from him.[11] According to Masson, we could interpret this to mean that the dog had some kind of moral sense of what was licit and what was not, but we could also suppose that it was simply obeying the police code of conduct.

Darwin believed that some individual dogs are capable of even higher order emotions. Some dogs are particularly faithful to their masters, while others have a particularly strong love for them. This feeling is somehow a precursor of what humans feel toward their god.[12] Darwin emphasized—and I agree—that the acquisition of morality by humans is the result of complex social relationships of a very high order, and the potential for morality might just as well be left to humans. If dogs take up speech someday, about which writers have often fantasized,[13] and develop the ability to think at length about social relations and their own feelings, then and only then will there be a basis for their developing moral behavior. Until then, let us be satisfied that in contrast to all other animals, dogs are capable of following rules, as I will show in the next chapter; but of course, emotions are not the only factor in this.

Chapter 6

Obeying the Rules

Personal Rituals and Stereotypes

Humans develop personal habits, and somehow these become ritualized and develop into rules over the years. Psychologists refer to these habits as stereotypes. For example, when we get up in the morning and get ready to go to work, we do a number of things, and in a particular order, and these activities become a ritual. It does not make too much difference whether we drink our coffee first and then put on our clothes or conversely, but all of us have our habits concerning these matters and we stick to them. People feel at ease when they carry out their tasks in the right order. One great advantage of such rituals is that we no longer need to think about the tasks at hand; everything happens by itself, one does not forget anything, the glasses and the wallet are in the appropriate place, and we are not tortured by the thought of having forgotten something, because we know that if we unfailingly stick to the morning ritual, everything will be in order.

The formation of stereotypes can be observed among animals as well. Animals kept in a confined space often walk back and forth or engage in other systematic or regular behavior. But rituals are born not only from confinement. Rituals can develop among multiple participants and become a social behavioral pattern. This is most readily observed when animals play together, particularly in the case of apes.[1] Two individuals who often play together tend to learn the forms of behavior with which each can initiate or continue a habitual game, and each tends to respond to such an invitation with some predictable behavior. They observe each other and learn easily, as a result of which the game exhibits unified conventions and ground rules. Chimpanzee A knows exactly that the raising and waving of an arm by B will be followed by energetic tickling, which A accepts by exhibiting the appropriate learned sign, which has also been learned by B. The development of personal rituals makes it easy to forecast the behavior of particular individuals, because in repetitive situations they both conduct themselves accordingly.[2]

Dogs easily develop such behavioral rituals, too. We may not even notice them, but in our daily life—unless we lead a very disordered one—our dogs get used to certain ways of doing things, including when we do them and in what order. We will return to the question of rituals in the chapter about the minds of dogs[3] because rituals have a prominent role in allowing the mind to work independently of the environment. Here we are concerned only with the *development* of ritual behavior, because it is probably an important component of obedience to rules.

Jerry's Rituals

For the sake of illustration, I discuss and briefly explain below Jerry's daily rituals.

1. *The wake-up yip in the morning.* I tend to get up in the morning at different times, particularly if I have been working at night. Flip is happy to sleep till all hours, but by seven-thirty Jerry gets tired of lazing around and he comes into the bedroom to check on the situation. This usually wakes me, but I keep my eyes shut and listen to what he is doing. He first comes to the bed and checks whether my eyes are open. If yes, he begins to jump around as if to say "Let's go walking." If my eyes are shut, he quietly withdraws, as most dogs will leave a sleeping

person alone. He returns in about five minutes, and then again a little later, and finally he tries to wake me with a puppylike high-pitched
whine. If that proves to be unsuccessful, he comes right up to the bed
and wakes me with a peculiar and loud yip. It will be better if I do not
describe what happens if I am stubborn at this point, because the
reader would conclude that my dogs have been brought up very badly.

2. *The bedcover game.* When Flip, and later Jerry, were puppies, we often played the game (sometimes also played with children) of cover-
ing their heads with a towel and asking, "Where is the dog (or the
child)?" In such a situation, dogs remain motionless for a second or
two, as if they were saying, analogously to children, "Nowhere." Then,
suddenly, they will get rid of the towel and rejoice in the greeting
"Here is the dog (or the child)." Well, Jerry was two years old but
would not miss this game for the life of him. We always had to play the
game when I made the bed in the morning and placed the cover on
it. Before putting the cover on the bed, I had to put it over him with
the exclamation, "Where is Jerry?" Then, while I shouted, "Here is
Jerry," I helped him crawl out from under the heavy cover. If he were
elsewhere, with another member of the family, when I was making
the bed, he would listen to the noises emanating from my bedroom,
and as soon as he heard the noises characteristic of bed making, he
would quickly run to me lest he miss the morning bedcover game. In
the evening, when I turned down the bed and the bedcover was removed, he never asked to play the game.

3. *Requesting a cookie with growls.* After I get up, I usually go to the
kitchen. Jerry goes and stands by the cookie jar and waits. If this does
not lead to anything, he "begs" with a deep growl, the origins of
which I will discuss later. He does this repeatedly if necessary.

4. *The pulling of pants' legs.* When I have finished with my own bathroom rituals, I start to get dressed, and putting on my trousers is an
obvious part of that. That provokes an irresistible grabbing urge in
both Jerry and Flip. With deep growls they grab my pants' legs, which
obviously makes it hard to put them on. This gives them great pleasure, particularly when I am in a hurry.

5. *Good-bye bark for Bubu when he is not around.* Bubu is a Pekingese (also known as Peking Palasthund) that lives on the floor above us and usually sits in a window that is easily visible from our front door. When he sees that we are preparing to go on our morning walk, he greets us with indignant barking. Our dogs are not allowed to respond to this, and we usually depart in silence but with our pride intact. However, if Bubu is not at his customary post, Jerry will bark loudly, no matter what I do, and look toward Bubu's window. Sometimes, but not always, his barks bring Bubu to the window.

6. *Urinating at a certain point on the road leading to the bridge.* Voiding is permitted only after the dogs have been let loose on a hill that is five minutes away. That is the rule, but Jerry scent-marks on a little-used side road leading to the bridge, and always at the same spot.

7. *Leash pulling at the top of the hill.* When we get to the foot of the hill, I let both dogs loose and they can run around freely, socialize with other dogs, stay with me, or explore in the bushes. Every day, when we get to the top, Jerry joins me and unambiguously demands the leash that is in my pocket. I throw him one end of the leash and with deep growls he tries to catch it and take the leash away from me. As soon as Flip realizes this, he comes to my assistance and "attacks" Jerry; the chase and the tugging of the leash may last a minute or two.

8. *A leash game on the return trip, at the head of the bridge.* Afterward, they do not touch the leash again until the start of the return trip, when Jerry tries to play with the leash attached to his collar; for some thirty feet he tries to grab the leash, but in the end he leaves it alone.

9. *The bringing of a towel in rainy weather.* When we return home on a rainy day, the routine is to get toweled dry. Most often, Jerry will go to the bathroom without being told and bring his towel.

10. *Jerry's breakfast.* Jerry happens to be a thin dog who runs around a lot and the veterinarian suggested that he also get a morning meal. Jerry knows that he is supposed to get breakfast and if I am slow in giving it to him, he will sit down in front of me in a begging pose

characteristic of dogs and lick his lips. Only breakfast can make him stop this behavior.

11. *Calling to be caressed on the bed.* After his walk, no matter which one of us took him, I usually sit at my computer and do miscellaneous work. I soon hear Jerry "whistling" from my bed in a high voice like a puppy. This lasts until I finally get up and caress him and give him a good mauling. Afterward, he rapidly assumes his guard post in the front hall so that he may bark at the people passing on the other side of the front door.

12. *Invitation to an afternoon walk.* Around 3 p.m., if I have given no sign of preparing to go on a walk, Jerry will appear and look at me in a definitely questioning manner. As a rule, I try to gain time with the expressions "not yet," "right away," or "wait a little," but this gains me at most a few minutes. If I do not seem to be getting ready to go, Jerry starts to bark and demand his afternoon walk in an increasingly determined manner. If it happens that I have time for a walk only later, I can stop his pestering with a determined and loud no, whereupon Jerry, acting offended, returns to his guard post. In another hour, Flip will appear and urge me to go on a walk. Sooner or later we set out on our walk. Thus goes the hard life of our experimental dogs.

13. *Begging for dinner.* After the afternoon walk comes the evening meal. If it does not arrive promptly, Jerry poses the appropriate question by ostentatiously licking his lips.

14. *Begging for some dog food during dinner preparation.* It is a bit complicated to prepare dinner for the two dogs because they eat different food. Flip is on the heavy side and older, and he gets a light meal designed for senior dogs, which we soften with a broth. Jerry gets meat as well as high-carbohydrate dog food, which he consumes with soup. When I go to the pantry for the day's rations, Jerry always follows me and begs for (and receives) a bit of Flip's dog food, which he is reluctant to eat at other times.

15. *Asking for a walk after we turn off the computer or the television set.* The evening walk is usually short and takes place at an undetermined time.

Usually Jerry asks to go for a walk when he hears that I have turned off my computer. He rushes in from the front hall and indicates in all conceivable ways that we must absolutely go now. The same happens on those rare occasions when the whole family is watching TV together and at the end of the program I turn it off. Jerry responds to this signal by jumping around and generally acting in a demanding way.

16. *Asking for a walk in other instances.* If Jerry gets no signal from my turning off the computer or television set that it is time for a walk, nor from the departure of some guests, he usually tries for it anyway around 11 p.m.

17. *Asking to accompany a departing guest to the elevator.* Jerry listens to conversations with rapt attention, and when he thinks that they are over, he approaches, looks questioningly, and sometimes whines in a pleading manner.

18. *Asking for a blanket at nighttime.* In our country house, Jerry's sleeping quarters are in a room with a stone floor and he gets a blanket to sleep on. At night, if he is sleepy but nobody else seems ready to go to bed, he approaches and asks for his blanket.

19. *Asking for a game of hide-and-seek with a ball or a rubber toy.* We often play hide-and-seek in the evening. Jerry will bring us the object that he wants to play the game with and ask for the game to begin.

20. *Asking for an evening snack after the walk.* After the evening walk, the dogs look for a comfortable place to sleep. But Jerry still has one more thing on his agenda: he sits down in front of me and longingly licks his lips. Some time ago, after the evening walk, I had inadvertently given him a bit to eat from the refrigerator; since that time he asks for it daily, even though what he had gotten was only a tiny piece of cold cuts. This is a clear case of ritual consumption.

Some of the items in this list are tied to extraneous circumstances, such as pulling my pants' legs, for which I myself provide the provocation. Others depend on the order of events, such as the final snack after the evening

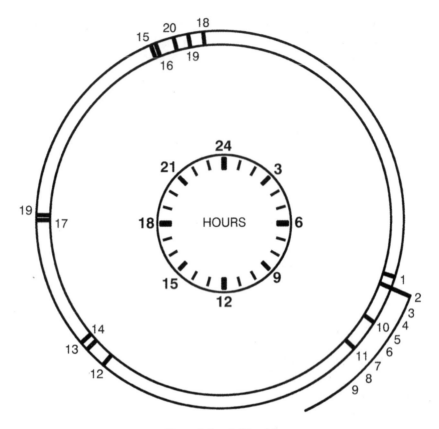

Figure 8. Jerry's Rituals*

*Numbers refer to numbered items in the text.

walk, and still others are connected to particular times of day, such as the walks. It is interesting to see the daily distribution of rituals (see figure 8).

These characteristics play an important role in the functioning of the canine mind. I shall return to this later, but suffice it to say here that these personal rituals can be defined as minor rules and, in contrast to taught behavioral forms that dogs are required to conform to, they develop by accident in the context of social activities. And the dogs themselves stick to them. One of my colleagues, Peter Pongrácz, is investigating the formation of canine rituals. So far, the data show that most family dogs have six to ten different rituals and that the development of rituals is as characteristic of dogs as it is of humans. There is no doubt that one can easily base the development of rule-observing behavior on such rituals. Thanks to the finely tuned emotions of dogs, they get easily attached to certain minor activities, which can be extended and made more complex through instruction. Finally, we may arrive at rule observing behavior that is quite humanlike.

Humans Observe the Rules

It has become clear from the analysis of the teachability of animals and humans that even the most developed animals are distinguished from humans by a peculiar sort of capacity to learn. Animals can learn signs and the relevance of points of time as quickly as we do and resemble us in associating signs with events or consequences. But only humans are able to learn and obey complicated social rules. This is a characteristic of our species. The experiments to teach language to the apes has revealed that a chimpanzee or a gorilla can easily learn a "vocabulary" consisting of a few hundred signs, but it is unable to learn the order in which words or signs must be used or the rules that describe the relationship among them. In other words, the animal mind is unable to learn grammar.[4]

I have mentioned that from the ethological point of view, obeying rules represents the capacity to subject ourselves to impersonal dominance. A socially accepted rule replaces the dominant individual, and the subordinated person carries out the instruction embodied in the rule. Humans have the ability to find the proper place in the rank order for the various rules. Thus, the rank order maintained in human groups has a dual nature and contains both persons and rules.

In an animal group, the behavior of the individual in particular situations is governed by the social rank order. This plays an important role among humans as well, but at times one finds that a certain position in the rank order is occupied by a *prescriptive rule*, which humans obey as faithfully as the instructions of a superior. It is quite certain that the development of rituals preceded rule-obeying behavior. This development was also influenced by certain rules, but even more by emotional triggers that do not need a rational explanation, but depend more on replicability and the precise repetition of some previous behavioral form. There is no accepted definition for rules, although there is a huge literature on the creation of rules, the obedience to rules, and the role of rules in the legal system and practical life.⁵ Equally relevant is the fact that language, the creation of objects, religious strictures, and practically any component of culture cannot develop or survive without rules. It is interesting that investigations into rules of various origins mostly begin with an examination of the system of oral or written rules, although it would be more exciting to ask how rule-obeying behavior developed in the course of evolution and how a biological foundation can be provided for this characteristic of ours, since its existence is by no means self-explanatory.

It makes sense to start out by asking how observed but unstated rules develop in small groups. Human groups that meet regularly quickly develop some local rules that promote order in communal living. For example, what, if anything, does one bring one's host? Nothing? Or perhaps a bottle of wine? What does one give the lady of the house? How do we dress for such an occasion so that we are neither excessively sloppy in our attire, nor overdressed? May one sit anywhere, or might a certain chair be reserved for a particular person? Does one have to be on time and when should one leave? Every small group develops dozens of rules without prior discussion and without even becoming aware that rules are being employed. From the point of view of an ethologist, it is unambiguous that the members of the group behave so as to minimize the possibility of conflict. If we violate one of the rules, minor unpleasantness may occur and we have to explain ourselves by saying, "The flower shop was closed" or "I am so sorry, but I completely forgot" and so on.

This type of conflict reduction manifests itself in all human groups, but this is only the simplest form of rule-observing behavior. A more highly developed form is that of the *explicitly stated rule*, which is drawn up by the group, and is thereafter treated as part of the group norm and followed by its members. Explicitly stated rules can come into being only after the development of language. Even more highly developed and complex behavior is demanded for formulating and instituting written rules. Rules for governing behavior are also very advantageous because they obviate the need for reexamining each time the appropriateness of various actions. It is entirely enough to just follow the accepted rules. Imitation and conforming to patterns also play important roles in the rule-following behavior of humans because they also enable group members of lesser ability to acquire complex and intelligent forms of behavior, which they could not do on their own.

Things do not work as smoothly in monkey troops. While the rank order determines what is permitted and what is not, the lives of monkeys are filled with conflict and they resolve their problems through continual aggression. According to F. De Waal, only chimpanzees have the capacity to avoid some types of behavior while actively engaging in others, that is, to follow rules. By doing so, they may avoid conflicts, although their behavior represents only the first steps in rule observance.[6] A chimpanzee can be taught many things, and with some practice can be taught to carry out some of the activities of humans living in small villages. But it would be useless to teach these activities to a few hundred chimpanzees: if we placed them in an empty village, they would never be able to develop the kind of social life that is characteristic of humans, because the members of the colony would be unable to obey the complex system of rules required for that. When they become hungry, they will sooner or later obtain food no matter what the cost, and they will satisfy their sexual urges immediately and by force if necessary. A human without money to buy food will often rather go hungry than steal from a food store. This would never happen in the case of an animal. Among humans hardly anything is more important than obeying the accepted rules. We breach them only in the name of an even more powerful system of rules.

Much social thought identifies the promulgator of the rules with ancestors or with gods, but the majority of humans are convinced by the notion that certain things "just have to be done this way or that." Obedience can be exacted even by referring to presumptive rules. Humans are very sensitive to relations of dominance, including those implied by paradigms of rules, and at the highest levels of obedience to rules they accept them as an inner moral imperative.

Dogs Also Respect the Rank Order and Readily Accept Rules

Every normal dog owner knows that a well-brought-up dog can easily be made to accept rules. This peculiar behavior rests on three auxiliary mechanisms. First is the above-mentioned conflict minimization: if we are consistent in teaching the dog, sooner or later it will act as we want. For example, it will walk on our left or our right, stop at the curb, and not jump on the table. We do not even need to provide special training or punishment; it is sufficient if we consistently and frequently reinforce the desired behavior. Dogs greatly respect the rank order and they are particularly obedient if their master is consistent. The second auxiliary mechanism is their characteristic of *following personal rituals*. If we carry out an activity with a dog several times in a row, at the same time, in the same place, and in the same way, then the dog will be inclined to carry out this activity on its own initiative and in the same way. The third mechanism is the dog's *pattern-imitating* behavior, which I will discuss in a later chapter.[7]

A dog brought up in a family environment realizes early in life how useful it is to minimize conflict. It may not eliminate indoors, it cannot go out when it wants, it may not chew shoes or carpets, but on the contrary, it is encouraged to chew its ball or other toys. The dog is encouraged to do certain things; for example, to come when called by the master, for which it is usually rewarded, or to fetch the leash when commanded, for which it is again rewarded. Sooner or later it realizes that among the many possible activities some are followed by conflict, such as punishment, while other actions, possibly quite similar, result in rewards. Dogs differ from other animals not only in their great interest in joint activities with humans, but also in the fact that through domestication they became, as we did, self-regulating. Dogs are also able to refrain from carrying out an action. For example, a puppy is easily taught to wait patiently until the food is placed in its dish and to start eating only after it has received permission to do so, no matter how hungry it is. To accomplish this, it is sufficient to restrain a puppy by hand a couple of times or to rebuke it verbally, and the relevant rules are rapidly instilled. It is a genetic characteristic of dogs to obey a person superior in the rank order. It will stop at the curb and look at its master, waiting for permission to cross the road. If this is reinforced over some years, it will act similarly when it becomes an adult and not even the greatest temptation will make it break the rule.

David Freedman examined in one experiment the extent to which dogs could internalize a rule they had been taught, that is, obey it even if there was no threat of punishment.[8] Pieces of meat were placed near the puppies and they were punished a few times if they ate them. When they had learned what was required and did not even look at the meat, Freedman left the room. The basenji puppies immediately attacked the food and ate it, while the shelties did not touch it. It follows that genetic factors play a significant role on obeying the rules and the behavior of different breeds can be quite different.[9]

An important role is played by the dog's environment, for example, by the consistency of the master. If the rule says that the dog must sometimes stop at the curb, but may sometimes cross the street without stopping, the dog will invariably select the most favorable alternative. Possibly it may learn that punishment is not such a big deal and that it is sometimes worthwhile to take a chance on it. This holds equally for children. It is simply not true that voluntary control of one's behavior is natural in the animal kingdom. If one tried to teach some of the behavior discussed earlier to, say, a badger, one would realize almost immediately that it is a hopeless task. If an otherwise tame badger is prevented from attaining its objective, it will attack immediately. It has its own ideas about possible activities, and these can be altered in minor ways only through very substantial rewards or punishments, which is the reason that we see trained dogs in circuses but no badgers. Badgers are not social creatures and are unable to develop conflict-avoidance behavior.

Our examples of decision rules are all of the simple "yes/no" or "permitted/not permitted" variety. Social life among humans is organized on the basis of much more complex rules.

A famous old experiment by psychologists was aimed at investigating whether children have any concept of the *permanence* of objects. The concept that objects are permanent is entirely natural for adults, but not so for a few-months-old baby or for an animal. If we show a toy to a three-year-old child and then, in plain sight, hide it under a blanket, the child knows that the toy did not disappear and that it exists somewhere. The child saw that we placed it under the blanket and it is therefore sure that the toy is there and will surely look for it there. This is an insoluble mystery for a few-months-old baby, because it has not yet progressed to having a concept of the permanence of objects. If an object disappears, it will not look for it, because it does not exist. Similar experiments have been carried out with animals and it turns out that apes and dogs have a well-developed concept of the permanence of objects and are able to successfully complete tasks related to this. We made a dog sit in front of three covered baskets and showed it a ball. We then hid the ball in one of the baskets, and showing our empty hands to the dog, told it to look

for the ball. The dog knew immediately which basket to look in. In a
more complicated version of this test we would place our hand holding
the ball under the covers of each of the baskets, one after another, showing the dog our hand after removing it from each basket so it could see
whether the ball was still in our hand. After the command to look for the
ball, the dog was supposed to go to the basket from which we withdrew
an empty hand for the first time. This more complicated task can be
solved by three-year-old children and by most dogs.

One day I wanted to see how Flip did in this experiment. I had never
done this with him and I thought it would be a complicated experiment,
because the dog has to sit quietly while one is hiding the ball and has to
pay attention so it can note from which basket the hand returns empty,
and even has to wait for permission to start the search. I thought that
Flip could learn this complicated game in four or five days. I confess that
I badly underestimated him: he needed no more than five minutes to
learn to find the hidden ball in the majority of trials. Then I became suspicious that I was not really testing his concept of the permanence of
objects but something entirely different. We were playing: Flip had to
sit, I hid the ball, and he looked for it. Perhaps he had learned only our
joint rules of the game? If so, the matter could be easily decided. If, after
some pretended hiding of the ball, I were to place it next to me and were
then to stick my empty hand in each of the baskets, then, even though he
would see that there was nothing to be searched for, he would still pretend to look for the ball, because that is what the joint rules of the game
prescribe. I tried this out, and to my great surprise, my theory turned out
to be right. Flip glanced at the ball lying next to me, but when I told him
to look for it, he searched all three baskets. Clearly, he was using the previously learned rules.

One experiment is no experiment, they say in my field, and therefore
one must not draw exaggerated conclusions from observing a single dog.
So we formed a small research team consisting of my colleagues József
Topál and Márta Gácsi and graduate student Zsuzsanna Sárközi and many
dogs, and they undertook unbiased repetitions of the rule-learning experiment. Since the permanence of objects is an important human mental construct and humans gladly learn the rules of a game, we thought it
would be most appropriate in the light of the advice of child psychologist György Gergely if we repeated the experiment with children as well

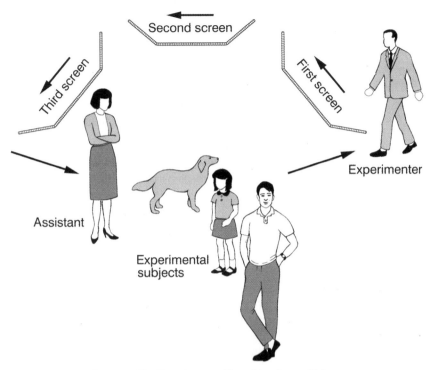

Figure 9. The Experiment of Searching for an Object

as with graduate students.[10] The participants in the experiments were 18 adult dogs, 24 children between the ages of 4 and 6, and 24 graduate students. We slightly altered the experimental setup. In essence, we set up three screens in a room behind which an object could be hidden. The role of the hand in the previous experiment (holding the ball or empty) was now assumed by a plastic bucket, and at the beginning of the experiment we placed in it the ball that was to be located. We showed this to each experimental subject, and then the experimenter would go, in turn, behind each of the screens, putter for a few moments, and then show the subject whether the ball was still in the bucket or not. While going behind the screens, the experimenter would leave the ball behind one of them and would then return to his starting point and exhibit the empty bucket (see figure 9). At that point, either he (in the case of graduate student subjects) or the children's kindergarten teacher or the dog's master would give the signal for the start of the search. Each experimental subject searched several times, and, of course, the ball was left behind

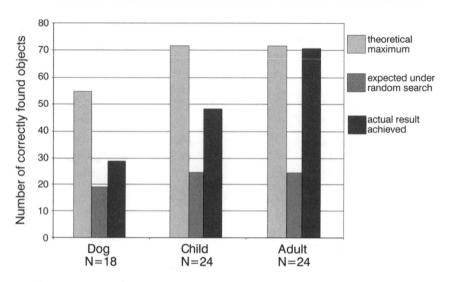

Figure 10. Results for the Experimental Subject in the Object Search Experiment

different screens from case to case. In order to ensure comparability, it was important that canines and humans have the same information set about the experimental setup. We therefore told the children and the graduate students—they had to be told something—only that this was an experiment, that they had to guess what they were supposed to do, and that anything that they did was a part of the experiment.

The next figure shows that the adults hardly ever made an error in searching, while the dogs and the children had a more appreciable error rate, but even the results for the dogs were statistically significantly different from those that could be expected under random search (figure 10). This part of the experiment shows only that humans and dogs are able to note behind which screen the experimenter has hidden the ball. Of course, there are dogs as well as children who perform exceptionally well or very badly, while the adults all scored the maximum number of points.

The most exciting part of the experiment came after the experimental subjects had learned in the first part of the experiment how they were supposed to search for the hidden ball. In the next experiment, the experimenter stood in front of the subjects and was quite obvious about putting the ball in his pocket. He then showed them the empty bucket and disappeared behind the screens, where he pretended to be hiding

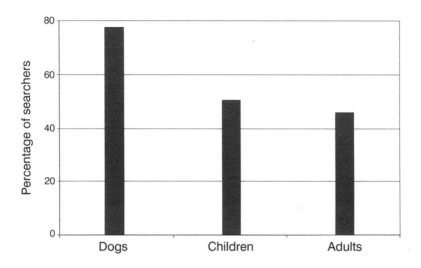

Figure 11. How Many Search for a Nonexistent Ball?

the ball. He then returned and gave the signal for the search to begin, and the experimental subjects could then look for the ball if they felt like it. All three groups—dogs, children, adults—had some smart participants who pointed to the experimenter's pocket: there is the hidden ball!

But cunning minds are rare: almost 50 percent of the graduate students pretended to search behind the screens, a somewhat higher percentage of children did so, and almost three quarters of the dogs (figure 11). We asked the students and the children why they did that, and all said that they had thought that searching behind the screen was the essence of the game, independently of where the ball really was, and they were just abiding by the rules.

I see no reason to doubt that the dogs had similar ideas. This is further supported by our examination of the videotapes we made of the experiments, from which it appeared that if the experimental subjects—the dogs, the children, and the students—saw the ball in the experimenter's pocket, their search for the ball behind the screens was of much shorter duration than when they believed it to be hidden there. They also looked at the experimenter more often when he had retained the ball than when he had hidden it behind one of the screens. It was very interesting—in the case of both the dogs and the humans—that when the ball was not in fact behind any of the screens, they seemed to be feigning the search.

They made exaggerated gestures suggesting search; for example, they inspected the corners of the ceiling to suggest that they were searching, although, as we know from our prior observations, they were all entirely clear about what the situation was.

This complicated experiment leads to a simple conclusion, namely that children as well as dogs are able quickly to learn and apply a set of rules, even if these rules have no apparent purpose or make no sense. In other words, *dogs are able to learn rules*, not only humans! Additional experiments have also shown that imitation and following patterns play a significant role in the formation of rule-obeying behavior, but I will discuss this later.[11]

If we reflect on our relationship with dogs from this point of view, it is not difficult to find further examples of their ability to learn rules.

Jerry is very fond of a particular rubber toy that consists of three rubber rings and that I call an "eared ball." Jerry's favorite game with it is to hold one end of it while I hold the other, and we play tug-of-war, during which he growls balefully and we try to take it away from each other. I tend to get tired of this game after a while, so I introduced certain rules. I first throw the toy and Jerry has to bring it back; but before the tug-of-war can begin, I throw it a second time, and it is only after Jerry has retrieved it a second time that the amiable but slightly aggressive game can begin. After a while I say, "I will throw it now," which indicates that two more rounds of throwing and retrieving must follow and the tug-of-war may continue only after those are completed. Jerry quickly learned the rules of this game.

Both dogs learned another game, of the hide-and-seek variety, very quickly, as a practical matter on the first try, when they were about six months old. I would take some small object and tell one of the dogs that we would play and would make him sit. I would then go to another room and hide the object and call out to the patiently waiting dog that he could come and search. Hearing the call, and only then, he would run into the room and excitedly begin to search for the object, which he would usually find. At times we played the game more than once. In the evenings, Jerry would often appear with an object in his mouth, and ask me to play the game with him by dropping it in my lap.

Sticking to the rules demands attention and a certain emotional state, which I can illustrate with another story. When Flip was a puppy, we often played hide-and-seek with him, too, but in those days Eve and I used to play the game together. One of us would hold Flip while the other hid the toy. This worked very well until, one day, I was at home alone and Flip was obviously bored. So the two of us tried to play hide-and-seek. He already knew the command "sit," which we employed when we wanted to prevent some activity: for example, when another dog was approaching on the street or we wanted to prevent him from stepping off the curb. So I took his favorite ball and commanded him to sit. Flip sat down, I hid the ball in the adjacent room, and then called him with "come and find it." Strangely, it took him some time to respond and he came very slowly and started to search very cautiously. I had to encourage him several times, and when he finally found the ball, he did not take it in his mouth and did not bring it to me; rather he just touched it with his nose and looked at me to make sure that I saw that the ball was there, and then he lay down. After that, no matter what I did, he was unwilling to start searching again. After long reflection, I realized that I was an idiot: the "sit" command, while not exactly a punishment, was certainly one with an unpleasant emotional content, and probably for that reason Flip did not want to play.

As I have mentioned before, dogs are very careful not to do things that provoke the master's displeasure. Except, of course, if the matter is very important to them. To see if we could prove this, we did not try to play hide-and-seek for three months, but in the meantime, we introduced another command, "csüccs" (chüch, meaning "sit"), which we associated with pleasant things.[12] We used it during the exciting moments before a departure or some carefree romping, in a friendly voice and as part of some jolly activities. Behavior corresponding to such an atmosphere developed rapidly and in three months came the iron test. Once again, I was alone with Flip. I took the ball, said "csüccs," and hid the ball in the adjacent room. Upon hearing the command "come," Flip rushed in and quickly found the hidden ball as of old. And it has worked like this ever since. As one may surmise, there exists a rank order even among rules, and for Flip, the first rule was not to do anything that might make the master angry or even seemingly angry.[13]

It is a tantalizing question whether a dog is capable of reflecting over the rule or whether the dog simply applies the rule automatically as the final stage of a learning process. I found this question truly exciting, and Flip and Jerry did give us satisfactory answers, although we still have to gather much experimental support.

For a long time, Flip was the only canine inhabitant of our country garden and soon learned to eliminate elsewhere; when he needed to, he would ask to be let out. Even more surprising to our neighbors was the fact that Flip never ran around in the flower beds, wherever he happened to be going, but always followed the narrow garden paths. We were indeed grateful to him for that. When Jerry arrived in his capacity as dog number two at the age of six weeks, it soon became clear that Flip's behavior in the garden was by no means natural. Jerry barged right through the flower beds when he was pursuing some desirable objective such as a bird or responding to the master's call. The straighter and the faster the better! We were quite irritated by this, but it turned out that we got good assistance from Flip in enforcing the rules. When I called the dogs and Flip rushed along the permissible paths, while Jerry started to trample our most beautiful flowers, he would get severely punished by Flip. As of today, Jerry also sticks to the regular paths, or to be quite accurate, he does not trample the flower beds but jumps over the narrower ones with six-foot leaps. Thus he sticks to the rules and is the first to get there.

Dog owners have known many similar cases in which the older, dominant dog "instructs" the younger: if it should violate a rule, the older one will growl at it and discipline it. From the point of view of studying evolutionary similarities, it is very important that dogs' observance of the rules is related to the rank order. It is therefore not far-fetched to say that the observance of rules among humans and dogs developed through identical mechanisms and similar forces of natural selection.

Chapter 7

Cooperation

Cooperation among humans is commonplace and is highly complex behavior. We shall describe it only briefly so that we can better understand the corresponding traits of dogs.

Human Cooperation

Let us imagine a tiny society, consisting of, say, two humans, who together have to solve a simple problem. Let us further imagine that the task at hand is to make a fire at the edge of a forest. First, they have to gather some wood; thin pieces as well as some thicker ones. They have to determine where the fire will be built and they may have to surround the fireplace with large stones so that the fire remains confined. Then they have to stack some wood in the fireplace, with thinner twigs near the bottom and thicker ones higher up. Finally, they have to light it with something such as a match or a lighter. If the wood used to make the stack is dry and if the twigs at the bottom are small, the fire will soon burn well.

If there are two people working at this, many of the individual tasks can be divided between them. One can collect stones, the other can gather the wood, but it is possible that both will work at every task. If a human ethologist were to observe their joint labor and document their activities, his report about their making a fire might read as follows.

Humans always start out by agreeing on a common goal and by recognizing the problem, and their objective is to solve it. For example, if they are cold or hungry, they will make a fire so that they can warm themselves or cook. They make a plan of action and subdivide the task into smaller subtasks, consisting in our case of determining the location of the campfire, collecting wood, stacking it, and lighting it. The subunits of the group complement each other in carrying out the jointly decided action. We may note that they observe certain rules in subdividing the tasks and in carrying out complementary actions. For example, they place the kindling under the thicker pieces of wood and they light the fire only after there is an adequate supply of wood on hand, and so on. It is an interesting characteristic of human cooperation that the identity of the leader of these activities frequently changes. Person A may give an instruction, "Please bring stones," while person B may say to A, "Put the wood behind the bush." A may ask for the matches and B may instruct him to light the fire from the other side. If an ethologist were to say that the person who gives the instructions for executing a partial task is the dominant one, the above form of cooperation would be seen to involve frequent alternations in the exercise of dominance. It is another characteristic of cooperation that much information is exchanged before and during the execution of the activity.

A conscientious ethologist would also have to note that this complex and harmonious cooperative behavior can occur only because human individuals are attracted to each other, tolerate the presence of others, like to participate in joint actions, are interested in the plans and actions devised by others, and in general are mutually quite willing to temporarily surrender their dominance. In other words, they obey a very flexible rank order designed for the particular objective.

We can summarize the characteristics of human cooperation as follows: (1) bonding, (2) recognition of the problem, (3) preparation of an action plan, (4) division of the task into complementary subtasks and the harmonious execution of these, (5) obedience to rules, (6) alternation in the exercise of dominance, and (7) information exchange.

Cooperation among Animals

An extended literature covers cooperation among animals, and we encounter joint activities among animals living in groups, beginning with insects and all the way to mammals.[1] This literature studies animal cooperation primarily from the point of view of evolutionary genetics. The most important question is whether it is worthwhile for an individual to cooperate with another. What is the distribution of costs and profits among the participants? In general, cooperation arises when each of the continually competing individuals benefits from it. In the case of insects—termites, ants, and bees—cooperation is the result of definite genetic factors. An ant colony is such a closed unit that it might even be regarded as a superorganism that has its own interests and without which the individuals could not survive on their own. Among higher animals, but particularly among monkeys and apes, there exists a genetic basis for the willingness to cooperate,[2] although learned behavior is decisive for cooperation. Among wolves, it is always the alpha male that leads the hunt. What is certain is that when they start out on a hunt, every individual knows what the activity is about. It is frequently observed that when they catch a glimpse of the prey and the alpha male begins to sneak up on it, some of the other wolves will circle around so that they can attack the prey from behind. This, too, can be construed as dividing the task into subtasks.

It is also the case that animals do not exhibit all seven of the characteristics listed above: among them we note only bonding, the recognition of the problem, and to a lesser extent, the subdivision of the action into complementary parts and the harmonious execution of these. What is missing is the preparation of a plan, the observance of rules, the alternation in dominance, and the exchange of information.

Dogs Cooperate Well with Humans

I have recounted many an anecdote the essence of which was cooperation among dogs and humans. There is a large professional literature on the day-to-day cooperation of dogs and humans and on the training of the various breeds, such as the herders, gun dogs, Seeing Eye dogs, and the helpers of the handicapped.[3] This literature says a lot about the rearing, training, and use of these dogs, but precious little about the interesting ethological implications of dog-human cooperation.

We actually started to investigate the capacity of dogs to cooperate from the ethological point of view, because numerous wolf researchers had claimed that wolves are able to carry out certain tasks much more intelligently than dogs.[4] The explanation was that during the process of domestication, dogs' intellectual capacity diminished, as it did among other domestic animals. But I could never accept this view, because it is precisely dogs that are used by us for numerous tasks requiring reason and intelligence. My collaborators and I had thought that the apparently superior performance of wolves might be due to the fact that dogs usually work in collaboration with humans but in subordinate roles.

The claim was seemingly supported by one of H. Frank's examples in which he reported that he kept a wolf, a malamute, and a wolf-malamute mix in his backyard. Its gate could be opened from the inside only by unlocking a complicated mechanism, which required a metal bolt to be retracted and then turned. The wolf needed to observe only once how the human unlocked the gate and was able thereafter to unlock it itself. The malamute never learned to unlock it, while the wolf-malamute mix needed to observe the process five or six times before it was able to master it. This seemingly proved that the wolf was very smart, the dog was stupid, and the wolf-malamute mix was in between. I am sure that Frank did not install the particular gate mechanism in order to enable his animals to come and go at will. The malamute, like any well-behaved dog, knew that it was not allowed to go outside, and accordingly obeyed the rule. The wolf, a self-reliant animal independent of humans, observed and learned how to get out, because it very much wanted to. The hybrid animal had both inclinations.

We were not inclined to try to replace Frank's theory with a new one by using the same data; rather we attempted to support our theory with experimental proof.[5] József Topál, Ádám Miklósi, and I carried out the following experiment with twenty-eight dogs of different breeds and their masters.

We brought the master-dog pairs into a room one at a time, where they first spent a few minutes together to allow us to make some prelim-

Figure 12. Analysis of How to Solve the Problem

inary observations. Then the experiment leader entered the room, conversed with the dog's owner briefly, and attempted to play with the dog. He then called both of them to an enclosed corner of the room in which the master was allowed to sit in a chair and the dog was confronted with a problem to be solved. The dog faced a firmly fixed wire fence with a gap at the bottom. Ten dishes with long handles and containing some cold cuts were placed under the fence just beyond the gap, with the handle of every other one pointing toward the dogs and the rest in the opposite direction. The dogs were able to grab the handles that pointed toward them and could thus pull the dish out and eat the reward, while they could not reach the other dishes. The experiment leader demonstrated the procedure by pulling out the dishes that had handles pointing toward him and eating the cold cuts (figure 12).

What did the dogs do? They were given three minutes to get hold of the cold cuts. There were some that got all the cold cuts and some that got none. There were a lot of differences among the dogs, but the results did not depend on their gender, age, breed, or whether they had gone to dog training school. The decisive factor was the relationship they had to their master. About half of them were chosen to be family dogs and half were "outdoor dogs," that is, guard dogs or dogs that had other tasks as a result of which they did not live indoors. It turned out that the dogs that were, in a sense, more independent, solved the problem with more verve and more successfully than those that lived indoors and were better

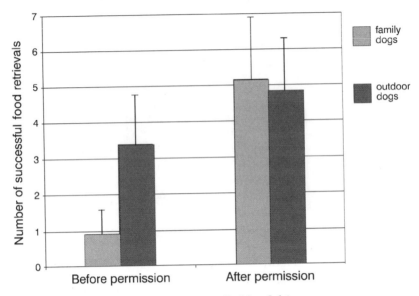

Figure 13. Success in Problem Solving

adapted to their masters; on average, the outdoor dogs obtained three times as much food as the others.

The masters of the dogs had to sit quietly for a minute and a half and not speak to their dogs. But in the remaining ninety seconds they could encourage their dogs any way they saw fit. The outdoor dogs did not wait for the encouragement and addressed themselves immediately to the task of getting the food, and soon got the hang of it. The indoor dogs, on the other hand, almost without exception waited for permission to start and frequently glanced at the master; they addressed themselves to the task only after permission or even positive encouragement had been given. But even so, there were some dogs that seemed to want the master to get up and help them (see figure 13). After permission was given, there was no difference in performance between the indoor and outdoor dogs.

I think that this result illustrates the methodological problem in the experiment that compared wolves with dogs. The wolf is independent, while the dog prefers to work under human direction, which is the source of the differential assessment of the intelligence of the two.

Four years have passed since the first edition of this book was published and we have learned a great deal in the meantime about the behavior of wolf pups and juvenile wolves. Enthusiastic graduate students, first and foremost Enikő Kubinyi, Krisztina Soproni, and Dorottya Uj-falusi, offered to participate in an experiment to rear a few wolves in an environment that guaranteed the closest possible contact between wolves and humans. We hoped that this experiment would highlight the behavioral differences between dogs and wolves. The pups came from the tame wolf pack kept by the animal filmmaker Zoltán Horkai. The pups were adopted by their human mothers even before their eyes were open and were kept in close physical proximity until they were three months old: at night they slept with their "mothers" and during the day they were carried around in baby carriers. Of course, in the daytime the foster mothers played with the pups a lot and took them on walks. They had daily encounters with the other wolf pups as well as with dogs, which displayed a lot of interest on these occasions. In the following periods, the close physical proximity was discontinued, but they were kept busy for several hours each day.

The pups grew rapidly and became very active as well as tame animals, although an outside observer might have doubted their tameness, mostly because they were very agile and tended to jump on everybody, and during their contacts with humans they occasionally emitted blood-curdling sounds that positively frightened inexperienced people. But we knew that the pups were extremely tame, which is confirmed by the fact that not once in their first two years did they bite or behave aggressively toward their foster mothers, in spite of the fact that by age one they were grown wolves. They frequently fought with each other and had to be separated in order to restore the peace. They bit each other on such occasions but never their caretakers. The situation was a bit different for others who worked on the wolf farm; several workers were slightly injured when they disturbed the pups' routine. One could probably attribute this difference to the fact that the foster mothers never forced the pups to do anything; everything was accomplished through persuasion and not by loud voices or physical force. We carried out a number of behavioral tests, and I shall report a few of these, but here I shall confine myself to a few general experiences gathered during the two years.

1. Wolves are much more independent and active than dogs of the same age. When a dog's master is not at home, the dog is no longer

on "active duty" and its activity level is low while it waits for its master's return. Not so in the case of wolves: they might look for something to eat, or an object to take apart, or something that can be destroyed, or, if there is more than one, they might engage in aggressive play.

2. Dogs are dependent on humans, while wolves are independent. They like their caretakers but do not bond with them. The bonding experiments have shown unambiguously that while wolves are very friendly toward everybody, in contrast to dogs, they do not bond with humans. They do not whine if the master leaves them and do not greet him or her when the master returns. One greeting a day is enough for wolves to express their affection toward the caretaker. But dog owners know that even if they leave their dogs ten times a day, their return will elicit delighted emotional outbursts in each and every case. In the so-called preference test, if six-week-old wolf pups can choose between physical proximity to a human or a strange dog, they will prefer the dog. Dogs, on the other hand, even if interested in another nearby dog, would first approach the human and only then, having established a secure base, go and investigate the other dog. Wolves are usually much more interested in an adult dog. Various communication tests have shown that dogs pay a lot of attention to humans and to their activities and await information and directives from them, but wolves do not. They may greet a human with pleasure, but are not interested in what he or she is pointing to or what activities can be undertaken jointly with humans.

3. Dogs can be inhibited in their activities; it is normally enough to tell them no, and the dog stops what it is doing. Wolves cannot be stopped in their activities in this manner. Contrary to other reports about tame wolves, our wolves responded to their names; however, in agreement with other reports, they are unstoppable when engaged in mischief. An attempt to stop them with force or dominance would elicit wild aggressiveness.

4. In general, wolves are much more aggressive than dogs. They become angry easily and attack each other with wild snarls and biting. One cannot take food away from them and they are quick to estab-

lish the power relations among them. In some Hungarian animal rescue organizations more than a hundred dogs are kept together and
are able to coexist peacefully. Under similar circumstances, wolves
would surely attack one another and probably only the strongest
among them would survive.[6]

On the basis of experience and some experiments, it seems reasonable to claim that bonding plays an important role in the collaboration
between dogs and humans, which is lacking among other animals, as does
the learning of rules, and to some extent, the identification of a problem.
Of course, in the majority of cases it is the humans who determine what
problem needs to be solved and dogs have no say in this. But collaboration can come into being only if the dog realizes itself what the problem
is. I cannot resist the temptation to recount here a childhood experience, which impressed me so deeply that I can still remember it in detail.
It supports the view that dogs are excellent at problem identification.

During the summer of 1946, a social service organization placed me
in the countryside with a well-to-do farm family for the summer holidays. The family had myriad animals: cattle, hogs, sheep, horses, geese,
and in general, everything one might encounter on a farm. Other children of my age or older were also participating in the holiday program
and I had numerous exciting and new adventures. One day, the women
were plucking geese; they would corner them, grab them one at a time,
and with rapid motions pluck their feathers. The plucked geese were let
go, and soon they congregated and awaited their friends with loud cack-
ling. There must have been some two hundred of them, and by late afternoon there was only one goose left that had not been plucked. But
they could not catch it; it kept escaping and mingling with the plucked
ones. The women were laughing and tried to catch it but could not,
while the other two hundred geese were running and jumping around.
While I was observing this vain effort, I had a brain wave and offered to
catch it with the assistance of Bugsy, a very smart and industrious puli,
with which I had excellent working relations, since we often herded the
sheep together. The women agreed to this suggestion. I called the puli
and we started to drive the by now rather excited gaggle of geese. Within
a minute, Bugsy caught the still-feathered goose and held it to the ground
until I arrived on the scene. I thought that this was entirely in order,

since I had told the Bugsy to catch the feathered goose. But even then, I was surprised by the dog's remarkable goal orientation that made him succeed at this task. He did not catch a single one of the plucked geese; in other words, it was not the luck of the draw. I realized then, as I do today, that he "knew" what the task was.

We will now turn to examples of more complex collaboration arising with Seeing Eye dogs that are able to recognize the objective of collaboration in very complicated tasks.

Dogs Lead the Sightless

Dogs have been guiding the sightless or vision impaired for a long time. The first clue to this is a fresco discovered in a Greek city, probably depicting a beggar with his dog. The first training school for Seeing Eye dogs opened in Germany in 1916, and since that time, an abundance of such schools have functioned. Their graduates are much beloved by and useful to vision-impaired people. Such a school operates in Csepel in Hungary. When we began our investigations into canine behavior at the Department of Ethology, we visited this school so that we could study the collaboration of canines and humans. Peter Vasteleki, the director of the school, was very helpful in our work. The studies were carried out by Szima Naderi, Antal Dóka, and, less often, by Zsolt Förgeteg, and we were also much assisted by interviews with dog owners, which had been designed by the psychologist Zita Fekete.

During the first few months, our chief tasks were to record a lot of video footage about the dog-master collaboration and to observe the training and how the trained dogs performed. It is quite easy to assess the performance of the dogs. The trainers often arrange contests for them, and at Csepel they have training grounds at which the quality of their performance can be judged by the number of errors committed. It soon became evident on the basis of our measurements and observations that there is a close connection between the dogs' performance and their propensity to bond. In contrast, laboratory tests show that new tasks are accomplished most rapidly by dogs that are relatively independent of their masters.[7] However, the study of Seeing Eye dogs demonstrated that the dogs that bond strongly with their masters are the most effective in leading the blind. In previous (non–Seeing Eye dog) experiments, dogs attained good results if they could distance themselves from the master's control. The job of Seeing Eye dogs is much more complicated and they are up to it only if they cooperate completely with their masters. Conversations with blind people revealed that they actually possess a great deal of information about their environment: they hear many more sounds than sighted people, and their other senses are at work as well. For example, a blind person can sense with his facial skin that he is passing along a wall, because it radiates heat, and he will also sense where the wall ends. They feel secure in the company of Seeing Eye dogs and consider well-trained dogs to be reliable guides.

We were curious to find out whether the dogs understood what their tasks were or whether they merely followed faithfully the few rules that they have been taught. Training schools give the dogs endless practice concerning the rules of how to get around with blind people; for example, how the dogs are to signal that they have reached a staircase, or the curb at the edge of the sidewalk, or an obstacle that is placed high enough so that it would not bother the dog but could be dangerous for its master. They have to obey the instructions of the master to stop, turn, start, or continue walking. They also have to learn to ignore cats or other dogs and to suffer in silence if they are hurt in a crowd; for example, if somebody steps on their foot. In a San Francisco training school, the dogs' test for graduation requires that each dog guide its blindfolded trainer over a two-and-a-half-mile stretch of the busiest streets in the city.[8] When a dog's training is finished and the prospective master arrives, the two of them spend two more weeks in intensive joint training, which is followed by another examination from which the school determines whether the particular dog-human pair is well suited for getting around independently. Of course, even after the master takes his dog home they still have a lot to learn. The dog needs to familiarize itself with the environment of the master's home and his customary routes, and it needs to learn the instructions for getting to this or that place.

Dogs learn these tasks easily and, for example, they will know precisely where a particular shop is located; some dogs can even find a particular department in a department store.[9] There are dogs that signal their arrival at a desired location. A Seeing Eye dog named Mike Tetley Sweep belonging to an Englishman learned to guide his master to the homes of specified friends of his after as few as one or two visits to them. Upon finding that the telephone in the master's favorite telephone booth was broken, another English Seeing Eye dog, Emma, would search until she found another one.[10]

One of the blind owners working with us, Zsuzsa Kroll, recounted the following story. Once she arranged to meet two friends, also blind, in the underpass of one of the railroad stations in Budapest. As she was leaving home, she suddenly realized that they had forgotten to specify exactly where they would meet, which was worrisome, because the underpass was not only very large, but usually very crowded, and they might have had trouble finding each other. She arrived at the underpass with her dog, Nancy, in a state of considerable excitement and boldly commanded her dog, "Go find the blind people." The dog started to lead her through the crowd, and soon they met up with her friends.

There is one fairly typical story, which we have heard, albeit with minor variations, from at least four different people who did not know one another. The story goes like this. It is obviously important to take Seeing Eye dogs for walks and perhaps to let them loose so that they can take care of their need to eliminate. In a well-known park, a blind person let his dog roam freely while he continued to walk slowly by himself along a well-known path. Suddenly, he realized that his dog had returned to him, pressed against him, and seemed to herd him in a particular direction. The master did not quite understand what this was about, patted his dog, and encouraged it to "do his business." They walked together a bit and after a while the dog ran off again. At that point, somebody approached the blind person and the following conversation ensued:

"You certainly have a very smart dog."

"Yes, he is, but why do you say that?"

"Because if he had not returned to you a minute ago, you would have fallen into the hole that was dug by Public Service this morning. I almost yelled at you, but at the last moment the dog led you away from it."

Of course, in the variants of these stories it is not always a hole that is a threat to the blind person; sometimes it is a tree blown down by a storm, or some other object obstructing the way. It is obvious from these conversations that at least some Seeing Eye dogs are quite clear about what their task really is. But this is not taught in the training schools. There the dog learns that when its harness is attached, it must obediently lead the blind person. The fact that a dog that was let loose returns to its master and begins to lead him without the harness, because he realized the impending danger to the person, proves that these dogs had a true understanding of the task entrusted to them. Only an animal with a high level of intelligence is capable of such actions.

We obtained some interesting results from an experiment in which we compared the performance of three groups over an obstacle course. The first group comprised experienced Seeing Eye dogs and their masters, the second, family dogs and their masters, while the third consisted of trained police dogs and their masters.[11] Each group contained ten dog-master pairs. Each dog had to navigate the obstacle course in the presence of its master but by himself and return to the starting point. After this, we blindfolded the masters, even the blind ones, and sent the dog-master pairs out on the obstacle course, trusting the dogs to take the lead. As expected, the Seeing Eye dogs had no problems at all. After the start signal, the police dogs obediently dragged their blindfolded detective masters around the obstacles. There were two exceptions, and those dogs were very surprised when their masters bumped into the obstacles. Afterward, they proceeded very slowly and cautiously and managed to avoid most of the obstacles with their masters. The behavior of the family dogs was quite similar. We developed a measure of the degree of bonding and applied it to each dog-human pair, and it became evident that the dogs that bonded most strongly with their masters were the most successful in the test. This was further underscored by the fact that the more successful dogs maintained a closer contact with their masters than the less successful ones (see figure 14).

In the past, the collaboration of Seeing Eye dogs with humans was attributed to conditioning and teaching; in other words, the dog only obeys a few commands. This is certainly not the case, and even the simplest explanation will have to admit that the dog acts according to certain rules; these are not merely the result of associative learning, because they are not rooted in fixed environmental factors as had been thought before. Our own observations showed, and we were rather surprised by this, that well-performing dogs were often scolded by their masters, and in spite of that, they did their jobs well. One of our video records shows that a dog and its master set out on a walk sometime after a summer shower, after the busy street had become more or less dry. But in the

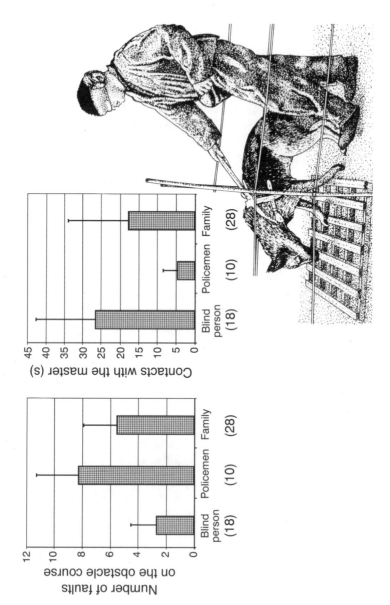

Figure 14. Leading the Blind: Results from Trained and Inexperienced Dogs

middle of a pedestrian crosswalk there was an enormous puddle. Naturally, the dog made a substantial detour to avoid it. The master did not understand the reason for the detour and felt that the dog was not behaving properly. He scolded the dog, and in order to teach him the correct behavior, he made them retrace their steps. The dog again avoided the puddle; this time the scolding was more emphatic and a new repetition followed. This time the master commanded "go straight"; the poor dog obeyed and they waded through the deep puddle. When the master understood what the dog was trying to accomplish, he immediately apologized to the dog and embraced it. From the point of view of a behavioral scientist, this can be interpreted to represent two instances in which the dog was punished for the correct behavior and one instance in which it was praised for the incorrect behavior. We were waiting with bated breath to see what would happen at the next puddle. Of course, the dog obeyed the rule and again avoided it, albeit anxiously. The simplest explanation for this is that dogs are able to conceptualize and understand at least a part of their task and to behave so as to aid in its completion. We are unaware of similar reactions on the part of other animals, with the exception of some apes that were brought up from early childhood in a human environment.

We saw and heard a great deal about the cooperation between Seeing Eye dogs and their masters, but we did not understand the essence of this until we started to examine Seeing Eye dogs that had several years of experience.

The Ability to Alternate Dominance

We were actually very curious to know how Seeing Eye dogs keep in mind the many rules and commands they have to learn. We recorded many videos of dog-human pairs that had worked together for several years and found, with some surprise, that the dogs were often doing things differently from the way they had been taught in school. For example, they did not always stop at the curb, but only slowed down, and sometimes not even that. But it was also evident that dog-human pairs that were well in tune with one another got around very efficiently. They walk fast, avoid obstacles with ease, and do not hesitate even at busy intersections.

Both the dogs and their masters appeared much more confident than the beginners, in spite of the fact that they have forgotten a goodly part of what they had learned in school or, as we thought at first, that they have relearned many of the original lessons in their own way. In other words, the masters may be retraining the dogs in some fashion to obey signals they like better. This seemed like a fairly good idea, but we did not understand the secret of pairs that had gotten used to each other, even after viewing hundreds of hours of video clips. I decided to look at those moments in which a significant change takes place or in which a major decision is made. In other words, they stop, they start, or turn, or avoid. It seemed useful to examine who initiated the decision: the master or the dog? We know that the master is quite aware of his surroundings and knows exactly where he wants to go; it is therefore certain that he has an influence on the collaboration, too. In any event, we thought that most of the decisions are made by the dogs, since, after all, that is what they are taught and that is their job.

When we were done with the analysis and the statistical calculations, we were in for a big surprise. It turned out that more than half the decisions were made by the dogs, with the balance by the blind persons, and that the "right" to make a decision frequently alternated. Sometimes the dog will decide what they will do several times in a row, after which the master retakes the initiative because, say, he wants to stop or turn at a corner. Following that, the dog may make the decision again, because it notices a car moving silently and does not permit the master to proceed. It also turned out that there were substantial differences among pairs. We have found pairs in which the dog made the decision 80 percent of the time as well as others in which the dog decided only 20 percent of the time (see figure 15). This latter group consisted mostly of people who had some vision and were thus able to evaluate their surroundings visually to some extent.

This is a very interesting result,[12] because it proves that dogs are capable of alternating dominant behavior in the interests of carrying out a task, a feature previously observed only among humans. In a sequence of partial tasks, the initiator is the individual "who" feels that at that moment he has a better understanding of the situation and of what needs to be done. But such an individual does not insist on this if his partner thinks otherwise, and easily yields the right to make a decision, which

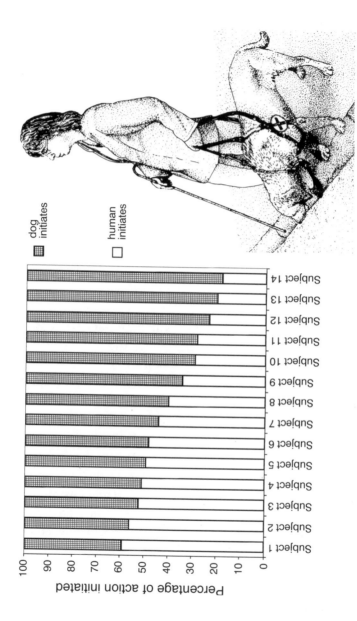

Figure 15. Distribution of Decision Making in Long-Standing Dog-Human Pairs

he may recapture later. We have heard many stories about Seeing Eye dogs to the effect that in critical situations they never yield the right to make a decision. This normally happens at street crossings, when the blind master feels that all vehicles have come to a stop. In other words, he feels that it is all right to cross and to command the dog to go. But the dog may not go and may be practically unmovable, and with good reason; for example, when a careless driver does not yield the pedestrians the right of way and threatens to drive right through them. The blind person then knows that the dog has saved his life once again.[13] These stories also support the previous hypothesis that Seeing Eye dogs have some conception or understanding of the joint tasks at hand. The dog will yield the right to make the decision not only because the master demands it, but also because it feels that the situation is not one in which it is more important to refuse to obey. However, if the dog's assessment is that this is important, it will do so.

Exchange of Information

Nearly continual information exchange is an important element in human collaboration. Information exchange was the subject of lengthy analyses in experiments with apes, because if we could determine that information exchange takes place, we would be able to provide proof of the existence of a higher order of intelligence.[14]

The term *information* refers to communications and signals by our fellow humans that convey knowledge to us about something that we did not know. The signal that mediates information is often very simple. If we ask an employee in a self-service store where the dog food is, he might indicate the direction silently by pointing. In other words, the signal is simple, but the framework is rather more complicated, because both of us are aware of what is involved. The questioner knows about dog food, assumes that the store carries it, and that it is on some shelf somewhere. The employee has the same knowledge or makes the same assumptions, and hence deems it sufficient simply to point; nothing more is needed. If we do not have such prior knowledge, the signal or the series of signals that mediate the information can be very complicated. If we inquire in an office how we could settle a particular matter, it is quite possible that the information would be provided through a conversation lasting several minutes, in spite of the fact that the two participants in the information exchange would be relying on much common knowledge. From the ethological point of view, one might say that human behavior in information exchange is characterized by intentionality, by the use of symbols and by each participant's assumptions about what the other knows. Information plays the role of enlarging the scope of what is already known or altering it.

Providing information occurs among animals as well, but it might not be the best terminology to call this information exchange. Birds use calls that signal the presence of danger, but the simplest explanation for that is that when they see a predator, they become scared and call involuntarily. The hypothesis of intentionality on the part of an animal requires proof. Even if we succeed in finding such a proof, we have not necessarily shown that the animal has taken into account the mental state of the other, but the usefulness of the intention is evident anyway. This latter assertion is very important for understanding the later discussion and it is useful to illustrate it with a simple human example. A child asks for a chocolate bar. Sometimes he gets one and sometime he does not. After a while, when he does not get a chocolate bar, he begins to cry, and when we get tired of that, we give him one anyway. From a scientific point of view, we might say that the child has learned that crying produces chocolate. This simple explanation is surely sufficient in the case of children, but will it be adequate when your wife or girlfriend sheds tears for the sake of getting a piece of jewelry? Probably not, because that matter is much more complicated. But the example shows that in the case of animals, as in the case of children, we must always seek the simplest possible explanation.

My dog Flip has the habit of asking for something that he cannot reach on a table by looking at the part of the table that is the source of the tantalizing aromas with which he would like to become better acquainted. I can signal Jerry as well as Flip by just pointing to where a piece of food has fallen on the floor. Every dog owner has made similar observations, but if we asked a behavioral scientist whether this represents information exchange, he would surely say that this is not the simplest explanation. What probably happened in the case of Flip was that he was trying to call attention to himself in various ways, and when he happened to glance at the appropriate spot, his master rewarded him; at the same time, Flip learned that his particular action would "mobilize" the master. This is called operational learning, and many animals with a simpler brain than dogs are capable of it. In the case of Jerry, a different type of association took place. The master often pointed, and the dog sometimes found something on the floor, and the two events became linked. Where in this is there proof of intentionality or of any kind of conceptualization by the mind?

The above-mentioned behavioral scientist may be right, although he probably never had a dog; nevertheless, we have to take his views into account.

Attention! There It Is!

To be sure, we cannot base theories that require too much from our four-legged friends upon such simple observations. Fortunately, the experiments conducted with monkeys and apes have led to methodologies that are suitable for a scientific investigation of these questions. For example, many scholars have examined whether rhesus or capuchin monkeys are capable of understanding or learning the significance of pointing with hands or eyes. The earliest experiments have shown that they are unable to interpret human glances as giving directions, but with great difficulty can be taught to understand the meaning of pointing. But even that can succeed only if the pointing hand is no more than eight to twelve inches from the object pointed to.[15] But chimpanzees, orang-utans, and barely nine-month-old children can be taught not only to understand pointing but also to follow a person's glance. They understand these signals even if the person who points is as much as three feet from the object.[16] These experiments were followed by protracted debates about the reasons for the monkeys' weaker abilities: whether this was due to the inability of their minds to comprehend the significance of pointing, or to their failure to accept humans as partners from whom something useful could be learned. The latter hypothesis is supported by the fact that among monkeys eye contact always expresses aggression, and consequently they avoid looking humans in the eye. Some experiments have been conducted in which rhesus monkeys were taught to follow the gaze of other rhesus monkeys on a video screen. This supports the view that following a gaze has many species-based idiosyncrasies and the absence of this behavior should not be used to infer the lack of certain mental abilities.[17]

The majority of dogs not only tolerate eye contact with their masters well, but often they are the ones that seek it, just like children. That is what they do when they ask permission to do something, ask a question, or when they want to call the master's attention to something. Many breeds have a white in their eyes like humans. All parts of a monkey's eyes are almost completely dark. The uniform eye color makes it difficult to guess where it is looking. This confers numerous benefits on a monkey; for example, if it notices a tasty morsel on the ground, it is to its benefit that its comrades do not figure out where it is looking. In human communication, however, it is extremely advantageous for us to be able to give eye signals to each other. Among dogs, the genetic changes accompanying domestication also started to develop the signaling role of the color pattern of the eyes. We have good reason to suppose that dogs use this in their collaboration and information exchange with humans.[18]

Recognizing all this, my colleagues and I launched a detailed and complicated series of experiments. We wanted to examine how easily family dogs understand or can learn the various forms of pointing.[19]

The experiment involved family dogs and took place in the apartments of willing owners, and as always, we recorded the experiments with video cameras. Several breeds participated, including Labrador, terrier, and sheep dog; in all, we had six dogs. We wanted to find out how easily the dogs could learn the various forms of pointing—ranging from obvious arm gestures to mere glances—or whether they could learn them at all if they were used sequentially.

A food reward was placed in one of two brown plastic containers and we wanted see whether we could make them select the right one on the basis of our signals. Both containers were smeared on the outside with the scent of the food lest the disparity in their odors provide a clue. The two containers were approximately five feet apart, with the master in the middle giving the signals, which alternately consisted of pointing with the arm, or the hand, or a finger, turning the upper body, nodding with the head, turning the head without nodding, and glancing at the container. In the last case, the master knelt down so that a smaller dog would see the clue clearly. The dog was positioned about three feet from the master and was shown the signal once or twice only after the dog and the master established eye contact. The signaling was discontinued when the dog started out to identify a container.[20] If the dog selected the "correct" container, it received the reward; if not, it had to go without it. The experiments stretched over many days, until the dogs could identify the correct container in two consecutive tries at least 80 percent of the time.

The experiments led to very interesting results. These dogs had probably encountered similar signals in the family environment, and it was to be expected that a sizable fraction would already be familiar with them and would rapidly learn them during the course of the experiments. That was the case for pointing with the hand, turning the body, and nodding with the head. The smartest subjects reached the 80 percent achievement level within the first fifteen tries. But a simple turning of the head or casting a glance proved to be signals that most dogs had to learn, and they indeed did so (see figure 16). We were also able to prove that they had begun to acquire an understanding of signals in the family environment. We repeated the experiment with the dogs of an Austrian dog-training center, in which the dogs were well used to humans, but in which they had spent the better part of each day with other dogs and not with humans. In other words, they were unable to form daily dog-human contacts, had no exclusive master, and during the experiments, the signals were given by an experimenter and not by the dog's master. These dogs also learned to accomplish the task, but there was only one among them that was able to do so right at the outset. It also became clear that dogs not only understand hand, head, and eye signals, but they understand and correctly interpret the very act of signaling. For example, it does not confuse them if one points to the left with the right hand.

The next logical question is whether dogs themselves have the ability to show something to their masters. Dog owners have long known the answer, since they know more about this question than scientists. I remember one morning when Flip woke me, although he generally respects my right to sleep. He called me, led me to the front hall, and pointed to a tick on the floor that had grown to gigantic size from gorging. It probably dropped off Flip during the previous night. I picked it

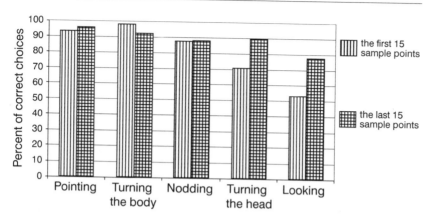

Figure 16. The Utilization by Dogs of Human Body Signals

up and got rid of it, to Flip's great satisfaction. I learned later that earlier he had shown it to Eve as well (but she hated to touch it and so I had to do the job).

Réka Polgárdi and I decided to undertake a scientific investigation of this question.[21] The experiments took place in the apartments in which the experimental subjects, all family dogs, lived with their masters. The master would first leave the dog alone in a room. Somebody else would then enter, and within the dog's sight would hide some tasty morsel, but in such a way that the dog could not get to it. This person would then leave, and soon the master would return, not knowing where the morsel had been hidden. The videos that were taken show that the dogs would initiate lively communication with their masters; they would run to where the food had been hidden and run back to the master. Most revealing were the glances by which they would first look at the master, then at the hiding place, and then at the master again. After this, the masters would easily find the hiding place and reward the dog with the morsel for sharing the information. We proved with these experiments that in the course of collaborating with humans, dogs are able to understand and employ signals as much as the most highly developed apes.[22] The latter experiments also revealed that when necessary, dogs are also able to provide signals and hence information, and that humans understand these just as easily as dogs understand the signals of humans. As I mentioned before, dogs perform much better than apes and also better than wolves. In

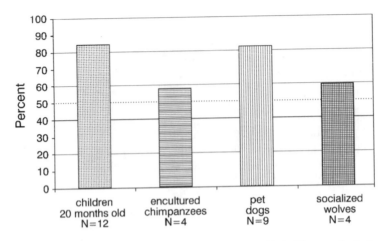

Figure 17. Correct Choice in a Two-Way Choice Task (N is sample size)

figure 17, we compare the performance of children, chimpanzees, our one-and-a-half-year-old wolves, and dogs in a pointing test in which a human is pointing to one of the two containers that contains a reward.[23]

It was still an open question whether dogs have any thoughts about the mental state of a signaling human. Are they contemplating what humans might be thinking during an exchange of signals? This is a hard question to which we found a very interesting answer.

Can Dogs Make Inferences about a Human's State of Mind?

Similar experiments with monkeys produced fairly negative results. However, apes—chimpanzees and orangutans—were able to exhibit behavior in some experimental situations that is most easily explained by assuming that they were able to make some inferences about the experimenting humans' state of mind. In one experiment, three persons were involved. One of these would hide a reward, but the chimpanzees could not see where it was being hidden. Two other persons were present during the hiding of the reward, but one of these had a paper bag over his head, so that he could not have seen where the hiding place was. The chimpanzees could observe these two people and could see that only one of them was able to observe where the reward was concealed. The animal had to choose the person from whom it wanted to learn the location of the reward. The chimpanzees acquitted themselves well: they always asked for information from the person who had observed the act of concealment.[24] Some people do not believe the outcome of this experiment and claim on the basis of other, similar ones that chimpanzees are unable to grasp that the person with a bag over his head *could not have seen* where the reward was being hidden. They prefer to think that the result is better explained by simple associative conditioning: the chimpanzee just learned that the person with the bag is not a suitable source of information.

Our experiments show conclusively that dogs are capable of similar inferences, but of course, they have had a hundred thousand years to adapt to humans.

The experiment was carried out by my previously mentioned colleagues as well as Zsófia Virány and consisted of the same basic situation as the ape experiment described above. A person hid a reward in one of several boxes while the dog's master was absent. In these experiments, the box and the reward contained in it could be reached only with the aid of a stick placed nearby. After the reward had been hidden, the master returned and awaited the assistance of his dog, which it promptly provided by alternately looking at the master and at the box in which the reward was hidden. If the master understood which box was the right one, he took the stick from its regular resting place, retrieved the box, and rewarded the dog.

After ten initial tries of this experiment, we divided the thirteen dogs into two groups. The first group consisted of six dogs, and what they saw was that before the reward was hidden, the master and the person who was going to hide it placed the stick in a new spot. The master then left, the other person hid the reward, and then he left, too. The master would then return, and the dog would signal the correct box. The master then looked for the stick in its original place, then hesitated a bit, and finally retrieved it from its new spot. He then retrieved the box with it and rewarded the dog. In the second group, the dogs saw their master leave and then saw that the other person hid the stick *in a new spot* by himself and then, of course, hid the reward as well. Thus, in this case, the master did not know the location of either the stick or the reward and could determine them only with the dog's assistance. When the master returned, he would first go to where the stick used to be and would pretend to be looking for it, whereupon the dogs would emphatically signal the new location of the stick and would glance at it more frequently than at the reward itself. If the master then found the stick, the dogs would indicate the location of the reward by alternately looking at the master and the correct box.

The decisive difference between the two experiments is that when the master participates in the placement of the stick in a new spot and upon returning first looks for it in its original position, *the dogs do not signal the new position of the stick*, but only the location of the reward. In the other group, the master does not know that the stick has been relocated and the dogs begin animated signaling, primarily *indicating the new location of the stick*: they alternate their glances between the master and the new stick location more than *ten times* as frequently as the dogs in the first group. In other words, the dogs are able somehow to conceptualize the minor difference consisting of whether the master did or did not participate in repositioning the stick (see figure 18).[25]

There is no doubt that dogs are able to decompose an activity into its constituent parts: that the master must first grasp the stick and only then can he retrieve the box. It also goes without saying that they provide information in a complementary manner and do so just when it is needed. It is very likely that they understand the part of the master's state of mind that deals with the location of the stick. In other words, whether the master does or does not know its location. We have several articles in print, in which we were able to demonstrate that dogs have a sensitive appreciation of a human's *quality of attention*. When they have the option of asking for something from one or the other of two persons, they always select the one who turns his or her face toward them and whose eyes are visible. They do not ask a person who turns away from them or who is blindfolded. If they are given a command by tape recorder, they carry it out only if one of the persons present actually looks at them.

This means that nearly all the characteristics of human collaboration can be found in dogs as well.

To be more precise, one characteristic has been left out, namely planning. Are dogs able to act on the basis of some idea or plan? And if yes, how would one prove that in a convincing manner? Or if not, how

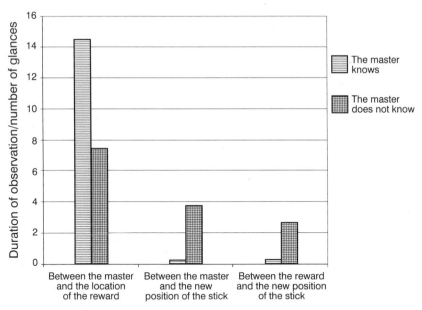

Figure 18. Relative Frequency of Alternating Glances

would one prove that? So far we have no experimental proof, but I can relate a Flip anecdote that convinced me that dogs are able to devise plans and are even capable of enlisting human help for their execution.

Our apartment is not far from a pet store, where we buy fish food for our goldfish. Of course, the pet store has many delectable tidbits that Flip enjoys greatly, and so a visit to buy fish food is often an occasion for him to get something as well. But Flip also likes to visit the store for other reasons: he loves to visit the section in which various small animals such as hamsters and guinea pigs are kept in cages. He eyes them carefully, sniffs at them, and then begs the store's owner for a little handout. These visits are very peaceful because Flip is a very well-brought-up dog. In the past two years we have also been accompanied on these visits by Jerry, who has a much wilder personality and gets so excited in the pet store that we could hardly continue our pleasant and calm visits to the store when he was along. But from time to time we would bring him anyway and then struggle to contain him. On one occasion, during an afternoon walk, Flip let us know in no uncertain terms that he wanted to go to the pet store by turning at a certain street corner. But I decided that on that occasion I did not have the stomach for a fight with Jerry and proceeded straight. I noticed after a while that we had slowed down considerably. Flip was walking with tiny steps, like an old and sick dog that can barely walk. He did not sit down and did not seem to want to go in a different direction; he just walked very slowly. I had been thinking of all sorts of other things and had not even noticed this. But after a while I caught on that Flip was dragging himself along because he wanted to go to the pet store. I quickly looked around to make sure we would not be overheard and said to Flip, "Listen here! If you pick up your legs and start walking normally, after the walk I'll take you to the pet store."

Flip listened carefully, tilting his head the way dogs often do when they are trying to discern the master's meaning. I repeated what I had said more slowly and we continued our walk. Flip immediately took up position in front and merrily led our little troop like a puppy at a fast pace. It is important for the story that for the time being we were not moving toward the pet store, but on the contrary, we were getting farther from it, because our immediate objective was a certain park where the dogs were allowed to run loose. The return trip was also quick, and when we reached a fork in the road, Flip determinedly took a branch of the fork that was an unusual route for us but was a shortcut to the pet store. At the time I was not sure whether I should be annoyed or rejoice. The cause of my annoyance was the fact that my old dog had outsmarted me and had, as a practical matter, forced me to accept his will, like a naughty child. My elation was due to the fact that I had been blessed with such a foresighted, intelligent, and communicative companion. I decided that I really felt the latter emotion, and I think it is time to report in more detail about my oft-mentioned dogs, Flip and Jerry.

Part
Three

The Diary of Flip and Jerry

In the study of animal behavior, we are trying to find answers from experiments conducted with scientific thoroughness. However, depending on the nature of the question, careful observation in nonexperimental settings can also be of great help. The observations of Konrad Lorenz and Jane Goodall, often anecdotal in character, have helped many a researcher to design a better experiment, at times just because they wanted to dispute the theories of these outstanding ethologists.

Quite some time before my colleagues and I started to do experiments, I began to write "Flip's Diary," which later became "The Diary of Flip and Jerry." At the beginning, I did not have the time to write a genuinely scientific diary, and I now think that such an effort would not even have made much sense, because I would have had to record every tiny variant in behavior and my whole life would have consisted of making minute observations. The bulk of the ultimately useless data would have consisted of which dog was lying where or doing what at every moment, and so on.[1] In the past ten to fifteen years, I would have collected a mass of uninteresting data. Instead, the diary records every observation I could make about the dogs that I considered unusual, surprising, or otherwise worth recording. I was careful to note the precise time and place of events and to provide a professional description. I have already recounted a few stories from my observations, but in this part of the book I will provide many more. I know that one dog or story does not prove anything; but a faithful record of a recurrent or peculiar dog story will surely help in the design of new experiments and theories.

I hope that the reader will delve into the stories in this spirit. I begin with the first entry in the diary.

November 26, 1989. Eve and I were hiking in the Kékes Mountains when we came upon Flip (a fuzzy male of low stature, surely a mixed breed) and Jenő, a small, black adult dog. According to the cafeteria attendant, Flip must have been abandoned and had been roaming around for the past three days. He was very friendly and quite unafraid. We started out on the return hike to Mátrafüred and Flip came with us. Before we entered the forest, Jenő tried to chase him back, but he hid behind us and plodded along in the deep snow. He stayed with us during the entire hike, never more than three to six feet from us. After about five miles he seemed very tired and I carried him for the final stretch. We returned home a day earlier than planned, because dogs were not allowed at the inn. During the return trip he slept. At home he was very obedient. He needed to be told only once not to do something. He slept in the kitchen and was a real sweetheart.

Flip was our only dog for almost eight years until Jerry arrived; why he did is a long and uninteresting story. The important thing is that he is here, and this is what I wrote in the diary.

June 27, 1997. Jerry arrived. He is a male and was born on May 17, so he is just six weeks old. His mother, Janka, is Uncle Vizi's purebred pumi.[2] His father is an unknown, stray husky. Jerry is a vigorous, independent little dog that eats enthusiastically, rather like a wild animal. He did not cry during the night. Flip seemingly cannot stand him, but they will make friends sooner or later. In the evening he tried to jump on the bed with a big towel in his mouth and almost succeeded.

Chapter 8

Dogs Understand a Lot

Of course, I did not learn canine ethology from Flip and Jerry alone. There was, for example, Balthasar, whom I mentioned before and whom I had brought up in the early part of his life.[1] Eventually, he got to the Department of Ethology, where he lived for almost the whole remainder of his life. Once, many years later, when he was no longer living with us, I had to take him home with me for some reason. I noticed that he was behaving peculiarly. At the time, we were living in a large five-room apartment, and Balthasar was following me around from room to room, like a shadow. A day later, he would get up only when I was getting ready to leave a room. It began to interest me how he knew that I was going to leave the room. I started to experiment: at times I would exit suddenly, or I would go to the door and only then decide whether to actually leave or not. But I was never able to fool Balthasar. He always knew exactly when I was going to leave. On the occasions when I was really leaving he would jump up and follow me. When I had decided not to leave, he would not even stir.

I am ashamed to have to confess that in spite of being an ethologist, I never figured this one out. Balthasar knew something about me that signaled my intention to leave, but I could never figure out what it was.

Dogs Are Good Ethologists, Too

We know for sure that apes observe the activities of their companions. The studies of C. R. Menzel revealed that captive chimpanzees observe each other carefully and gather a lot of information from the behavior of their companions.[2] In a study of the memory of chimpanzees, food was hidden at various spots in a large wooded area. From time to time, an individual chimpanzee would be allowed to observe what was being hidden and where. When this individual was allowed to roam the area alone, he would quickly and systematically gather up all the delicious morsels of food. At other times, the chimpanzee that observed the hiding of the food would be allowed into the area together with its companions. It soon became clear that the others inferred from its behavior that it knew where the food was concealed. The entire troop then began to follow the chimpanzee in the know, and they often got to the food before it did.

In another experiment, two different types of food were hidden and two chimpanzees were allowed to observe, but in such a way that one of them saw only where the first type of food was being hidden and the other only the second. When these two were let loose in the area with the rest of the troop, it turned out that the others followed the one that knew the whereabouts of the preferred food item. That chimpanzee was perhaps more excited, or perhaps the rest of the troop inferred in some other way from his behavior that he was the one worth following.

Dogs are excellent human ethologists, too; they continually observe us, and are much helped in this by the fact that they strongly bond with humans. They also have an excellent understanding of human body language. I have had countless opportunities to note how carefully Flip observed us and how well he could figure out what was likely to happen. There was a period when Eve or I made frequent trips abroad, and Flip was very upset about this. As soon as one of us started to pack a suitcase, Flip went into a funk; he became sad, and no matter how much we consoled him and how many delicacies we gave him, he continued to grieve until the person who had been away returned. The first summer we planned to spend a holiday of some weeks in the Bükk Mountains, and when the large suitcase made its appearance, Flip again became upset. It did not do him any good to see that the excitement of the trip prepara-

tions made us happy; he crawled into a corner and moped. At that point
I had a great idea.

> July 1, 1990. We were preparing for our holiday in the Bükk Mountains,
> in the town of Szilvásvárad. When we brought out the suitcase, Flip be-
> came agitated and then lay down sadly. On a sudden impulse, I showed
> him my walking stick and explained to him that we were going on an ex-
> cursion, and then I hung the stick on the door handle of the front door.
> He looked at me, went to the door, touched the stick with his nose, and
> looked at me again. "Yes," I said, "we are going on an excursion, and you
> are coming, too." This quieted him down, and he then started to frolic
> around and even jumped into the open suitcase.

I am sure that Flip knew the walking stick well, because I always took it
with me on weekend excursions. But it was an experience of lasting value
for me to see how he achieved an *understanding* while he was alternately
looking at me and at the stick. As we saw in the previous chapter, the alternation of glances plays an important role in human communication and cooperation. I could see that as he switched from sadness to elation, he
understood that we were going on an excursion. I very much felt as I did
when I tried to explain something to a small child and the child understood
what I was saying. I had no doubts that I was dealing with a "person."

Dogs have this outstanding ability to continually "read" us, and this
talent can be exploited for serious tasks. There are many places world-
wide where dogs are trained to signal their master's impending epileptic
attack ten to fifteen minutes before the onset. This is of enormous help
to an epileptic, because it gives him time to withdraw to a place of safety,
lie down, and notify those around him of the impending attack. His sense
of security is also enhanced by the absence of such a warning from his
dog, because it tells him that he need not fear an unexpected attack. The
remarkable observational ability of dogs is also useful in animal husbandry.
It is important in artificial insemination that one know the cows' time
for ovulation, but this is difficult to determine. Dogs can probably determine this by smell, and if they are taught to signal it, they will.

If several dogs live together, they will observe each other. When Jerry
came to us at the age of six weeks, he did not pay much attention to what
we were saying to him. In about two weeks he more or less figured out that

he needed to pay attention to human speech, and started to do so, but he did not understand a thing we were saying. We came to that conclusion because when we spoke to the dogs, Flip would pay attention to us, and Jerry would look at Flip and seemed to be waiting for Flip to show with his body language what was about to happen: a walk, food, a car ride, visitors' arrival, or any other activity of interest to dogs. We were much amused that Flip seemed to be taking on the role of an interpreter. Within two weeks, Jerry knew himself what kinds of sounds precede the activities most important for him.

Often we were unable to determine how Flip figured out the state of affairs, and I am quite sure that verbal language was as important in this as body language. A relevant section of the diary follows.

> March 7, 1992. We were planning to pick up at the airport our friend, Gerhard Schaeffer, a German professor of biology. We first had lunch at Eve's parents' and afterward drove home with Flip. While we were driving, we discussed, in words that Flip did not understand, whether it might be better not to take him with us to the airport. We got home and opened the front door to let Flip in—we did not even take our overcoats off. But much as we looked, Flip was nowhere to be found. "He probably lay down somewhere in the apartment," said Eve. I wanted to be sure that he was around and kept calling him, but there was no sign of him. I called again and accidentally looked toward the open front door. I saw that he was cautiously sticking his head in the door from the stairwell, where he had been waiting to go out again for some time. We had no choice but to take him with us.

When Eve and I straightened out who was where, it turned out that Flip never came into the apartment. Since he wanted to make sure that he would come with us again, he remained in the stairwell. In other words, he knew in advance, probably from the conversation we had had in the car, that we were planning to go out again. And this in spite of the caution we used in discussing it!

Of course, observant dogs do not passively wait for things to turn out all right, but try from time to time to influence the course of events. This also proves their insight into human ethology and their understanding of what it is that might make humans understand their desires.

All owners of strongly bonding dogs know that their intentions, questions, and requests are easily understood from their body language. For the sake of those readers who have no dog, I will summarize the most important signs that give clues to the dog's state of mind:

Tail wagging
Nudging with the nose
Pointing with a glance
Glancing
Eye contact
Pointing with the head
Requests
Questions
Complaints
"No"
Vocalization
Immobility
Resentment
Miming

The most important function of *tail wagging* is to let us know that the dog is paying attention to us. This applies to all living creatures with which the dog communicates, not only us. Once Flip was in the next room and I heard a strange growl. I opened the door and saw that he was standing in front of the wall, vigorously wagging his tail, and was growling in an increasingly menacing manner. It turned out that a huge fly was sitting on the wall and Flip was communicating with it. If a dog wants to call our attention to something, it will usually *nudge* our leg or knee or other suitable body part with his nose. This indicates that we need to pay attention to it, because it is signaling something or asking a question or asking for something. After a nudge, a dog will establish *eye contact*, about which we have already spoken several times. Eye contact may be followed by looking back and forth; for example, when the dog wants to call our attention to an object or a place. Pointing may take place by turning the head. If something worthy of our attention has taken place, or a visitor has arrived or a stranger has passed outside, dogs will often signal with a yip or a loud bark. The nature of the signal will depend on the state of their excitement: the greater the excitement, the more emphatic the signal.

At times, the signal provides important information:

October 23, 1997. Today we were in Nógrád. In the morning, Peter and his family came over with their dog Cricket to take a look at our stove. Cricket was left below because he is afraid of Flip, but Jerry ran down to him to play. After a while, when the visitors were getting ready to leave, Jerry appeared and went up to Peter and whined at him. Peter and I both thought that he wanted to be caressed or get a good mauling, but when we got downstairs, it turned out that the gate was open and Cricket had disappeared. At that point, Jerry stopped whining. He was probably just signaling the departure of Cricket, who had quietly walked home.

And then, when the information is important only to them:

November 22, 1997. We were visiting Laci Elek with the two dogs. From time to time we put the dogs outside, because our hosts' Newfoundland female reeked of wet fur. On one of these occasions, Flip succeeded in staying inside, and after a while, he came to me and asked me to come to the glass door with him. Jerry was standing on the other side of the door. I opened it and let Jerry come in. At that point, Flip went to lie down in some corner.

Flip can also express his desire *not to do* something. For example, late at night, I might want to go on a little walk and call him. Most of the time he would come merrily, but sometimes he is not in the mood, and then he will remain motionless, but indicate with wags ever so small that he is listening to me. *Becoming motionless* always means some kind of *no*. When we are on a hike and get to a fork in the road, I may choose one branch, but Flip may want to go in the other direction. In such a case he would stop and remain motionless while staring at me. If I insist on going my way, he will naturally follow me. But if I want to please him, I go back to the fork and take a few steps in the other direction. If this does not please him either, he will not budge, but if he likes that direction, he will immediately follow me.

A relevant entry from the diary:

March 27, 1993. We returned late at night from a concert, and it was raining gently, which Flip hates. I took him out for a quick walk and we passed by a small park. He ran into the park, but I went on and called him to come. He came out but just stood there stiffly, which I did not understand, because our walk was so brief. But it turned out that he had had enough, because when I turned around (I thought he wanted to go in the other direction), he ran back into the park, voided, and when he was finished, led me home. This is interesting because he was signaling that he wanted to stay there; in other words he was not signaling a direction.

In time, I introduced the signal for "where" into our communication. Flip quickly learned that when I ask this question, he might choose the direction. When I ask "Where?" he usually holds his head up and sniffs around, and the odors are probably decisive in his choice of the direction in which he then sets off. We have had occasions on a hot summer day, after a longish trek, when the "Where?" question seemed to plunge him in deep thought, after which he selected a nice shady tree and lay down for a rest, watching all the time whether I accepted his suggestion. I did.

Jerry also learned very quickly that he may make choices, but he indicates his choice with a yip. When he approaches with a begging mien, I usually know what he wants, but sometimes I am wrong. In such a case I enumerate the possibilities, such as walking, eating, playing, and so on. When I reach the item that he has his heart set on, he will indicate it with a loud bark. But sometimes the dogs express their desires in a much more complicated way. The diary contains a few pertinent illustrations.

January 16, 1992. For the past several days, we took our evening walk with Eve. Around 10 p.m., Flip may come and nudge me with his nose, urging me to go for a walk, and I always say to him that we will go with Eve. But today he did not come, because he was sleeping in Eve's room. Eve had phoned to say that she would be late and that we should go walking without her. I called Flip and he approached slowly, stopped in the front hall, and conspicuously looked out the window. I sent him to fetch his leash, and he started to amble toward it in a leisurely fashion. On his way to the leash he passed a chair on which Eve's sweater was lying. Flip stopped, touched it with his nose, and looked back at me questioningly.

"Go ahead and fetch the leash, Eve is not coming," I said, whereupon he brought me the leash.

A very nice and excellent dog groomer, Bea, visits us from time to time. She is much beloved by our dogs, although they would just as well not have to undergo the ordeals of brushing, clipping, and bathing. Bea's arrival has been accompanied several times by boisterous greetings, after which Flip rushes to me in my room and begs with imploring looks that I should be present at the horrors that are about to be performed. My calming influence is really needed at some point during the grooming. If somebody else arrives on business unrelated to the dogs and I am not there, the dogs will indicate that somebody has arrived but will not call me. Once, a workman, well known to us, was fixing the outer iron door. The front door was open and the workman was going back and forth between the iron door and the front hall where he had left his tool kit. I was working in one of the other rooms. Flip was observing the workman's activities with rapt attention, and every time that he crossed the front door threshold, Flip ran to me and signaled with a bark that he had come in again.

A *call* by a dog is an unambiguous signal: the dog is usually standing, ready to move and with an urgent look about him. If I budge, he moves in the chosen direction. Anyone who has seen this a few times cannot mistake it for anything else.

A request can happen in several ways: it is usually accompanied by vigorous tail wagging, but sometimes the dog sits and has an urgent look. I have two examples from the diary.

November 5, 1991. Today we had a completely unambiguous request. In the afternoon I fed him. He ate his food with gusto, sat around for a while, and then he came to me in the kitchen and sat down in front of me in the usual begging position and looked at me. He had just eaten, so I asked him what he wanted but I could not figure it out. I happened to look at his water bowl and realized that it was empty. I filled it; he was obviously very happy and drank at length.

November 27, 1991. It was raining today and we were wet when we returned from our walk, but I had forgotten to dry him. Flip ran after me, got in front of me, stopped, and started to dry his head on the rug. Then he stopped and looked at me questioningly. "Do you want a towel?" I asked. At that he jumped up and ran to the bathroom where his towel hangs.

This latter case is actually a case of miming behavior. It does not happen all that often, but it is an important category of making a request, because it presupposes a well-developed intelligence. For the sake of scientific accuracy, I interpreted only the first appearance of the wish as miming, because if it happens more than once, it is possible that the dog has learned that I respond to some given action of his in the manner expected by him. In any event, miming accompanies quite a few different requests, and I relate another two below.

August 26, 1996. In the garden of our country house, a mole had dug a large hill under a mulberry tree. Eve, our friend Paul, and I were just standing there, when Flip gave his growl that characterizes a request. When I asked him what he wanted and where, he sort of howled, went to the mulberry tree, looked at me, and carefully drew his paw twice over the molehill. He was not digging at it, but just touched it and looked at me while he was doing so. Since our rule is that he may not dig up molehills in the garden, I said no to him. He gave a big sigh and lay down next to it.

It should be added that when we go on walks in the country in nearby fields, Flip and Jerry dig up molehills with glee, but I do not allow them to do so in the garden.

September 11, 1996. For a few days, Flip has been carrying around his ball for us to hide it so that he might then go and find it. I found out that while he is waiting for me to hide the ball, he listens carefully and knows exactly where I have walked in the adjacent room; he then looks for the ball by retracing the steps he heard me take. He wanted to play the game again today, but the ball was missing, and so he "asked" for it. When Eve asked him what he wanted, he sat and looked left and right as if he were searching. Eve guessed immediately that he wanted the ball.

It happens often that he supports his request by pointing to a place or with some other signal.

February 10, 1993. My daughter, Julie, and her family were here with their cat, which evokes violent feelings in Flip. He was licking the cat and seemed intent on picking up the poor animal with his mouth. We had to lock the cat in the bathroom. But from time to time we would look in on it with Flip. In the evening, after the guests had departed, we turned on the evening news, after which we usually go for a walk. Eve asked him, "What does the puppy-dog want?" The answer was a groan and a sighlike whine, which we first heard while he was bothering the cat. I could barely believe my ears and thought that he urgently needed to go out; but when I got out of my chair, he did not run to where the leash is kept, as he would normally do, but went to the bathroom, where the cat had been before. In other words, he was fantasizing about the cat.

A few days later, Julie came by herself in the morning, and Flip explained to her, too, that he would very much like to see the cat. Again, he sighed and whinnied, and then led Julie to the bathroom where the cat had been.

The most exciting thing is when dogs ask questions. It is strange that it has not been reported in the scientific literature that this type of behavior exists at all. Highly trained and disciplined dogs are often inadvertently discouraged by their owners from asking questions. One must pay very close attention to the requests of and questions posed by dogs, because if one does not react appropriately, they soon stop asking. Dogs are very committed to following the rules and wholeheartedly accept their subordination. If life is to be orderly and if the master demands that the dog be obedient, then that is what happens, and the dog does not ask questions and does not make requests. My dogs are relatively ill-mannered, and that is probably why they ask so many questions and request so many things.

We have already discussed requests. When a dog asks a question, it sits down in front of us and—I cannot describe it in any other way— looks questioningly. We can verify that it was actually asking a question by noting that it seems satisfied with the answer, goes away, and behaves accordingly. The most frequent question that our dogs ask when we are getting ready in the morning is who will take them for a walk. If they ask me, and I tell them that I will take them, they stay with me and do not bother Eve. If I tell them that Eve will take them, they go to her.

On those occasions when we are preparing to go at an unusual time, one or the other dog will briefly ask what is going on. There are two possible answers. The first one is, "We are leaving but you are staying behind." In that case they become visibly sad and go to find a place to rest. If the answer is, "We are leaving and you are coming, too," they break into boisterous behavior. If Jerry asked the question, he would normally run to find Flip and signal him with a peculiar yelp, and then Flip would arrive himself to witness the departure preparations.

I will never forget the time when an English friend of mine, Peter Saunders, was staying with us for three weeks. Peter developed a very good relationship with Flip during his stay. I have already mentioned that Flip always gets upset if we bring out the suitcases, because that means a trip. When, on his last day, Peter started to pack his suitcase, Flip became very excited, continually ran to me (I was fussing with something in another room), circled around me, sat down, and questioned me. I replied, "Peter is going but I am staying." He turned his head, as if to make sure that he had understood, and asked me at least three times until he finally quieted down; he did not show the sadness that normally accompanies the departure of a member of the family.

Dogs are not only able to formulate such definite questions or requests, but are able to express emotions as well. I have already mentioned Flip's complaints; but Jerry frequently complains as well, for example, if I accidentally step on his foot or if on one of our walks we meet a threatening and dangerous dog, with which Jerry might have a difference of opinion. After the event, Jerry will come to me, rub himself against my leg, and emit a peculiar, emotional, and deep growl that can last as long as a minute. In such cases I console him as much as I can.

A more difficult situation arises if dogs *take offense*. Young dogs are particularly prone to taking offense, particularly if something happens that they consider unjust or distressing, in which case they may temporarily suspend their relationship with their master. They go off somewhere, they pout, and they can become reconciled again only after a longish time and with great difficulty. Once they are reconciled, they show with their behavior that the bad patch is over.

January 29, 1992. During our evening walk, Flip bit Freddy, a small pup. I scolded him and gave him a slight swat. After a few minutes the same thing happened again. I swatted him again and we went home. He acted offended all evening. He accepted food, but if I bent down toward him, he turned his head away. He carried out all my commands with remarkable zeal, but initiated no communication with an emotional content. Eve tried to reconcile us by stroking my hand and calling Flip. He came and licked her, but not me as he would normally. His resentment dissipated only by the next day.

That is what taking offense means among dogs. Real dog lovers, among themselves, swear that dogs have a sense of humor. I personally doubt this, because primitive humor always rests on some form of aggression, and dogs are not sufficiently aggressive toward their masters. But in spite of this, I have a little story (not for scientists but only for dog lovers). One summer we spent a few weeks on holiday in the countryside and often took a walk in the village, which was full of dogs. As we passed them, they hurled themselves against the garden fences with loud barking. I commanded Flip not to respond to the provocations, and he accompanied me silently, not even glancing at the nasty dogs. After a long walk we came to a house whose canine inhabitant did not leap at the fence but rather accompanied us on the other side of the garden fence silently, with measured steps. During the last few feet Flip moved from my side and gave the dog a loud bark, whereupon the surprised dog maniacally attacked the fence. Flip silently returned to my other side and, after establishing interesting and meaningful eye contact with me, continued our walk with studied indifference.

Dogs Make Inferences

Monkeys, but particularly apes, are able to figure out simple causal connections. Humans do the same with a passion from childhood on.[3] I think it is clear from the canine experiments and various stories that dogs are able to do likewise.

I would like to illustrate this ability of theirs with a few anecdotes. On one occasion, Flip's leash broke and we bought him a new one, but it turned out that the old one could also be repaired. This gave me an opportunity to find out whether Flip can account for the various parts of his har-

ness—the leash and the collar—or whether he is simply obeying commands when before a walk he first fetches the leash and then his collar. I
experimented with this by placing the two leashes and the two collars in a
single pile and asked Flip to bring me the leash. He went to the pile and
with some difficulty untangled a leash and brought it to me. Then I asked
him to bring me a collar, and after some hesitation he brought me one.
Then I asked him again to bring me a leash. He became bewildered; he
looked at me, looked at the items that he had already brought me, and
then suddenly picked up the leash that he had already brought me and
placed it in my hands. In other words, he did not want to bring me three
separate items. We repeated the experiment that evening and the next day
and it became clear that he did not care whether the leash was new or old.
He would only bring me one leash and one collar. In other words, he knew
exactly that these items belong together and are sufficient for a walk.

Dogs are very conscious of having a leash, and for them this is not a
form of restraint or a symbol of slavery as is believed by enthusiastic lib-
erals who know nothing about animals. On the contrary, it is a symbol of
love and of belonging to the master. This is supported by the story of our
summer holiday one year, which we spent with some friends who had
three children between the ages of four and nine. We often went on
hikes together and I always carried the leash. From time to time, one or
the other child would ask whether they could carry the leash, but when
they did, after a while Flip would take the leash away from the child in
question with a soft growl and bring it back to me. On another occasion,
I took Flip to the groomers for his spring haircut, where a bunch of nice
ladies took charge of him. Just then, an already shorn spaniel escaped
through the open door, which upset the staff, because both employees
were doing something that could not be interrupted. I was about to go
after him myself when the spaniel unexpectedly returned, rushed to the
chair on which his leash was lying, grabbed it, and set out for home once
more. We barely managed to catch him at that point. In other words, he
remembered that he had *forgotten* his leash and he came back for it. Has
anyone heard of an *animal* doing such a thing?

It is clear that Flip understands the dual significance of the leash and
the collar. That raises the interesting question whether dogs are able in
general to distinguish the whole from its parts. After all, the leash and
the collar are each a separate thing and only careful thought allows us to

infer that they are component parts of a single thing. I hope that the reader will not consider this train of thought just so much abstract reasoning, because I have made observations that prove that dogs are able to contemplate the problem of the whole versus its parts.

November 3, 1990. Whenever I sit somewhere, Flip is likely to bring his rag for playing tug-of-war and put it in my hand so we can play. He brought it again today. I was sitting in an armchair, with my stockinged feet on a table. Flip stopped and alternately looked at my hands and my feet, and after a short while pressed the rag against the soles of my feet.

Unfortunately, he had to learn that my soles are not well adapted for grabbing and has never tried that again.

Dogs are able to recognize the connection between objects and actions and their memory about these is quite fantastic. Not long after we found Flip, we moved into a new apartment, and in the process I packed up a whole lot of junk, intending to take it to the basement for storage. When I was ready to go, I took the basement key from the little cabinet in which we keep keys and invited Flip, who was watching, to accompany me. We went down and stowed the junk. More than a year later, during which time I had not visited the basement, I had to go down for something and, once again, I took the key from the cabinet. Flip was all ready and rushed forward. I was thinking that this silly little dog was expecting to go for a walk and would be disappointed. I was intentionally walking slowly so I could see where he would run. If Flip was thinking of going for a walk, he would go through the corridor in the stairwell to the outer gate. But Flip did not hesitate even a second: at the bottom of the staircase he did not go toward the gate, but turned to the next flight of stairs down and was waiting for me by the basement door. The single occasion a year earlier was enough to make him remember the function of the key.

A similar event took place on the occasion of our excursion to the Bükk Mountains, when we also visited Aunt Gizi, whose guests we were for a few days. We were staying in a room on the second floor, and every morning we would go down to the kitchen with Flip to have breakfast. Then we would use the key to the courtyard door to let Flip out so he could do his business. One day, I had to get something from our car before breakfast and I started to go down, holding the small door key in my hand. As I got to the door, I saw that Flip was going in an entirely different direction, namely toward Aunt Gizi's separate kitchen, where I had never been. "Damn it," I thought while opening the courtyard door, "he has no business going there." But Flip was already outside, because it turned out that one could also get to the courtyard through the other kitchen, the door of which was open from early morning on.

Flip is not only able to infer what will happen from seeing the key, but he knows the word *key* itself. Once we were at our country house and we were in the garden, preparing to go home. At such times, Flip lies down somewhere and patiently awaits the denouement, which consists of our opening the garden gate and going to the car. When we were almost finished with packing, I yelled to Eve, "Do you have the key?" "It's in the lock," she replied. But as soon as Flip heard the word *key*, he went to the gate and looked back at us impatiently, waiting for us to come.

The most cunning key story from the diary is the following.

September 7, 1995. We had been at our country house for some time, and on that occasion, Flip was lying next to my chair. Our friend Zsuzsika has a summer house in the neighborhood but was not in residence. Her carpenter, Gábor, arrived by car in the afternoon and came to ask me for the key to her gate. I had it all ready and waiting on my desk and I gave it to him without mentioning Zsuzsika's name. Flip accompanied him all the way to the gate and then came back. A while later came the painter, Gábor's colleague, who was also working at her house, and I chatted with him for a few minutes. Still later I was talking to Eve on the telephone when the painter reappeared to return the key; seeing that I was on the telephone, he deposited the key on my desk. When I finished talking, Flip vehemently called me to the gate, and through the gate toward Zsuzsika's house. He wanted to get inside at all costs. I said, "Zsuzsika is not here; let's go home." I even called him twice but he would not come. "OK," I said. "I'll get the key." Hearing this, he immediately came with me for the key. I took it from my desk, whereupon Flip rushed back to Zsuzsika's house and again wanted to go inside. We entered, looked around, and he sniffed around quite thoroughly, after which he calmed down and we went home.

I have no idea how and when Flip learned that there was a connection between the key, Zsuzsika, and Gábor. But I think it is certain that he somehow understood this. He probably also understood that these workmen had been in her house and he just wanted to check out what they might have done.

The four stories together show that dogs are quite advanced in their analytical abilities, because they cannot be explained in terms of simple associative learning. We probably need to assume more complex mental processes.

I also believe on the basis of similar observations that dogs easily take note of the *order* in which certain events occur, even if they do not all pertain to them. On one occasion, Flip wanted to go for a walk at an unusual time, and since it was a nice, sunny day, I told him to fetch the leash. In the meantime, we went to the front hall where the leash was lying. In our new apartment I was not in the habit of asking him for the leash before a walk, but this time I did. However, he did not bring it. We bickered about this a little and I said that we would not go until he fetched the leash. At that point, Flip went to my shoes that were standing in the front hall and, with a reproachful look at me, nudged them with his nose. The light dawned: I always put my shoes on first and only then ask for the leash. So that is what happened: I put on the shoes, Flip fetched the leash, and order was reestablished. It often happens in Göd that I am busy with something and Flip is pestering me to go for a walk in the park. When I pretend not to understand him, he goes to my coat and nudges it, watching me to see whether I have seen him do it. Of course, first comes the coat.

All these cases revolve around the recognition of connections between objects, actions, and persons. The most convincing example happened with my father-in-law, whom Flip was particularly fond of. He was playing ball with Flip in one of the rooms and after a while he came out astonished and explained the following: "You won't believe this, but the ball rolled under a bureau and the dog showed me how to retrieve it. I tried to get it with my hand but couldn't reach it. He then came to me, nudged me, and led me to a corner where a walking stick was standing in the umbrella stand. He touched it as well and alternately looked at me and at the bureau."

So far, the dog was always an interested party in these anecdotes. But dogs note the order of events in other cases as well. Once, my son Gábor and I were trying to take some pictures of Flip. Gábor was busily snapping away while I was giving commands to Flip, like "Sit," "Stand," "Don't move," and so on. All of a sudden, Gábor exclaimed, "Listen, this dog does not move until he hears the snap of the shutter." We tested this several times, and it turned out to be true. In other words, he figured out after a few pictures were taken that he was allowed to move after the sound of the shutter, and that we thought it important that he not move before. I can still remember how I tortured my father when I was a child because I always moved before he snapped the picture.

I also wrote some notes in the diary about how Flip solves a logical problem involving cause and effect:

July 14, 1994. This morning, when we were getting ready to go for a walk, I asked Flip to fetch the leash as usual. The leash was lying on one of my shirts on top of the laundry hamper, which is very easy to knock over. Flip got on his hind legs and stretched for the leash but could not reach it. He sat down and thought about it; he then started cautiously to pull the shirt, which he could reach because part of it was hanging down, until the end of the leash was in sight. He then got on his hind legs again and grabbed it. This was an outstanding solution to a logical problem.

Sometimes the dog's ability to use logic proves useful:

December 6, 1994. The telephone rang and Flip ran to me barking loudly. When I finished my conversation, he started to bark again and insisted that I go outside. I did not understand what he wanted, and having finished my telephone conversation, had no particular desire to go outside. At that point I heard the soft ringing of the intercom from the gate, and it soon turned out that it had rung before. In other words, the two instruments signaled at the same time, and he waited until I was finished with the one before he called my attention to the other.

There have been also very complicated situations in which I was unable to figure out how Flip made the correct inference. Here is a pertinent story:

July 11, 1993. In the evening, I took Flip walking by myself. Our first-floor neighbor, Erika, spoke to me from her window and said that we should stop in when we returned because she wanted to give him something. During the walk I had completely forgotten the matter and started to go upstairs, but Flip stopped at Erika's front door and kept looking at me. I went back and rang the doorbell. She gave me a large plate of chicken giblets. I asked her whether it was all right for me to return the plate the next day. She said I should rather return it in two weeks, because she was leaving on a trip early in the morning. "Well, in that case," I said, "I'll bring it back right away." We went upstairs, Flip tagging along, and after I transferred the contents of the plate to another container, I noticed that he did not come into the apartment, but stayed at the front door. When I returned to the front door with the plate in my hand, he jumped up and started to go downstairs toward Erika's apartment.

We have not yet studied scientifically the range of dogs' inferential thinking and the complexity of situations that they are able to figure out. And the last two stories suggest that this will not be an easy task.

I have mentioned that my dogs are ill-mannered. This is partly because they are relatively independent, which gives rise to many interesting situations. For example, they are permitted to beg for food when we are at the table and we give them many a tasty morsel. When we get tired of Flip's begging, we stop it with a characteristic hand gesture: the hands are rotated at chest height, which means "no!" And he understands this, because we use it consistently. Once, a good friend of ours, Ernő, visited us for lunch in our country house. Flip set out on his round of begging by first turning to me, then to Eve, and finally to Ernő.

"What am I supposed to do?" Ernő asked.

"Copy what I am doing and he will leave you in peace," said Eve while showing the "no" sign with her hand above the table.

What does the reader think happened?

I posed this question to several friends in behavioral research and I usually got one of two answers: either that the dog stopped begging, because the right signal was given or that the dog continued to beg from Ernő, because the signal was not given by the person from whom he was begging. Well, it turns out that both replies are in error, because these replies assume that learning the signal "no!" was simple conditioning. What actually happened was that upon seeing Eve's hand signal, Flip became extremely angry and barked at Eve mightily, which he had never done before. After that he turned to Ernő and continued begging. They may throw me out of various scientific societies for this, but I think Flip understood the situation exactly right, namely that Eve was teaching Ernő the signal for "no!" and that is why he became mad. "I'll thank you not to mess around with my affairs!" I need not dwell on what high order of intellectual ability is needed for this: about that of a four-year-old child.

Dogs have some problems with names and do not particularly care about the proper terminology. It takes a great deal of teaching for them to learn the names of two or three objects sufficiently well so that they will fetch the correct object from another room at least 80 percent of the time. But there are cases when they do not even have to learn the name of something but can infer it from the subtext or the context of the action.

November 15, 1993. On our walk on Castle Hill, we found a pigeon under a bush that had been hit by an arrow, still alive but in bad shape. The struggling bird elicited Flip's keen interest. We took it home and determined that an arrow made of a six-inch-long knitting needle had pierced its chest. It could not even stand and I had no choice but to perform minor surgery on it. It was so thirsty that it drank at length from a glass I held for it. Afterward, I put it in a small, covered cage, which I placed on top of a kitchen cabinet. Flip was watching the action with considerable attention. After I had taken care of the bird, I had to go out and Eve asked me what we should call the bird. I said we would call it Dodó and left on my business.

November 16, 1993. Eve left early in the morning and I was taking care of the bird by myself. I was the first one home in the afternoon and I saw that the bird's condition had improved and it ate some of the bird food I had given it. When Eve arrived home, I said to her, "Guess what, Dodó is eating." Upon hearing this, Flip rushed to the kitchen like greased lightning to where the cage was and started to watch the bird.

Afterward, Dodó was with us for about six weeks,[4] and we often saw convincing proof that Flip remembered his name well, because upon hearing it he would always rush to the kitchen. We also tried to see whether Flip would do likewise upon hearing the bird's name after we released it, but he would not even budge. In other words, he was able to associate the unknown word heard just once with the star of the event, purely on the basis of observation. This is also a remarkable achievement.

Chapter 9

Dogs Imitate but Have No Hands

Unfortunately, there is no precise and generally accepted definition of imitation or aping. In animal experimentation, imitation usually refers to conscious copying, which occurs when one individual copies the behavior of another exactly, down to the last details, in order to accomplish some objective. Human imitation is classified by psychologists in a separate category and does not require consciousness, exactness, or even the presence of a goal. It is a highly developed mechanism for achieving reconciliation and harmony and can be analyzed only in the context of a group's organizational structure. Imitation also requires a well-developed intellect, because the brain has to "translate" the movements and activity of another person or animal into commands that move one's own body parts.

Dogs Imitate but We Rarely Notice It

Our observations and experimental results suggest that for some reason the ability to imitate is a necessary condition for a well-developed social lifestyle, because dogs have this ability, too. At least, that is what we think. We will start with a few observations from the diary of Flip and

Jerry, and then discuss some experiments. But first, let me again cite De La Malle, who described a case of imitation more than one hundred years ago.[1] He described a spaniel whose master let him into a warm room on a cold winter night. After a few hours, the dog wanted to go out and the master explained that it was fiercely cold outside and it would be better if the dog just stayed put. But his argument was in vain and the dog continued to beg to be let out. Thinking that the dog only had to urinate, the master then had a great idea. He took a chamber pot from under the bed and placed it in front of the dog, and to make sure that the dog understood what it was for, he himself urinated into it. The spaniel understood the matter and followed the master's example. When I first read this story, I was not inclined to believe it, but since I read an account of a Seeing Eye dog that was able to do its business along with his master in a men's toilet,[2] I started to think that the story might actually be true.

I have frequently observed that dogs imitate each other, and the imitation probably occurs because it involves the mechanism of stimulus enhancement. The meaning of the term is that the activities of another member of the species call the animal's attention to some aspect of its environment, which produces a stimulus leading to a parallel reaction. At our country house, Jerry is the bane of summer residents, because at each house where there is a dog, he lures the other animal to the fence and then the two run back and forth along it, barking wildly. In the meantime, as an ethologist I am embarrassed that I have such an ill-mannered dog. But there is nothing I can do, because in these cases Jerry is so excited that he simply stops obeying. Another similarly temperamental dog, Toto, lives near us and it not only races along the fence but in its rage it sinks its teeth into it as well. Jerry learned this behavior from Toto, and he, too, bites the fence (from the outside), but only at Toto's house.

Another frequent occurrence is probably caused by the same mechanism. When our neighbors in the country, Péter and Éva, arrive with their nice little white Bolognese, Cricket, in their arms and greet us at the corner of the garden, Jerry becomes restless, barks and jumps on me, all the while nodding toward Péter and Éva, until I pick him up as well. Then he quiets down, but I become restless, because he weighs about fifty pounds.

Dogs like to imitate children best.

February 5, 1993. A very strange thing happened today, and if I had not seen it myself, I would not have believed it. We went to Castle Hill, toward the funicular railway, and two little girls were sledding on a slope. They called to Flip, and when he ran to them, they caressed him. Then they sledded down the slope and Flip ran after them. We then continued our walk for a while. On the return leg of our walk he started to run toward this slope from quite a distance away. The girls were still sledding and they and Flip again went through the ritual of greeting, tail wagging, and caressing. Flip ran after them every time they slid down the slope. When I tried to resume the walk, Flip just stood there and looked at me and at the sled, and I got the feeling that he wanted to go sledding. I asked one of the girls whether they might take Flip for a ride. They looked at me a little strangely, but finally said OK, if Flip was willing to sit between them. "Very good," I said, and turning to Flip, "Go, they will take you." The three of them went to the top of the slope, then the two girls sat on the sled, making a small space for Flip between them, and said to him, "Sit here." Flip immediately jumped on the sled in the appointed place. The child behind him put her arms around him and they slid to the bottom. When the two children got off the sled, Flip remained in his place and did not want to get off the sled. I asked them whether they would take him for one more ride. This time they laughed and agreed readily. Flip ran after them and when they called him, he immediately jumped on the sled and they slid down together again. By that time I had to hurry home and as soon as I started out, Flip came right away. On the way back he was walking between my legs, yanking on the leash and pulling my hand, generally behavior that he engages in only when he is very happy. A fantastic, unambiguous case of imitation! There are very few examples of this [except for the jumping from the woodpile—see below], because he has no hands.

February 6, 1993. Today we again walked in the direction of the funicular, and Flip ran ahead toward the slope where the sledders had been. He stopped, looked around, and was manifestly very disappointed.

Another case of imitative behavior arose in connection with the woodpile. This event took place when we were on summer holidays with the friends I have mentioned before and their three children. At the place where we lived, there were three piles of neatly stacked long logs in the courtyard. One afternoon, Flip and I went for a walk, while Eve stayed behind with the children. When we got back, we saw that the three children were standing in a row by the smallest of the woodpiles, and one after another they climbed on top of all three. Eve was standing before the tallest of the woodpiles and each child would jump into her arms and then run to the end of the queue. Flip observed all this for a while and then he also queued up. He then climbed up, but with some difficulty, because dogs' feet are not made for this type of terrain, and then he, too, jumped into Eve's arms. What I found most surprising in this was that he took his place in the queue and patiently awaited his turn (he learned the rule).

For a long time I thought that Flip was an unusually gifted dog and my coworkers seconded that with gentle irony whenever I tried to egg them on in their experiments with my detailed observations. But it eventually turned out that Flip did not represent a unique case.

October 14, 1998. Today we visited some friends and took both dogs along. At the beginning of our visit, their three-year-old son, Bence, drove into the room in his big, red, pedal-propelled car. Both dogs ran to the car, looked at it, and when Bence got out, they indicated that they wanted to sit in it. I first asked Jerry whether he wanted a ride and I picked him up and put him in the car. But his feet were getting stuck, so we gave up on that. Then came Flip, and I also asked him whether he wanted me to put him in the car and he indicated that he did. He was very calm and placed his hind feet on the seat and his fore feet on the hood and I pushed the car along. He looked positively triumphant. Then, of course, Jerry wanted to ride again and the two dogs had a row about it. Jerry let me pick him up again, something that he normally hates, and finally I was able to position him like I had Flip and pushed him around a bit. Later, Bence sat on my lap, whereupon Jerry jumped up, too, and sat on my lap for a while.

Since dogs have no hands and their feet do not much resemble those of humans, I would not want to assert on the basis of our observations that they satisfied all the necessary conditions for a scientific definition of imitation. But I do think that we are dealing here with a high-order activity—at a minimum, with *role-playing*. The intellect of dogs is able to evaluate what it is that the person demonstrating the pattern is doing, and to realize that they, too, would like to do the same or something similar. For this to be possible, the mind must be able to imagine that its body could be placed in similar circumstances. It is important to note that many kinds of dogs probably often attempt to imitate children or their masters, but most of the time this behavior remains unnoticed. The mechanics of the human and canine bodies are so different that it is very difficult to realize that a four-legged dog running around really wants to go sledding or ride in a car or on a swing. (Once, Flip managed to climb into a children's swing and was very worked up by this, but he tried it out like a true hero.) If we pay attention, we may often catch on to these desires.

An old game we used to play with Flip may provide further proof of role-playing. We used to say to Flip, "I'll blow into your ear," whereupon he would respond with angry growls; at such times we would not touch him because it appeared to make him really angry. But this was only a game; if I really touched him and hugged him, he would immediately become as friendly as ever. In other words, he was able to play the role of an untouchable, angry dog, but at the same time he knew that he really loved us and would die for a hug.

My colleagues Márta Gácsi and József Topál started a very promising experiment in which the master places his backpack in front of the dog and attempts to make the dog understand that it is to play a game of defending it, not even letting his master touch it. While this seems like a difficult assignment, many dogs can be made to understand it in a few minutes. Videos taken of this experiment show that they defend the backpack by pretending to act very aggressively with fierce barks. But when the master finally does take the backpack away, they suddenly become their customary gentle selves. In other words, dogs understand that they were merely playing an aggressive role. We have not yet done experiments with role switching, but they are in preparation.

Imitation in Experimental Settings

Needless to say, these observations inspired a number of different experiments. Our biggest problem was to design tasks in which the person demonstrating a pattern of behavior would not have to use his hands.

The first series of experiments employed the same arrangement, in simplified form, that we already described in the discussion of obedience to rules. We again set up three screens along an arc of a circle; the experimenter showed the dog a ball, and then deposited the ball behind one of the screens. He then returned to the dog and asked it to fetch the ball. The dogs would comply enthusiastically. In some cases we also placed a large box behind the screens, which the experimenter would just walk around before hiding the ball. This was an action without any purpose or function at all: if somebody wanted to retrieve the ball, it was entirely unnecessary to undertake it. The experimental results showed that the majority of dogs (twelve out of fourteen) nevertheless undertook the small extra trip, in other words, imitated the experimenter. Once the dogs had learned well to fetch the hidden ball, the experimental task was changed: within the dogs' sight, the experimenter would give the ball to the dog's master and then go behind the screens with open hands. He pretended to be looking for something, and when he returned, he asked the dogs for the ball. It was again the case that more than half the dogs (fourteen out of seventeen) did the same, searching quite overtly. The three that did not conform to this pattern went to their master and asked for the ball. Here, too, is a case of imitation, which is an important element in the development of obedience to rules.

This experiment led to another observation, which is mainly to be credited to our Ph.D. candidate Enikő Kubinyi. On one occasion I asked her to use her vizsla for trying out a situation with a potential for imitation. I suggested that after she returned home from a walk with the dog, she should not go directly to her front door, but should proceed in a superfluously roundabout way; perhaps climbing an extra flight of stairs above her apartment. While doing this she should not call the dog, not praise it if it happened to go with her; then she should return to her front door and open it as usual. Enikő started to make the necessary observations and I, like the proverbial absentminded professor, forgot all about

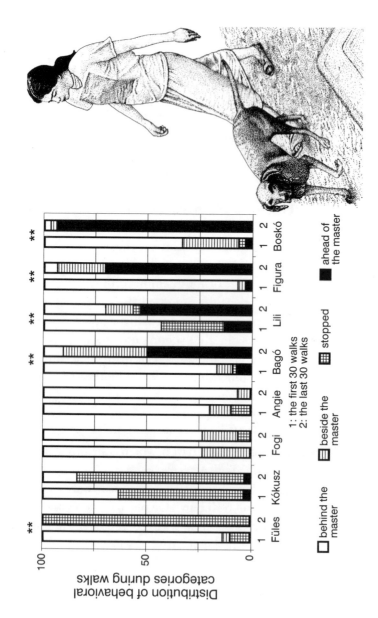

Figure 19. Percentage Distribution of Behavioral Categories
Dogs imitate their master at the end of the walk. Asterisks mark columns showing statistically significant differences.

it. If, say, a month later she had reported that the vizsla always waited for her at her front door and exhibited no inclination to imitate her, I would have said fine, stop the experiment because this idea just did not work. But Enikő is an outstanding and persistent experimenter. She presented herself after some three months and told me that after the 180th trial the vizsla normally preceded her and undertook the roundabout way independently of her. After that, the vizsla behaved in that fashion with increasing regularity until its behavior became perfect imitation. We were very glad that Enikő was so persistent, but thought it a bit strange that it took so long to develop the imitative behavior. For that reason, we decided to study the situation further with the aid of dogs owned by eight cooperating dog owners. The dogs included vizslas and shepherds, and the results are shown in figure 19. Some of the imitating dogs followed their masters, some went ahead and covered the superfluous distance before the master, and some stayed beside their master as he performed his walk. Of course, there were some that simply stopped and did not cover the extra distance.³ There is also a simpler variant of this task. In an open space, one places two ten-foot fences at right angles to each other so that they form a "corner" and one places in this corner an object of interest to the dog, usually a ball. The dog is kept on a leash a small distance away on the "outside" of the corner and can clearly see where the ball is placed. The dog is then taken off the leash and the master asks the dog to retrieve the ball. At first, this represents a serious challenge for dogs; they tend to rummage and dig around the corner and it takes a long time before they realize that they can just walk around the open end of the fencing. But of course, after five or six tries they learn how to do this. However, if the human experimenter calls the dog's attention to himself before it makes its first try, points to the ball in the corner, and walks around the fence, thus showing the dog how to retrieve it, most dogs are able to solve the problem quickly on the basis of the demonstration.⁴

Up to this point, the experiments show that dogs easily imitate their masters if a path is to be chosen. In the next experiment, we examined the dogs' abilities to imitate in a more complicated setting requiring some manipulation. Canine sports enthusiasts will be familiar with the apparatus that shoots balls for dogs to catch. We used similar equipment for the following experiment. We divided twelve dogs and their masters into two groups. In the first group, the masters took their dogs to the equipment, which had a prominent lever. Making sure that the dogs were paying attention, they moved the lever, which delivered a ball, and they then allowed the dogs to play with it for a while. Ten trials were carried out. The masters in the other group merely played with their dogs and a ball during this period. Then the dogs were left alone with the ball equipment and their masters encouraged them to get a ball. There was a major difference in behavior between the dogs in the two groups. The dogs that saw how their masters got a ball by operating the equipment were themselves able to do so and quickly obtained one. After much encouragement, the dogs in the other group—which had no model to follow—got the idea that they needed to get hold of a ball, but could not figure out that they had to activate the lever; they would only paw at the device or simply knock it over and in the end obtained many fewer balls in the stipulated time than the dogs in the first group.[5] There was one other important difference between the two groups: if a dog that did not have a model to imitate nevertheless managed to obtain a ball, it would subsequently get other balls much more rapidly. In other words, it *learned* during the experiment. Those that had observed the master obtain a ball from the equipment got their first ball very quickly and could not improve their performance noticeably in subsequent trials (see figure 20).

These successful experiments raised the possibility that dogs might be able to carry out the most complicated tasks of imitation. The essence of these is to internalize the rule that in the given situation the most diverse actions of the human model must be imitated as precisely as possible. Behavioral scientists characterize this task as "do as I do."[6] Thus far, it can be experimentally proven only for dolphins, chimpanzees, and one orangutan that they are able to reliably copy actions even if they have not received prior training for that particular action. The essence of the procedure is to first try to make the experimental animal understand what is expected of it. Work of several weeks is required to induce the animal to observe the trainer while he performs some tasks; for example, turns a full circle, jumps on a chair, bends his upper body, picks up an object from the floor and places it in a bucket, and similar things. After these activities are completed, the trainer returns to the starting point and tells the animal, "Do as I do." The animal has no other clue for solving the problem than what it has seen in the previous moments, provided that it was paying adequate attention.

Figure 20. Imitation of the Act of Getting the Ball
*In one group of dogs, their masters showed them how to operate
the equipment that delivered the balls.*

After long training, the smartest of the above animals understands
the task and carries it out. When the experimenters believe that the animal has had enough practice in this, it is subjected to the decisive experiment: the trainer carries out actions that the animal has never seen in
this context. For example, the trainer may get on the floor and lap some
water from a dish or he may climb up on a piece of furniture. If the animal acts likewise after it hears the "do as I do" command, the experiment is deemed to be successful; it is then plausible to argue that it has
understood the essence of the game of imitation. The task can be made
more complicated by having it demonstrated by another person who is
known to the animal but has not been in close contact with it. If the animal also imitates this other person, we have solid proof that it understands this complicated task and has the ability to carry it out. This is no
mean accomplishment: it must not only observe and remember the various actions, but somehow it has to translate them so that they apply to
its own body and limbs. Only a mind of a very high order can do that.

I have to confess that we substantially underestimated the corresponding abilities of dogs and continually delayed starting the relevant
experiments, which required complicated preparations, many types of

controls, and hard, precise, methodical work lasting many weeks. But once we bit the bullet we started experiments with Philip, a dog trained to assist the handicapped, whose master, Richard Mányik, had worked wonders with it. Philip's performance was miraculous and was not based on months of training. Philip understood what was expected of him within days and he carried out his tasks even when my colleagues József Topál and Ádám Miklósi, with whom he was acquainted, were the ones who demonstrated what the task was, and he did so even when the task was brand new. His imitation was completely accurate in 60 percent to 70 percent of the trials and his error rate corresponded to what has been experienced with the very best performing chimpanzees. There were some tasks in which Philip was almost always successful and there were harder ones in which he succeeded on average only half the time. These exciting experiments are still ongoing, because it turned out that Philip is able to observe an action with several (two to three) elements and replicate it precisely on command, even if the given actions had never been used before in this imitation game.

For a while we believed that Philip is a kind of "wonder-dog" who acquired his abilities as a result of his regular and busy daily routine. We were wrong again. My dog Jerry understood within three days what I wanted from him and can successfully carry out the "do as I do" tasks. Right now we are working with several dogs and are trying to investigate whether the successful completion rates show any differences among the various types of tasks. It seems that there are such differences because dogs have no hands and have to solve lots of problems in different ways. Activities involving objects are easier for them, while actions involving their own bodies are harder. But whatever the case may be, the results to date prove that their imitative abilities are far better than those of other animals and only human children are much superior to dogs. I need to add that all dogs love these tasks once they have understood what the game is about.

This chapter summarizes the state of knowledge in the scientific investigation of dogs' ability to imitate models. It is quite certain that additional interesting insights will be gained in the future, but the results to date prove that dogs are able to imitate humans. This ability is an important evolutionary consequence of the domestication of dogs.

Chapter 10

Can Dogs "Speak"?

A nimals long ago discovered how to communicate, or at least to exhibit the kind of behavior that we call communication, but contrary to popular belief, they do not hold conversations.

In ethology, we define communication as *an animal's behavioral act that alters the probable conduct of another animal in a manner that, on the average, is advantageous for the communicating animal's survival and reproduction.* This definition says nothing about messages, signs, or conversations. Unfortunately, these notions emerged from the forms of communication prevalent among highly developed humans and particularly from descriptions of language use, and their role in ethology is purely as analogies or as elements of explanatory models. It is not literally true, as one might be tempted to say, that a courting peacock conveys a "love message" with his courtship to a peahen; our calling it a "love message" is merely a reference to a phenomenon well known in human behavior. In other words, it is "as if" the human pattern were taking place. It is a physiological phenomenon of the peacock's biological functions that when it is mating time and it catches a glimpse of a hen, it spreads its tail feathers and struts before mating. We tend to call that courting, because we are thinking of our own actions that have a similar function, even though they manifest themselves differently.

The model of communication can also clarify the functions of glandular secretions. For example, if we say that in the face of a fear-inducing event the adrenal gland sends an urgent "danger message" to the heart and other organs, so that they may prepare for coping with additional challenges, the message itself is just a hormone, namely adrenaline. I hope that nobody would interpret this statement to mean that the adrenal gland plants itself by the side of the highway represented by the blood vessels and eagerly waves a handkerchief soaked in adrenaline, meaning "Attention, trouble is brewing!" All this is but an analogy. Animal communication is not a conversation, but rather control carried out with the aid of behavioral patterns and anatomical signs.

Animal communication, as it is called in the final analysis, regulates or controls the recognition and identification of individuals and of the rank order within a group; it also regulates aggression, facilitates the avoidance of fights, helps the maintenance of contacts, and serves numerous other functions. But it fulfills these tasks in such a manner that the animal is not conscious or (in higher-order animals) not necessarily conscious of carrying out an act of communication. It also follows that animal communication is a limited system and the number of different "messages"—of behavioral signs that perform a regulating function— does not exceed twenty to forty on the average.

I have mentioned several times the behavior that consists of a dog's approaching its master and giving it a push with its nose. This is genuine communication, because afterward the dog looks at the master, establishes eye contact, and asks for something, or merely indicates that it had been away and is back now and wishes to resume contact. The crucial element of this behavior is that it elicits their joint attention, indicates an *intention*, and conveys information concerning something beyond them. In scientific language this phenomenon is called referentiality. This phenomenon simply does not occur in most cases of animal communication; with few exceptions, the communication of even our most developed relatives is a limited set of behavioral patterns that regulate the life of the group. The vervet monkey possesses a highly developed system of vocal signaling and indicates with different sounds whether the approaching predator is flying, has four legs, or is snakelike.[1] However, this danger signal does not, strictly speaking, communicate information, but is a regulator of behavior, as is the case with many other animals.

During the course of human evolution, probably in its earlier phases, genuine communication appeared as a result of a need to communicate. The signals of genuine communication were purposely paired with and matched to alterations of the state of mind or of the brain images of the individual group members. We may call a type of behavior genuine communication only if we can exhibit intentionality in it, if the initiator intends to affect the mental state of the recipient of the communication, and if the latter intends to pay attention to the content of the communication.

Of course, intentional communication did not start with humans. Its most elementary forms have been observed in nature: for example, in the begging behavior of chimpanzees, when they extend their hands toward a dominant individual or toward a person from whom they might receive something. It can be proved unambiguously that the participants in communication mutually pay attention and they recognize each other's intentions in the same way that dogs do. It is also certain that our distant relatives were able to use an array of very simple forms of communication consisting of touching, the gestures of holding back or pushing away, eye contact, pointing, or dismissive waves of the hand. Also, they were able to express their feelings, such as affection, anger, joy, and sorrow.

Of course, these refined modes of expression perform a real function only among those species in which the individuals continually and persistently strive to get clear about the mental states of the others in their group. Humans are a species that acts like that: a good part of our day is spent observing others or being observed by them. Humans are incredibly excited about knowing what others are thinking about, what they are planning, and what their opinion is about sundry matters. We have said the same about dogs on several occasions, and so we plan to examine in this chapter whether dogs have "conversations."

Teaching Chimpanzees to Speak Human Language Fails

A genuine examination of animal conversation began with the experiments to teach chimpanzees language. The experiments lasted a number of years and were accompanied by horrendous debates. In the 1950s, K. J. Hayes and C. H. Hayes were the first to attempt to teach English to a chimpanzee.[2] The result of many years' instruction was a vocabulary of four simple, one-syllable words, which the animal, named Vicky, was for the most part able to use actively and appropriately.

In the next famous experiment, another American team, B. T. Gardner and R. A. Gardner, taught a simplified form of sign language (called American Sign Language, ASL) to a chimpanzee called Washoe.[3] This experiment was followed by the work of David Premack, who taught an artificial sign language to his chimpanzee Sara.[4] In another experiment, the Lana project, chimpanzees communicated with computers, using keyboards and monitors.[5] In addition to the chimpanzees, there was a gorilla named Koko, who was taught sign language with great success.[6]

In two years, Washoe had learned and actively used more than a hundred signs. Experimental techniques have developed rapidly to the point where today the same result could be obtained in a few months. Videotapes, computers, and hundreds of thousands of data points confirm the results of these experiments.

After the publication of the Washoe experiments, it seemed that proof was at hand that chimpanzees could learn a language, and that laboratories engaged in animal experimentation would soon be populated by "talking" apes. Well, this did not come to pass, because chimpanzees do not have a linguistic ability that matches or even approaches that of humans.[7] The heightened expectations were not fulfilled, but even so, the experiments provided a great deal of interesting data. They proved the existence of an animal consciousness, they created the most appropriate methodologies for these studies, and they contributed to our understanding of the function and development of human language usage as a peculiarity of our species.

Let us briefly assess the results. The aptitude for language consists of several components. Among these, the most important is that the user of language be capable of *symbolic representation*—that is to say, have the ability to internalize the linguistic signs for objects, phenomena, and relationships. Chimpanzees are able to learn a few hundred signs, among them nouns, adjectives, relations—such as *"if . . . then," "same," "different"*— as well as negation. It is essential that the sign not simply reflect association, since even lower animals are able to learn signs by association. We can speak of genuine symbolic representation only if the sign symbolizes the object, the action, or the concept. A good portion of the experiments with chimpanzees' language learning is concerned with discovering the extent to which a learned sign is actually a symbol.

An analysis of the properties of objects is helpful here. Premack's chimpanzee, Sara, was willing to regard a rectangular, blue piece of paper as red and round if the paper denoted an apple. That is to say, the rectangular blue paper evoked in her brain the true internal "representation" of an apple. The sign thus mobilizes in the animal's brain not the response that corresponds to the immediate sensory observation, but one that corresponds to the properties of the object that is being symbolized. Thus, the use of signs among chimpanzees goes beyond purely associative learning and involves more complicated symbolic learning.

Researchers have also proved that under suitable experimental conditions chimpanzees are able and willing to use signs to ask each other for objects. In other words, a need that arises is capable of activating through the sign the internal representation of the desired object. It also follows from the examples above that the chimpanzees are able to recognize causal connections mediated by the signs.

In other respects, the linguistic abilities of chimpanzees are much more modest. It appears that apes are unable to form ordered sequences of signs according to rules that might basically correspond to the syntax of human language. In chimpanzee communication, we most often encountered sign combinations with only two elements, and even these were used in arbitrary order. We can infer from this finding that the human aptitude for grammar is probably a genetically determined characteristic of our species. Equally modest is the chimpanzees' aptitude for creating new linguistic constructs: in other words, they very rarely create new combinations or new signs. It is no accident that the linguistic experiments with chimpanzees failed.[8]

After the chimpanzee experiments, it became clear that a lot of other animals are also capable of learning signs and using them meaningfully. Later we shall discuss in detail Irene Pepperberg's parrot, Alex.[9] R. J. Schusterman and K. Krieger taught various signs to two California sea lions. The sea lions were able to learn almost two hundred signs in a short period and were also able to make sense of combinations (e.g.: "Take the white ball to the left corner of the pool").[10] L. M. Hermann taught signs to dolphins.[11] Not very long ago, it turned out that bonobos learn sign language spontaneously and without practice much faster and much more effectively than chimpanzees, and moreover, they can learn and understand the English words corresponding to the signs by just hearing them.[12]

Of course, psychologists have also studied the sign-learning ability of dogs.[13] According to a fairly thorough 1928 report of psychology professors C. J. Warden and L. H. Warner, the German shepherd Fellow, who was featured in many Hollywood films at that time, was able to understand some fifty-three verbal commands, even if these were uttered behind closed doors. All these commands were meant to result in the execution of some concrete task. For example: "Walk around the room!" "Touch the man!" "Bark!" "Go in the water!" "Turn your head!" and so on. They also tried out fifteen commands that instructed the dog to carry out a task in some particular direction or particular place. For example: "Jump on the table!" "Look out the window!" "Put your head on the chair!" and the like. But the dog obeyed these latter commands only if his master was physically present and indicated with looks or body language how and where the task was to be carried out. They also undertook a searching examination of the number of names of objects that a dog can distinguish. The owner gave the researchers a long list of names, but they determined only the proportion of cases in which the dog, confined to a separate room, selected the correct object when hearing its name. The results showed that if there were three objects in the room and thirty-six trials, Fellow selected the correct object twenty-one times, significantly surpassing the result expected under random selection, which would be twelve. The researchers were very careful and noted that there were numerous extraneous influences in the experiment. Occasionally, Fellow was made to work for two to three hours, even though it was soon evident that he was tired. He also had to obey in situations with which he had had no practice. It also became evident in the object selection tests that when, for example, they asked him to select a brush, he would retrieve it only if the bristles did not point upward, presumably because they hurt his mouth. It is interesting that these experiments took place much earlier than the ape experiments, and reading about them today is at least as interesting as reading the about latter, although they had been nearly forgotten in the meantime.

To summarize: highly developed animals' brains are able to carry out a certain transformation of the cerebral representation of signs they employ, and therefore, by all standards, are capable of a type of thinking. But they lack the special ability to create *their own specific, self-contained system* of these representations, which humans are able to do on the basis of their linguistic aptitudes and with the aid of symbols. An evaluation of the tests must also take into account that the researchers were actually interested in only one question, namely whether animals are able to approach the level of humans in linguistic capabilities. When they determined that the answer is no, they lost interest and discontinued any further experimentation. The "top-down" approach, which compares animal accomplishments to those of humans, is heavily burdened with ideology. Humans seek scientific proof of their superiority, and thanks to their idiosyncratic methodology, they find it easily.

Of course, there are other avenues as well. We could examine, for example, how animals, or even humans, *understand* how one should behave in a small community. The question is not whether the animal speaks a language, employs symbols, or interprets signs, or whether it simply associates them with something—these are all details—but how it manages to prosper, with whatever means. A true evolutionary characterization would adopt such an approach.

Dogs Excel in "Social Understanding"

People who own dogs have tremendous practical experience in how dogs adapt to their everyday life and how they understand their masters. Unfortunately, this does not mean that we can account for these special abilities of dogs scientifically. The majority of owners speak to their dogs largely the way we normally speak to a two- or three-year-old child. For their part, dogs look on with attention, listen to their owners' speech, and then do something, this way or that. The master does not expect the dog to answer, but does expect the dog to understand him, and demands that the dog do as it is told. Dog owners' theory thus is that dogs understand human speech, at least parts of it. If this conception were not prevalent, we probably would not speak to our pets. It follows that the precise definition of social understanding in the case of a dog is this: in a social situation, *the dog behaves in such a manner as to make its master believe that it has understood the situation.* Of course, we can probe further to see what the basis is for this belief in understanding and what behavior of the dog elicited it in the master. We can also examine what mechanisms were activated in the mind of the dog when the master came to the belief that the dog had understood something.

Fellow obeyed some sixty to seventy commands, and psychologists verified much of this through controlled experiments. It turned out—not surprisingly—that information for a dog is contained not only in words and in speech, but also in the master's looks, his movements, and the way he holds his body. A more modern analysis is undertaken by S. Coren,[14] whose dogs are able to interpret some sixty different communications, and he also notes that dogs interpret words together with body language.

In what follows, we shall mainly deal with the conceptualization of the social situation and dwell less on how the dog understood it. I will mention only one counterexample for cooling the ardor of those estimable dog owners who are convinced that their dog understands words the way humans do. On one occasion, we clipped Flip's fur and saved the clippings in a bag that we placed in a closet. It turned out that he very much enjoyed sniffing the bag, and occasionally we had to take it out of the closet to let him get a really good sniff. We decided to give the bag and its contents a name and called it "the other dog." Later, when we asked Flip, "Where is the other dog?" he would immediately run to the closet and beg with vigorous tail wagging that we open the closet door so that he could carry out the ritual sniffing. Once we demonstrated this to a guest, and he noted that Flip was very intelligent because he understood what was said to him. My son Gábor and I looked at each other and we both had exactly the same idea, except that he beat me to it. He turned to Flip and said in English, instead of Hungarian, "Where is the other dog?" whereupon Flip ran to the closet. "You see, he understands English as well," we said to the guest. But the poor guest did not understand. The essence of the matter is that the most important ingredient is the *situation*. A moment before we had performed the ritual, and we do not know which word or which questioning intonation triggered Flip. When the question was repeated in English, both the situation and the intonation were the same as before, and this sufficed for producing a repetition of the action. This is precisely the essence of social understanding: both communicating parties have something in mind, and they attempt to provide signals that will make the other party think of what they are thinking of. This type of communication is a process of harmonizing and synchronizing that promotes joint action. In the relationship between dogs and humans, this harmonizing works very well in certain realms of cooperative action, and at times even words can play a role in this process.

My colleague Peter Pongrácz and I began a scientific investigation of social understanding. In the pretest phase, a sizable sample of dog owners reported that their dogs understood some forty commands, with a minimum of eight and a maximum of seventy.[15]

Let us look at the simplest case. Sharon, a two-year-old Irish wolfhound, responds not only to her own name but also to the following seven commands: "sit," "down," "up," "stand," "stay," "walk," "come." The eight expressions actually fall into three categories. The dog's name, "walk," and "come" express the master's desire to interact with the dog. We shall refer to this category as invitation. The commands "sit," "down," "up," and "stand" are all instructions concerning the dog's posture, which is how we shall refer to this category. Finally, the "stay" command has the objective of inhibiting an action initiated by the dog and we shall refer to this category of commands as *action inhibition*.

When we deal with a dog that understands many more expressions, we have to introduce some new categories. Flip and Jerry understand approximately seventy expressions. We first look at the categories discussed before.

INVITATION: *Jerry,*[16] *Dogs, Come, Let's go, Back, Let's walk, We're going, Here*.

It is obvious that there are many words with comparable meaning.

POSTURE: *Sit, Down, Roll over, Up, Paws, Give me your paw, Beg, Bark*.

The commands to vocalize produce a deep growl by Jerry in response to *Beg* and a bark in response to *Bark*.

ACTION INHIBITION: *No, Enough, Gone, Stay, Wait, There is no more, Don't bark, Shame, Watch out*.

The command "no!" is fairly generally used and means that the dog must stop whatever it is doing. In general, dogs understand this command very well. The command "gone" refers to a situation in which we come home but Eve is not in: the dogs would run around to find her, but when they hear the command "gone," they stop their futile quest. Jerry learned the meaning of "There is no more" much faster than Flip, for whom rotating both hands at chest height became the action inhibitor.

INDIVIDUAL ACTIONS: *Let's take a bath, I'll dry you.*

I have no idea what the dog would think if I uttered these words, say, on the street. But in our apartment, near the bathroom, he understands them and starts for the bathroom, if not enthusiastically. Toweling produces more enthusiasm; if we return home after a rainy walk and I do not happen to say anything, Jerry will himself bring me the towel.

NAMES: *Eve, Willie, Tom, Stephen, cat, rabbit, bird, car, leash, shoe, ball, box, water, bone.*

Names can be those of persons or living creatures, and they can also be the names of various objects. Dogs learn the names of objects easily if they are associated with some exceptional activities. Peter Pongrácz showed in addition that they learn the names of living creatures, such as rabbit or pig, much faster than the names of objects. But in spite of their ability to learn names, I believe that dogs really dislike them, and one can teach them only with protracted effort to distinguish similar types of objects on the basis of their names.

PERMISSION: *Yes, OK, You can come, You are coming, too.*

These words are always tied to a particular situation. For example, Jerry always likes to accompany departing guests to the elevator. He is always asking to do so, and the reply is sometimes "No!" and sometimes "You can come." The latter is a permission that is probably tied to a context and is valid only in the given situation; for this reason I see no point in a scientific investigation that would attempt to explore the difference between "You can come" and "You are coming, too." The latter is relevant if I call Flip somewhere, and Jerry asks me what will happen with him. My reply can be either "No!" or "You are coming, too." In the latter case, elated leaping is the sign that he understood.

PROVIDING INFORMATION: *Somebody is coming, Guests are coming, You'll go with Eve, You'll come with me, I am coming, Right away, Not yet, You'll get something, Here's some food, You get a treat, There, Here, Look!, Coming right away, If . . . then . . .*

Dogs love guests, and if we announce that someone is coming, they show countless signs of heightened attention. This lasts fifteen to twenty minutes, and if the guests do not come within that period, they will ask about it once or twice more, but after a while they tend to lose interest.

Then, if the guests arrive after all, we can tell from the excited greeting that they were really waiting for the guests. Both Jerry and Flip react immediately to the words *there, here, look* by attempting to orient themselves, whether we are at home or in the open air. They will quickly look around to ascertain what this is all about and most often they will find what I am trying to point out.

The construction "if . . . then . . ." refers to a complicated set of events, but is understood by not only Jerry, but Flip as well. I discovered that they really understand this on an occasion when I was waiting at home for my son Gábor. In the meantime, the appointed hour for our walk had arrived and Flip was urging me to get going. "If *Gábor comes,* then *we shall go.*" I really did not expect him to understand this, but after I said it he quieted down. I thought that he understood me to have said no. After about half an hour, Gábor arrived, we got involved in an intense conversation, and I quite forgot about the dog. Hardly any time passed before Flip trotted into the room with the leash in his mouth, which he dropped at my feet, and started to bark angrily. It was quite unambiguous that he understood the "if . . . then . . ." construction. I have used it successfully since, and Jerry understands it, too. I will confess to my fussier readers that I do not believe that dogs understand conditional sentences; I rather think that they accept the inhibition of an action that is tied to the occurrence of some event. In other words, Flip has a continual desire to go walking, and what he understands is that the answer is "No!" until Gábor arrives. The essential difference between the human conditional statement and the dog's understanding of "If . . . then . . ." is that the dog must be continually motivated to carry out a particular action. This action can be temporarily inhibited, and the inhibition, or rather its lifting, can be tied to some signal. If in the meantime the motivation evaporates for whatever reason, the dog simply forgets the whole thing. Conditional statements of the kind "We shall go walking if the sun comes out" or "You'll get a treat if you behave" make no sense to dogs, because they do not know what it means for the sun to shine or what it means to "behave." In contrast, humans understand these constructions with ease.

COMMANDS CONTAINING TERMS OF REFERENCE: *Call* . . . (a person), *Bring the* . . . , *Grab the* . . . , *Put it inside, Drop it, Look for* . . . (some object). These commands are very specific to a situation. The "Drop it" makes sense only if the dog is holding something in its mouth. "Put it inside" makes sense only if there is a vessel or a box in the dog's visual field and it has something in its mouth or if there is an object next to the vessel. In these cases therefore the dog has to figure out and actually carry out an executable action.

QUESTION: *Where is* . . . (person or object)? *Which way?*

We have already seen that one can play a wonderful game of hide-and-seek with dogs, or ask them where a particular person or object is. Right away they set out to find the person or object. I have also mentioned the question "Which way?" and I am rather proud of it. I started to ask this question first with Flip, but Jerry also understands it. They learned the meaning of this question relatively slowly. When I pose the question "Which way?" the dog selects the direction in which we shall take a walk. At other times, and this case is more complicated, the dog may demand something, but I do not know what. When I ask "Which way?" in such a case, the dog provides additional information. For example, he may lead me to the door, because he wants to go out, or take me to his water bowl, because it is empty, or go to the container where we keep treats, because he wants one.

In order to illustrate the basis of the vocabulary I discussed above, I provide a few examples of understanding from Flip's diary.

1. Anywhere. *Come!*—He comes. (Flip, 1990)

2. The dog is on my lap and I am caressing him, the other one is at a distance of about fifteen feet. *Go play with him!*—He jumps off and goes to the other dog. (Flip, 1990)

3. We are walking on a street. *Look for the car!*—He approaches a car. (Flip, 1990)

4. We are standing in the apartment. *Look for Eve!*—He searches the apartment. (Flip, 1990)

5. We hide an object in another room and when we return we say: *Search!*—He goes to the room where I hid the object and starts sniffing around. (Flip, 1990)

6. We are standing on a street. *Where is the cat?* — He runs around and searches. (Flip, 1990)

7. Anywhere. *Cat.* — He searches. (Flip, 1990)

8. The dog is standing. *Sit!* — He sits. (Flip, 1990)

9. We are walking on the bank of a brook. He looks at me questioningly. *OK.* — He jumps in the brook. (Flip, 1990)

10. We are standing in the kitchen and a wasp is buzzing around. He is trying to catch it. *Careful!* — He slows down and becomes visibly careful. (Flip, 1990)

11. During a hike, Eve is lagging behind and is out of sight. *Get Eve!* — He runs back to Eve. (Flip, 1990)

12. On a hike, Eve gives him an object to hold. *Take it to Willy!* — He brings it to me. (Flip, 1990)

13. During a walk we encounter a fork in the road. *I point with my hand.* — He follows the indicated direction. (Flip, 1990)

14. We are getting ready to leave and Flip is inquiring. *You are coming, too!* — He runs for the leash. (Flip, 1990)

15. We are standing in the apartment or in a road. *Sit!* — He sits. (Flip, 1990)

16. We are in the kitchen. *Guests are coming.* — He runs to the front door. (Flip, 1990)

17. Flip's shorn hair is in a bag hanging in the closet. *Where is the other dog?* — He runs to the closet. (Flip, 1990)

18. We are playing hide-and-seek. I make him sit and I hide an object in another room. *Search!* — He goes and finds it. (Flip, 1990)

19. We are in our apartment, Eve in the bathroom. *Where is Eve?* — He goes and finds her. (Flip, 1990)

Detailed reflection on the above categories permits us to construct a very simple dog grammar.

1. Communications understood by dogs always deal with actions.

2. There exist innate and desirable actions for dogs that reflect the idiosyncrasies of the species. These are the actions that correspond to go, catch, chase, seek, eat, bark, sniff, as well as the actions that are involved in making social contact with the master, other persons, and other dogs.

3. There are learned actions corresponding to the signals "up," "down," or "fetch."

4. There exist signals that provide directions for the action, such as names or the commands "here," "in," "there."

5. Actions may be directed or inhibited.

6. The signals may be sounds, motions, or objects.

Most instances of social understanding can be explained as consisting of inhibitions of innate actions, understandings of directives concerning learned actions, and the meaningful use of directives concerning learned or innate actions.

For example: "*Search* (innate action) *for the cat* (an animal identifier as a term of reference) *in the box* (an object as a term of reference)!" "*Fetch* (learned action) *the towel* (object as a term of reference)!" The dog is begging (innate reaction modified by some learning): "*No more!*" (inhibition of action).

Giving information and asking questions are not quite this simple to explain, and I shall return to this topic promptly. But in the meantime, let us reflect on the extent to which the few rules and forty to fifty expressions enable understanding. Imagine a traveler who does not speak the language of a country but knows the most important words. Such a person is likely to agree that if one knows the customs of the country, one will get along quite well with a few basic words. Of course, he will not understand what is being said if his interlocutor says: "Sir, it appears that you have ignored the published timetable, and hence you are waiting for the last train in vain, because it has just left. Unfortunately, there are no more trains today, and I therefore respectfully recommend, if you see there are no obstacles to such a course of action, that you continue your trip in the morning, for which, in the name of the local office of the railroad company, I wish you a pleasant journey."

But as soon as they realize that the person does not speak the language, they will say "No train!" And if the person providing the information is reasonably clever, he will incline his head over his two folded hands to indicate sleep and may poke our traveler to help explain the situation with body language.

If we know that there is a last train, if we listen to body language, then we can determine from relatively few signs what one is trying to communicate to us. Dogs are in exactly the same position. With the exception of working dogs, most dogs do not have to exert themselves particularly to acquire food, water, and a place to sleep. If they need to do something at all, they will be taught at length to do so, and most often the important thing is that they should not do something.

This line of argument does not imply that dogs have poor intelligence, but only that their requirements for communication are modest. Even so, their need to communicate is greater than that of any other animal, although it does not even approach that of humans. Moreover, and this is the point that I shall try to prove in the next chapter, the intelligence of dogs is of a higher order than one would expect on the basis of their communication.

I have to make two further important remarks about communication. The first is about the class of signals for *giving information*, the discussion of which was postponed earlier, and the second concerns the interpretation of "Which way?", which belongs to the category of *questions*.

I begin with the latter. The dog has to understand that the master is asking a question, and the dog will decide which action desired by him will be realized. This is not a simple thing. If, upon hearing "Which way?" a choice has to be made among several alternatives, one can observe that dogs are thinking; at a fork in the road they sniff in both directions, and sometimes a whole minute elapses before Flip or Jerry decides which way to go. In part 4 we will discuss in more detail the role of secondary representations in the functioning of the human mind. It is very probable that some form of secondary representation appears in the mind of the dog, too. For example, by being able to think simultaneously about two possible courses of action, perhaps by pondering their relative advantages, and by being able to conceptualize that it, namely the dog itself, may decide. These are extremely important mechanisms—if, indeed, they exist in dogs' minds.

Giving information presupposes that the recipient accepts or asks for information and that, in certain cases, the recipient is satisfied with the information. If one pays attention to dogs, one can make the very important observation—long confirmed by the observations of my collaborators—that dogs ask *questions*. If Flip asks in the morning who will go walking with him, he accepts the reply. He cannot speak, and his question can be interpreted only within the framework of my human, social understanding, but his understanding follows unambiguously from the conformity of his behavior with the reply.

Teaching animals by using associative learning has a long history, and many have studied this scientifically. But there never was an animal psychologist who reported that his rat asked him: "Hey, who will conduct the experiment today?" I think the phenomena of posing questions and giving and accepting information reveal a great deal about the inner mechanisms of the canine mind.

In order to bolster this, I present below a few excerpts from my diaries (a few of these have been discussed before). What they have in common is that in these excerpts the dogs themselves initiated the communication. I have already emphasized that intentionality is the basis for communicating one's thoughts.

1. Because of an injection of steroids, Flip needs to urinate. He goes to the window, stands on his hind legs, wags his tail, and fixedly stares out the window. When I ask, "Shall we go out?" he runs to the door. (Flip, 1990)

2. He brings me the leash, indicating that he wants to go out. (Flip, 1990)

3. At the dinner table, he pushes against me with his nose to indicate that he wants food. (Flip, 1990)

4. At a Diósgyőr[17] campsite: somebody brought a bone and placed it in his dish. Flip asks whether he may eat it. The person who brought the bone also noticed this. (Flip, 1991)

5. I call him to go for a walk, but he does not want to come; he is pushing at Eve and goes with her. (Flip, 1990)

6. Eve is lagging behind. I send Flip to fetch her. He goes to her, pushes her with his nose, and growls, then runs back to me. (Flip, 1990)

7. In the morning, he sits impatiently by my bed and pushes my bathrobe with his nose, urging me to get up. (Flip, 1990)

8. We are in my room in Göd. Flip wants to take a walk. He goes to my overcoat and pushes at it with his nose. (Flip, 1990)

9. We are getting ready to go out; Flip approaches, sits down, wags his tail, and looks questioningly. If we say "You can't come," he goes away, but if we say, "You can come, too," he runs for the leash. (Flip, 1990)

10. On a hike, when we come to a fork in the trail, he stops and looks back. With my hand I indicate the right direction and he proceeds. (Flip, 1990)

11. I am sitting at my desk, Flip approaches, pushes me with his nose, and looks out the window. I stand up, he runs to the front door and grabs the leash. (Flip, 1991)

12. One morning, Eve was preparing to take him out, but Flip probably wanted me to come, too. Several times he left Eve standing and came to me in the bathroom and looked questioningly. When I told him that I would not go, he stopped coming. (Flip, 1991)

13. A story told by my father. A while ago, we were visiting my parents and my mother gave Flip a cheese-flavored biscuit, which he likes very much. On our next visit, my mother called Flip to the kitchen and offered him a cookie. He took it, put it on the floor, sniffed it, but did not eat it. My mother broke it in two and offered him half of it by hand, but he would not take that either and just looked out the window. Then my mother started to coax him quite emphatically to eat it, but Flip got up and went to the shelf on which there was the empty paper bag that had contained the cheese biscuits, touched the bag with his nose, returned to the cookie, and waited. Since my mother was busy talking, Flip stared out the window for a while and then left the kitchen. We were not present on this occasion of his pointing to an object. (Flip, 1991)

14. One morning, while I was dressing and getting ready to go out, Flip came to me and asked me whether I would take him. I told him that Eve would take him out, whereupon he left me and went to Eve in the bathroom. (Flip, 1991)

15. Around mealtime, he came to my study, sat down in front of me with vigorous wags and a questioning look. When I asked him, "Do you want to eat?" he immediately jumped up and rushed out of the room, where-upon I followed him to the kitchen and gave him food. (Flip, 1991)

16. Eve went to the kitchen to prepare breakfast. She worked at making breakfast for a while, and eventually everything was ready. At that point, Flip, without having been sent by Eve, came to me and started to call me by poking me with his nose. (Flip, 1991)

17. At a Diósjenő campsite: This morning he poked me with his nose at 5 a.m. and went to the door. I let him out. (Flip, 1991)

18. We had noted at times that Flip was a little overweight. When I fed him, I removed a portion of his food and put it in the refrigerator. In other words, he got less than his usual portion. After our walk in the evening, I sat down to work. After a while, Flip appeared and decisively poked me with his nose and looked at me. I asked him

what he wanted. In reply, he quite unambiguously nodded toward the kitchen by moving his head in a broad arc. I was so startled that I got up, whereupon he started to run toward the kitchen. I offered him a cookie, but he did not take it; he lay down in front of his dish, with his head pointing toward it. The request was unambiguous; I fetched the confiscated portion of his dog food, which he consumed with relish. (Flip, 1991)

19. It was raining today and we got quite wet. Flip stopped in the entrance hall, assuming the pose with which he usually indicates on the street that he wants to go in a different direction. I asked him whether he wanted me to dry him, whereupon he ran to the bathroom and stopped in front of the towel rack. (Flip, 1991)

20. The intercom from the front gate was defective and its sound was barely audible. Flip began to bark in the front hall, but since nobody reacted to this signal, he came to my study and called me by barking. (Flip, 1991)

21. Ernie was here to repair the front gate. Whenever he stepped inside through the open front door, Flip ran into the hall and barked at me. (Flip, 1994)

22. Flip got less than usual to eat for his evening meal, and I decided to take a nap. He came to me, pondered this for a while, and then woke me with his growls and led me to his dish in the kitchen. (Flip, 1994)

23. Flip was constipated for several days and we put him on a strict diet consisting of canned dog food, which he does not like very much. Today was the third day. In the evening, he ate very little. A good hour after his meal he called me. I followed him with Eve. He stopped in the front hall and started to vocalize plaintively. This went on for quite a while, and then he lay down in the kitchen near his dish, but facing away. Eve promptly gave him some ham. (Flip, 1994)

24. During the Christmas holidays in Göd, I received a big box of goodies in which there was also something for Flip to eat. I gave it to

him yesterday. This evening he came to me and led me to the closet
in which I had placed the box, and he started to indicate that he
wanted some of it. (Flip, 1996)

I think it is clear from these incidents that communication with dogs
is not one-sided; it is not the case that only humans speak, point, or ask
for something, but dogs do, too. Communication is two-sided. Dogs
make an effort to give us understandable messages about things that are
important *to them*.

In the preceding examples, human speech and body language were
used as signals, but one can communicate with dogs through other
means as well. It is easy to invent gestures for signaling. For example:
Flip is a bit overweight for his age, while Jerry is so active that he needs
more than a normal amount of food. But if I call him for his extra portion, Flip will hear me, too, and he will also come eagerly, lest he miss out
on something. Well, it did not take more then two or three tries for Jerry
to learn that if I beckon to him with my curved index finger, he should
come with me to a remote room where I can quietly satisfy his gluttony.

Objects can also be used as signals. When the Department of Ethology was first established, we experimented with dogs for a brief period.
My friend and colleague Anthony Dóka worked with a small, three-
month-old puli[18] and his experiment is noted for two things. The first
was object-based communication. My friend Tony carved a few pieces of
wood into different shapes, which became a vocabulary. There was a
piece of wood that connoted asking for something, one for inviting play,
and one for going out; there were other pieces of wood that corresponded
to particular persons or to certain other objects. The puppy quickly learned
the meaning of the pieces of wood and readily brought the appropriate
piece for asking something. He did not have to be taught to realize that
the piece of wood denoting a food request could be used to beg from anybody: as soon as he saw somebody eating, he would go and find the right
piece of wood and take it to the person. If the person failed to understand the request, the puppy would bark angrily. He also quickly learned
the signs for objects. We had examined the connection between eleven
different objects and their corresponding signs. This association was
studied in two ways: either the puppy had to select among the pieces of
wood the right one that corresponded to a particular object, or, from

among a set of objects, he had to select the one that corresponded to a particular piece of wood. Successful identification hovered between 40 percent and 70 percent, while the corresponding percentage in the case of random selection would have been less than 10 percent.

The other noteworthy characteristic of this dog was the set of sounds it would make to promote communication resting on reciprocal vocalizations. In my childhood, we once had a dachshund that regularly announced arrivals at our house, even before we could hear any noise. In such cases it would emit a peculiar whimper and run to the front door. My brother Laci and I once decided to test whether the dachshund would understand this sound. In its absence, we practiced until both of us excelled at whimpering. In the decisive experiment, we emitted the appropriate whimpers, whereupon it ran to the front door, and then looked back at us with a withering look that I have not been able to forget ever since. I persuaded Tony to try the same and he succeeded. The puli and all the researchers at the Biological Research Station were able to produce two characteristic sounds. One of these was a deep growl that indicated the arrival of a stranger. If we produced this sound, the puli would jump up, start looking for the person who might have arrived, and bark. When he was the first to notice the arrival of a stranger, he would signal with the same sound. The second sound was a call to the dog and was a kind of panting, and hearing it, the puli would run to us. He also called us in the same way. Everybody, of course, knew this signal in the Department of Ethology, and we always reacted to the call by going to him. The researchers at the Biological Research Station gave the call signal to the dog with great relish, but unfortunately, for understandable reasons, they did not respond to his call, and in a few weeks the dog got out of the habit of calling them.

I also observed with Jerry that if I could imitate dog sounds well, we could easily create six to eight signals. The problem is that it is difficult to find vocal signals that the dog is capable of emitting and learning through repetition. At some point, Flip learned, probably by accident, to make requests with a deep growl. First he would ask for a cookie, later a ball, a rag, a nocturnal walk, whatever. When Jerry was a puppy, he would ask for things in a high-pitched, whistling kind of voice; but since Flip asked for things with a growl, Jerry learned from this model and from time to time he, too, started to demand things with a growl. It is difficult to train a dog to growl, and Jerry would more often employ the puppy whimper for making a request. He also employs other sounds, such as the wake-up yip I mentioned before. More recently, if we lock him in or out of some room, he signals with precisely the same yip that he wants out (or in).[19] He also has a peculiar, whistling kind of high whine that differs from the demand whimper. This is the sound that he emits when he wants to be caressed. In general, what happens is that he jumps on the bed, arranges himself comfortably, and whistles until I start to stroke him. After he has gotten what he came for, he proceeds to his guard post by the front door and lies down there. He has one more peculiar sound in his repertoire. Jerry frequently asks for something, and if I do not know what he wants, I enumerate the various possibilities: *go out*, *play*, *eat*, and so on. When I mention the item that he has in mind, he breaks into barking. This is clearly the signal for "Yes, yes!" Overall, we have established five vocalizations for communicating, and I am sure that this repertoire could be extended.

A final observation shows that dogs have started to use symbols: I tried object-based symbolic communication with Jerry, and he learned it just as fast as the puli.

September 10, 1997. Today we went on an excursion to Királyrét,[20] which was enjoyed by all. Jerry got a few hot dogs because he was very hungry. In the evening, we gave him only canned food, which he does not like very much. As soon as he tasted it, he brought me the appropriate piece of wood and dropped it in front of me. He then repeated this several times, indicating that he had something else in mind. He simply would not eat the canned stuff. Later, he placed the piece of wood in front of him and pondered it for a while; he then took it and threw it off the balcony.

One important factor that made us abandon the experiment with the shaped pieces of wood was the need to have them available at all times, so that the dog could select the appropriate one. Unfortunately, Jerry started to chew the wood and we were unable to break him of this habit. In a few days, we had no more shaped pieces of wood. We might have solved this problem with some material more resistant to chewing and it might be worthwhile to investigate this further.

To conclude out discussion of canine communication, let me note that we know precious little about it and we are continuing our scientific investigations.

Part
Four

Scientific Study of the Animal Mind

Readers who are interested only in dogs may find the remaining part of this book more challenging. What we will discuss here is how the animal mind can be studied from a scientific point of view. Brave readers who plow ahead will learn how to evaluate and analyze the results of the observations and experiments described earlier. At the beginning of this book I stressed that the recent theoretical analyses of the canine mind suggest various similarities between the thought processes of dogs and humans. The time has come for a more searching and detailed examination of these matters.

Chapter 11

Observation, Theory, and Proof

Dogs That Read

T he other day, I got a phone call from a very excited man who told me that he had a dog and that he had taught the dog to read. He just wanted to know from me whether this was a *big deal*. I asked him a few questions to see what this was all about; in other words, I tried to clarify what this dog was really capable of doing.

"Well, it reads," said the man.

"But what does it do when it *reads*?" I asked.

"It looks at the letters which I have placed before it and then fetches the ball."

"In other words, you place large, easily visible letters next to each other, the dogs looks at them, and then fetches. Or, one could say, it fetches in response to the combination of letters."

"No, no; it reads, it reads the letters and understands them."

My further questions increasingly enraged the man because he felt that I did not believe him and he curtly said good-bye. But my questions were simply probing the circumstances surrounding his observations: who was present, where did this "reading" take place, how many errors the dog made, and how sensible the symbols were. I have also talked with owners of "counting" dogs, "talking" cats, and the like. In similar instances I am always somewhat embarrassed, because the well-intentioned owners who call me or write to me have truly observed something and are eager to find a nifty explanation for the observed phenomenon, while I, disgustingly, insist on applying the rules of the game employed in scientific investigations and thereby deprive them of the uplifting experience of providing a successful explanation.

The first report of a "reading" dog was published in 1885 by Sir John Lubbock in the proceedings of a British scientific society. He presented his poodle, Van, with cards on which certain words had been written in large letters and had taught it to select the right one on command.[1] I am doing something similar here by entertaining the reader with my own observations and accompanying explanations, and it behooves me to explain the rules of the game that scientists have developed over centuries, which must be observed by all researchers in accordance with the written and unwritten laws of the discipline.

Scientific thinking is not as remote from natural, day-to-day thought processes as some people think. Through evolution, humans acquired the marvelous capacity of language, and this enabled them to record the events and phenomena of the world and even their inner experiences. Symbols enabled them to condense these constituents into stories, descriptions, and explanations, which can serve as raw material for further thought. When the human mind is at work, it generally examines or works on stories that have happened and that it remembers. Any kind of information or knowledge about ourselves or our experiences invariably turns out to consist of little stories. In these, there are always actors, perhaps ourselves or others, and there are objects, animals, and plants as well as actions; in other words, something always happens to the actors. If we think of an object as mundane as a ballpoint pen, we immediately think of little stories about it: we wrote with it, it ran out of ink, somebody gave us one, and so on. These stories partly elaborate our own experiences and—this is very important—partly recall beliefs and knowledge that we hold in common with others. When we look out the window in the morning and notice that the sun has risen, we become aware not only of our own experiences connected with sunrise, but also of the belief that the earth rotates around its axis, which explains the sun's reappearance. I referred to this as a belief because we do not directly experience it, but we have heard it from our parents, teachers, or others, or have learned it from a book. Since the story agrees well with our own experience, we believe it; that is, accept it as an explanation.

The human mind is able to accommodate an incredible quantity of similar belief-based stories as well as personal experiences. It is characteristic of the mind that when it encounters a new story, it contrasts the story with the existing ones, and accepts the new one as true or good or as an *explanation* only if it does not contradict previously acquired experiences. If somebody were to claim that the fiery ball we call the sun revolves around the earth because it sits on a huge carriage pulled by six horses, we would not believe the assertion, because we believe that it is a huge celestial body with a surface temperature of thousands of degrees Fahrenheit, and this negates the possibility of any kind of "carriage story." But one or two thousand years ago, it was an entirely plausible one.

The mind not only stores thousands of stories, but also continually renews and recombines them in the context of everyday experience. Everyone is an observer: we observe ourselves, our companions, and the world around us, and the data we acquire steadily influence the mind's story-building activities. The observations sometimes contradict existing stories, and in these cases new stories are concocted, but proof is needed before we can say that they are true. In other words, a new story must somehow fit into the matrix of existing and accepted stories.

Our child has been coming home from school later than usual and we find a spot on his shirt that looks suspiciously like strawberry ice cream. But he claims that he came straight home, did not stop for anything, and did not see any ice cream. Our theory is nevertheless that he ate some ice cream somewhere en route, but we have little in the way of observational data and have no proof. The next day we go to fetch him at school and when we meet up we see that he is holding a huge ice cream cone. This confirms our theory that the rascal is spending his allowance on ice cream.

In other words, we had an initial theory, namely that the kid comes straight home. Then we made a few observations: he is late and there are spots on his shirt. We then formulated a new theory: the rascal is eating ice cream! The additional observations then confirmed the new theory.

Of course, it is possible that the child is dawdling on the street and that the spots have a different origin. In that case, an alternative theory will be right. We could even be facing the annoying circumstance that the day on which we caught him eating ice cream was the very first time that he did so, and that our theory concerning his past misdeed is false, in spite of catching him in the act. It is often the case that several different theories can be constructed from the same data, although only one of them can be true, and it may be difficult to determine which one.

The mind of a scientist works basically the same way when he is doing research. Perhaps the one difference is that a good researcher does all this consciously and is very careful in fitting his observations and the theories built on them into his prior beliefs.

In the earlier story, the dog's owner believed that his dog could read; in other words, that was his theory. What is it in our daily life that we refer to as reading? The commonsense answer might be that reading is a phenomenon in which a human, observing a series of abstract symbols, uses his mind to *interpret* a communication. When, for example, he reads the words "the horse drank water from a container," he is able to comprehend what happened and knows precisely what the elements of this story have to do with one another and with other stories. He knows, for instance, to what category of object a horse belongs. It is living, it is an animal, a mammal, but it is not Dapple; it is a generic horse that reflects all the characteristics of its class, without any specification whether it is a concrete horse or just generally a horse. Nor is the concept of a container all that simple. It is obvious from the above sentence that the container is one that held water; but what kind of a container is it? If we went to a store in which many kinds of containers are sold and asked for a container, we would probably get some funny looks. They might ask, "What kind of container do you want? A frying pan, a pot, a salt shaker, or a tub?"

The category of container comprises hundreds of different objects. A person who reads with understanding has to know that. For example, the fact that the horse drank from the container means that it must be fairly large to accommodate the head of the horse. It must surely be quite a bit larger than a mug, although that is a container, too. It must further be the case that the container cannot be made out of straw or cane, because it could not hold the water. In other words, a person who can really read must have a lot of complex information available to him and he will steadily use this information while reading. For example, such a person could unambiguously differentiate the above sentence from the following: "It seemed as if the horse were drinking from the container." This is also interesting because if *the horse seemed to be drinking*, then what the observer saw was that the drinking really took place, but the reader can easily tell the difference between the two stories.

The assertion that somebody or something *reads* is the result of an *inference* in which the observation that he is looking at written symbols is merely one element. More important in this inference is the belief that the person has the capacity for language, that he can reason and interpret and that he is familiar with the letters of the alphabet. If we assert that a dog can read, then we must have a theory about dogs that is compatible with their possession of all these abilities and knowledge. The question is: can we prove all that?

When a fly alighted on the newspaper, did it peruse it or did it just want to rest? There is no way of knowing. In everyday life we are not always eager to find out the whole truth. The most important thing for a scientist is to confirm or disprove the theory. Every science rests on an enormous repository of knowledge and beliefs that the scientific community has accepted as either true or false. New beliefs and theories can enter this repository only if they do not contradict the previous ones, or if they do, then their truth must be supported by massive amounts of observational data. In general, what happens is that we find the connections between a new theory and the older ones and demonstrate that the suspected contradiction was only apparent.

Scientific Questions

The repository of scientific beliefs is huge, and it is certain that a substantial portion of theories in this repository rests on bad or erroneous data; it is therefore easy to identify contradictions or murky connections among them. If we discover such a contradiction, we may formulate a *new scientific question*, which may often be a minor theory in itself and may differ from previous ones. We would seek the answer to such a question with new observations and new theories based on them. If we succeed in this endeavor, we will have weeded out an irritating contradiction from our common scientific repository.

It follows that a scientist always undertakes observations on the basis of some prior theory, assumption, or hypothesis. A prior theory will guide his selection of the object of his observations and of the methodology he will employ for making observations: that is, whether he will look with the naked eye or with a microscope, or telescope, or perhaps some other instrument. It is also important to select appropriately the target object's unit of observation. What that unit should be will depend on the question to which we are seeking an answer. Thus, one could observe one wolf, or two, or perhaps a whole pack, or even a population consisting of many packs. But one could also observe a part of a wolf—its tail or its ears, or perhaps some nerve cells in its brain that participate in activating the tail. Whatever we choose among the many possibilities, we choose it on the basis of some theory or hypothesis, and this choice will largely determine what we observe. If we select a single wolf, it could be an adult or a pup, a male or a female. If, for example, our theory were that the wolf catches its prey by itself, it would be a waste of time to observe a pup. If we are inquiring into maternal care, we need at least two wolves: a mother and its pup. It is also important that one rely on previous beliefs and knowledge when one begins to make observations, and this will have a large influence on what one finds.

Let us assume that we start with a suitable theory and that we have selected the objective of our observations appropriately. This may be followed by the accumulation of the appropriate quantity of observations, from which we will formulate a new assertion, which is, in effect, always a new theory. This will be a description that uses our preceding theories to interpret the new data and confirms the new interpretation.

In the case of "reading" dogs, my observations pertain to the connection between the written text and the behavior of the dog. To get proof I have to carry out a very detailed procedure; otherwise I could not prove my theory scientifically. If the dog can really read, then it might be sufficient proof to show the dog a whole variety of texts that deal with various tasks that need to be carried out. If the dog reads these texts and then carries out the tasks, even when I am not present, then—and only then—I may conclude that it can really read. In other words, I may consider my theory as proven only if it is in agreement with every essential observational datum. No one has so far succeeded in producing such proof, although quite a few people have thought that their dog knew how to read.

There are many stumbling blocks. If I write the word *bone* on a piece of paper and teach the dog that he should fetch the bone after I show him the piece of paper, I have not proved that he can read. I have to content myself with a much simpler assertion, namely that the dog is capable of carrying out an instruction after it recognizes a written symbol.

Theories are built upon data permitting manifold interpretations. Proof is the instrument with which we can select that one theory from among numerous alternative ones that provides the ultimate or best explanation.[2] There is no scientific methodology that could simplify or possibly automate the creation of a new theory or the selection of an appropriate one from among many possible ones. The correctness or the truth of a theory is proved not by its beauty or simplicity but by its practical value. In general, this means that a correct theory can be used effectively as a presupposition in dealing with the next observation. To put it differently, with a good theory one can make predictions. If we are familiar with the properties of powdered sulfur, charcoal, and nitrates, then we can predict that if we mix these substances in certain proportions and heat them in a closed vessel, the mixture will explode. In other words, we have discovered gunpowder.

Humans have not only scientific theories, but also various other beliefs: superstitions, magic, necromancy, and religious faith. In themselves, these can be attractive and comforting, but it is quite certain that they cannot be used to make predictions. It is all right to believe in angels, but this belief will not produce a prediction of even a single observable and verifiable event that would prove the existence and the activities of angels.

The relationship between beliefs, theories, observations, and practice is similar in all the natural sciences, but especially interesting problems arise when the object of the scientific investigation is the human mind, or as in our case, the animal mind.

Chapter 12

The Clever Hans and Alex,

the Parrot That Understands Words

At the beginning of the twentieth century, the newspapers frequently wrote about an extraordinarily gifted horse, the clever Hans, a stallion owned by an Austrian named von Osten. According to contemporary reports, this horse was capable of carrying out rather complicated arithmetical operations. He was able to convert from hours to minutes, he could correct erroneously played chords of music, and he could spell words and even sentences. The credibility of his performance was greatly enhanced by the fact that his owner had no interest in realizing a financial gain from his horse's abilities. The horse did not become a circus performer, the owner did not charge the audience an admission fee, and anybody who expressed an interest was given the opportunity to observe the horse's marvelous talents. The owner was even willing to let people check the horse's performance in his absence. In other words, it was highly probable that this was not a swindle for personal gain.

The sensationalism surrounding the case caught the attention of the experts, and the mechanism underlying the peculiar talents of Hans was clarified through bona fide scientific investigations.[1] The owner had considered his horse remarkably intelligent even in its youth. For many years, he spent several hours a day honing his abilities. He first taught

Hans to recognize numerals and to stamp his hoof as many times as shown by the numeral. Later, he established a correspondence between numbers and letters of the alphabet and the animal learned to express his recognition of letters and even words by stamping the appropriate number of times. The experiments were very straightforward. If somebody approached the horse and said, "Dear Hans, how much is five times three?" the horse would begin to stamp his hoof and stop after he had stamped fifteen times.

This is an excellent example of a scientific theory, of observation, and of proof. The initial theory is that Hans knows how to do arithmetic. The observation employs a simple experiment: we tell the horse what the arithmetical problem is and then we count the number of times it stamps. In this process, everything works out as we assumed, but the problem is that on the basis of this simple experiment we are forced to accept a *new* theory, namely that a horse is able to do arithmetic. This is difficult to reconcile with our prior beliefs, because a horse with that much intelligence has not been seen before. Many people have worked closely with horses, but no one has ever observed that they have such an enormous intellectual capacity. If it should turn out that the new theory is correct, we need to explain why all other horses are not equally intelligent. Might that be so because, perhaps, they were not treated correctly? Perhaps most horses can be taught to do arithmetic if only one would teach them the right way? Could it be that horses are just as intelligent as humans, but nobody has noticed this in the past five thousand years?

Or could the new theory be wrong? Perhaps the observations are faulty, or the inferences drawn from them incorrect? In such cases we must continue to observe until we find a rational connection between the observed phenomenon and our prior knowledge.

The horse was first examined by an ad hoc committee, the members of which included Paul Busch, a famous circus director and animal trainer; Heinroth,[2] Nagel, and Stumpf, distinguished professors of the University of Berlin; and others. The committee took as its principal mandate the discovery of a potential swindle, but after some tests, the members of the committee declared their considered opinion that the case involved no intentional deceit or swindle. They could not unlock the secret of the horse's performance, however. Somewhat later, Otto Pfungst, a psychologist of good reputation, succeeded with some appropriately designed experiments where the others had failed. First, he made the tasks more difficult; it turned out that Hans not only knew the four basic arithmetic operations, but was also able to exponentiate and to extract roots, although he had never been taught these operations. This made the achievement of Hans even more incredible. Then came a brilliant experiment in which the complicated problems were posed to Hans by persons who themselves did not know the answers. In these cases, Hans would stamp for a long time and eventually stop, and in many cases not even start to stamp his hoof. This observation led to two new theories; first, that the horse really does not know how to do arithmetic, and second, that in the earlier trials, when he gave the correct response, he had received some signal from the person who was posing the problem. And these theories were actually confirmed. It turned out that the persons who were posing the problems to Hans, who knew the correct answers, were themselves excitedly doing the arithmetic along with Hans, since they wanted to know whether Hans would succeed or not. When Hans reached the right answer in his stamping, they would suddenly relax and imperceptibly nod their head or give some other practically unnoticeable sign of their contentment, whereupon Hans would stop stamping.

During the long periods of instruction, Hans would be rewarded with bread or carrots whenever he stamped the correct number of times, and the horse somehow figured out that he would receive his reward if he stopped stamping as soon as he noticed the teacher's hardly perceptible, involuntary nod. After the horse made this discovery, he succeeded in applying it to other persons as well. During the experiments, Pfungst found out how to direct the horse's stamping with tiny but intentional movements. The nervous system of even a snail is able to recognize the connection between a reward and an immediately preceding tiny change in itself or in its environment. This is the ability to make associations, which every animal has, and is an extremely simple learning process that does not require any kind of conscious insight or thought. In other words, the observations are completely explained by a relatively uncomplicated theory that fits neatly into our repository of knowledge about animal psychology without presupposing any special talents. We need not assume that the basis of Hans's or possibly other horses' arithmetic ability is previously unrecognized genius.

Nevertheless, the story of the clever Hans took its place in the annals of animal psychology, and to this day the term "clever Hans effect" refers to a situation in which an experimenter involuntarily communicates small signals to an experimental animal and thereby influences its behavior. The clever Hans effect even occurs among humans. The reader has surely read about, heard, or seen performances in which a magician asks the audience to hide some small object on the body of a member of the audience while he is out of the room, and promises to find it upon his return with the aid of his magical powers. These tricks are usually successful, because all he has to do is to observe the participants; their state of excitement and their tiny, involuntary movements indicate quite accurately when he is near the person in question. One might call this a cheap trick, but actually it is smart psychology.

Since that time, we have found many instances in which the participants in an animal experiment were able to influence the experimental result in numerous ways, even involuntarily. At an American university, the students were asked to perform maze experiments with two groups of rats. Rats easily remember the structure of a labyrinth, and their ability is usually quantified by the number of errors they commit in repeated trials, that is, how often they enter dead ends. Psychologists have bred strains of rats that perform very well and strains that do poorly; but in the present experiment, both groups of rats were of average ability. Accordingly, their performance should have been rather similar. But according to the students' measurements, one group performed extraordinarily well, while the other did very poorly.

The differential performances had a very simple explanation: when the faculty member who led the experiment handed the rat cages to the students, he noted quite matter-of-factly that one of the two groups of rats consisted of famously intelligent animals, whereas the rats in the other group were all rather stupid. The students were supposed to treat the rats in the two groups identically. Each rat was taken out of its cage and placed in the labyrinth, and during its run the students counted the number of errors it committed. Finally, they removed the rat from the last compartment of the maze, which contained a food reward. This whole operation was repeated four or five times so that they could study the amount of learning that took place. But the students themselves were secretly under observation, and it turned out that contrary to their explicit instructions, they treated the putatively smart and stupid rats quite differently. The ones that were thought to be smart were removed from their cages gently, they were fondled and caressed, they were placed in the labyrinth with a great deal of care, and during the rats' run, the students rooted for them, encouraged them, and in some cases assisted them in selecting the right path by knocking on the wall of the maze. In contrast, the rats believed to be stupid were handled roughly and were tossed into the starting gate of the labyrinth and were often marked down if they as much as looked into a dead-end corridor. The final result after such differential treatment was quite understandable. The animals that had been treated roughly were afraid and this deteriorated their performance. This example is a nice illustration of how prior beliefs and theories can influence the outcome of observing something.

Are Animals Intelligent?

People throughout the ages have held many different beliefs about the intelligence of animals. In antiquity, people believed as a rule that animals were just as intelligent as humans, but just could not speak. According to the ideology of Christianity, the difference between animals and humans is the *immortality* of the soul: humans have one, but animals do not. For this reason, animals were considered lower order beings, quasi-machines that did not think or feel, had no reason, and were soulless mechanisms.

The field of psychology was primarily interested in human behavior, and the experiments in animal psychology were really only models for the study of human psychology. Darwin's work introduced a decisive change. His views on this subject were already expressed in his principal work on evolution[3] in which he stressed that the properties of animals and humans can be arrayed along a continuum and that there is no discontinuity or leap between animal and human characteristics. He devoted an entire book to the expression of human and animal feelings, which he based on numerous observations that prove the continuity of evolution.[4] Maternal love, anger, and fear are emotions, he wrote, the biological foundations of which are present in both animals and humans. His book on human evolution frequently refers to the common evolutionary origins of the mental abilities of humans and monkeys, but particularly of humans and apes.[5] It is of particular interest to us that in addition to the monkeys and apes, Darwin also mentioned dogs as possibly having a conscious mind, of perhaps more modest capabilities. Darwin was an exceptional genius, and even in the light of today's knowledge of biology, his works contain very few errors. His amazingly accurate conjectures have been verified in a number of instances. I believe that his remarks concerning the mental abilities of dogs fall into this category.

George Romanes, who was Darwin's friend and intellectual inspiration, was an assiduous researcher of the evolution of the animal and human minds and wrote several books on the subject.[6] But Romanes was not a genius and did not succeed in chronicling the history of the mind's evolution, even though he used evolutionary theories still valid today, because he made a number of elementary logical errors. His mistakes are regarded as classic errors in the behavioral sciences and are often used to illustrate how the relationship between observation and theory can be misunderstood. He employed many anecdotes in trying to prove his theories, although experimental psychology was already fairly advanced in his day and one-time observations did not count for much.

The star of one of these anecdotes was a cat that happened to be owned by the wife of the Turkish ambassador to London. (This minor detail was important for Romanes because he believed that the reports of highly placed persons were scientifically more credible than those of others.) In any event, one day the cat was scratching at her mistress' gown and mewing. The ambassador's wife then followed the cat out to the kitchen where, to her surprise, a pot of milk on the stove was about to boil over. This smart cat was signaling the impending danger, or at least that is what the ambassador's wife and later Romanes believed.

The logical error is obvious. There could be multiple connections between the observed events, namely between the scratching, mewing, and the milk boiling over, and they might be explained with several different theories. One of these theories is, of course, the one espoused by Romanes; but an equally good theory would be that the cat smelled the milk and was asking its mistress for some. It is also possible that the cat's mewing at the same time that the milk was starting to boil over was pure coincidence. Of the three theories, the latter two are easily compatible with our prior knowledge about cats, since they rarely exhibit a level of intelligence that would do a four-year-old child proud. If we were to accept Romanes's theory, we would have to reevaluate our prior beliefs about cats, all on the basis of the Turkish ambassador's wife's story.

Morgan's Canon

The psychologists who were Romanes's contemporaries were much annoyed by his stories, and to this day, annoying his contemporaries is regarded as his greatest achievement. They wanted to refute his theories, and in the process they started to work out appropriate procedures for observation and experiment in animal psychology. In contrast to Romanes's theories, which rested for the most part on hearsay observations and theories, the outstanding English psychologist C. Lloyd Morgan emphasized the importance of *direct observation*. He maintained that scientific theories should be built only on carefully checked and described observations and on data generated by experiments. One of his most famous scientific principles for building theories was the *principle of parsimony*. To this day, this has been universally accepted in the behavioral sciences dealing with animals. It is known as Morgan's Canon, which states that the explanation of behavior must not posit a higher degree of intelligence when a lower degree is sufficient. In other words, in explaining animal behavior, we should always seek the *simplest possible explanation*.

Psychologists who adopted Morgan's Canon in their work disproved the levels of animal intelligence hypothesized by Romanes one by one and showed that animal behavior is explained by random trials, simple reflexes, and primitive learning processes rather than conscious activity. The English psychologist L. Thorndyke introduced a device called the *problem box* into the study of animal behavior. The problem box was normally a cage that was locked with a bolt but that could be opened from the inside. An animal placed in the cage could come out only if it was able to solve the problem, that is, open the bolt. According to Thorndyke's observations, the experimental animals, dogs and cats, did not display any behavior that could be classified as deliberate or goal oriented, but moved and jumped around at random in their efforts to get out. If they accidentally triggered the opening mechanism and were subsequently placed in a cage again, however, they found the way to open it much faster and in a much more goal-oriented manner than before. In other words, they learned from their experience. Even so, one could not have said that the opening of the cage was the result of conscious activity. What the animals had learned was what kind of bodily motion in which part of the cage was necessary for opening its door. If the locking mechanism was relocated, they had to learn everything anew, because they did not recognize the causal connection between their own movement and the mechanism. Because of the initial random movements that are involved, this phenomenon was called *learning by trial and error*.

Is It Possible That Animals Are Only Complicated Machines?

Animal psychologists were so mesmerized by methodological problems that they neglected to make sufficient progress in the theoretical realm. As a result, their investigations did not assume their proper place in the biological sciences. Animal psychology, a laboratory-based behavioral science, was born, and its principal objective was to carry out experiments that were designed in an artificial environment, could be reproduced exactly, and were based on an extremely simplified theory. This objective was successfully accomplished.

Animal psychology came under the influence of behaviorism, the main trend in psychology as practiced at that time. The fundamental proposition of behaviorism was that all animal behavior is essentially a response to environmental stimuli. However, the behavior of an animal is decisively influenced by its past experiences; hence the most important thing in the study of animal behavior is the analysis of learning mechanisms that were (erroneously) believed to be identical in all species. Only thus would one be able to discover the reasons for particular animal behavior. Behaviorists such as the American psychologist B. F. Skinner tried to apply the most objective experimental and descriptive methodologies and eliminated from their analyses the potential effects of subjective factors, emotions, thoughts, plans, and so on. They essentially regarded animals as machines that might be moderately complicated, but were nevertheless reasonably transparent in their basic organization. This trend was reinforced in neurobiology by the theory of reflexes that was based on the analyses of an English and a Russian scientist, namely C. S. Sherrington and I. P. Pavlov. They hypothesized that the behavior of an animal is reducible to a simple, innate reaction or reflex, or to *conditioned reflexes* and their concatenation, acquired through learning. It followed that if one knew precisely the history of rewards and punishments in the past, one could predict the animal's future behavior.

While biologists succeeded in proving that biological phenomena can be understood only in a general evolutionary framework, the activities of psychologists led to a basically anti-Darwinian behavioral science. The methodological preconceptions of behaviorism precluded the use of *observations made in nature* in its analyses, and consequently of the study of genetic diversity, and restricted itself entirely to the study of behavior that could be produced in the laboratory: learning. Moreover, the younger generations of behaviorist researchers began to reinterpret Morgan's original and well-founded recommendation that higher-order behavioral phenomena, such as thinking, emotions, insights, and consciousness, should be excluded from the analysis because they are too complicated and unsuitable for scientific investigations. Their reinterpretation took the form of asserting that the various higher order phenomena in fact did not exist, and thereby these researchers lost touch with reality.

Behaviorist psychology had some truly extreme manifestations. It was considered scientifically incorrect to use in the description of an animal's behavior, say that of a chimpanzee, expressions such as *it wanted*, *thought*, *felt*, *desired*, or *imagined*, because behaviorists believed that these expressions are only suitable for describing the human mind. Any researcher who dared to believe that an animal could feel or want something was branded as being anthropomorphic. (Originally, the term *anthropomorphism* was employed by the ancient Greeks to denote the custom of endowing *gods* with human traits. Later, people were branded with this term if they believed that animal behavior exhibited *human* characteristics.) According to well-known gossip in the profession, a certain professional journal did not want to accept for publication the first article written by Jane Goodall, who subsequently became the famed chimpanzee researcher, because she gave the chimpanzees individual names and referred to them with pronouns usually reserved for persons—*he* or *she* rather than *it*. The article was nevertheless published.

The Theory of Animal Consciousness

In the meantime, a lot of new things had happened, and more and more psychologists began to criticize behaviorist theory, because orthodox behaviorists objected even in the case of human behavior to the analysis of states that could not be directly observed, such as desires, wants, or thoughts. But it was obvious that these terms substantially simplify descriptions of behavior and have great practical value for formulating theories that can be used to predict behavior. This development greatly boosted the cognitive trends in psychology, which began to freely use indicators of states that are not directly observable but can be inferred from behavior. Of course, these trends did not affect the study of animals, because most psychologists believed that it would be an anthropomorphism if they were to attribute to animals a state that was similar or identical to that of the human mind.

Donald Griffin's famous book on animal consciousness was soon published, and it strongly endorsed the existence of an animal mind and the possibilities of studying it.[7] Griffin is a well-known American ethologist who discovered the echolocation mechanism of bats, and his support for accepting the notion of animal consciousness proved to be very effective. Many ethologists participated in the development of the science of the animal mind, referred to as *cognitive ethology*. As in all new fields, some extremist points of view appeared here as well. Many researchers hypothesized that animals engage in thinking, planning, hoping, or even plotting crafty moves and that they get disappointed and can daydream, just as humans, whether one is talking of chimpanzees or of ladybugs. At that point, the earlier behaviorists rejoined the fray and established what they thought were necessary conditions for the existence of shared characteristics in the animal and human minds, which could be fulfilled only if the animal were able to speak a human language.

A respectable middle ground has been developing in the past few years among those ethologists whom we could most appropriately call the *new anthropomorphists*. They classify researchers who hypothesize without any analysis that animals behave like mindless machines as mechanomorphists and consider them to be as much in error as the older anthropomorphists who believed without analysis or proof that humans and animals share numerous mental characteristics.[8] According to current views, initial descriptions of phenomena should be as simple as possible and the technical terms in them should or may be regarded as similes or metaphors, but the prior hypotheses of the analysis and the true scientific significance of similes must be *verified* with observations and experiments. While this provides the researcher a great deal of freedom in describing perceived behavior, it forces him to *verify* the content of his description. Earlier researchers who based their theories on little stories and anecdotes were roundly criticized, but the current view— as shown by the broadly accepted work of Konrad Lorenz and Jane Goodall—is that the individual observations of trained researchers are acceptable as scientific proof if the theories based on them fit well with the rest of our knowledge. For example, two primate researchers collected several hundred anecdotes from colleagues working on monkeys, which conclusively prove that these animals are capable of deceiving their mates.[9]

Alex Speaks

The experiments with Alex, the famous parrot that understood words, also rest on individual observations and a whole series of anecdotes. The observations were made over a number of years by Irene Pepperberg, a famous American researcher, with strict attention to the mandates of behaviorism.[10] Animal psychology experiments that investigate the learning of signs or signals face the big problem that it is very difficult to get convincing evidence in favor of one or the other of two competing hypotheses, namely whether the animal merely associates a sign with some reward or whether it is able to learn the connection between the sign and what it signifies, independently of any reward. This problem would admit an easy solution if animals could speak, because we could then simply ask them. But even the clever Hans could indicate its answer only with its hoof, which is the reason that its master could delude himself for years that it was capable of intelligent answers.

Pepperberg noted that the larger parrots generally appear to be rather smart and it is fairly easy to teach them words. She conjectured that if one experimented with such parrots, one might discover that they can use words meaningfully. Accordingly, she applied for a grant to the National Science Foundation and described in her proposal what methods she would use to study the mind of an African gray parrot. Her proposal was promptly rejected on the basis of scathing evaluations by the referees who pointed out that the existence of a mind had not even been proved for apes, let alone for birds. But she was stubborn and submitted another proposal in which she promised to undertake some associational experiments with an unspecified small species other than rats. This proposal was duly funded.[11] The experiments, conducted over many years, proved that her parrot, Alex, was able to meaningfully learn more than one hundred English words. In one experiment, which was also seen on television, a tray holding twenty-three different objects was placed in front of Alex. The objects had different shapes and colors and were made of various materials. The experimenter would pick up an object, say a red wooden triangle, and then ask, "What is this?" Alex would reply immediately, "Triangle." "What is its color?" would be the next question. Alex's reply, "Red." "What is it made from?" the experimenter would ask. Alex would then peck at the object a bit and then say, "Wood."

Alex was also able to pick out from among the many objects the blue metal square or the white leather circle. Alex was subjected to many similar tests, which were analyzed statistically, and it is generally accepted nowadays that the African gray parrot is able to learn and meaningfully use a few words pertaining to objects and their properties. This seems to be a fairly meager result after nearly twenty years of work, although it agrees well with the spirit of the American form of behaviorism that is free of anthropomorphism.

I was curious what this was all about. A few years ago, during a coffee break at an ethology conference, I asked Pepperberg about Alex's daily life and what he was doing. I did not really think that Alex would be practicing his boring but meaningful and statistically measurable vocabulary.

Pepperberg recounted that her research support was only for experiments of that type, and so she had to continue with these experiments, but that on the whole, Alex's life was much livelier than would appear from the reports of the experiments. Alex continually talks with the people around him; with her, an assistant, a veterinarian, and a young psychologist. He has various desires: when he sees her wearing a new piece of jewelry, he asks for it, he wants to go for a walk, he asks for various fruits he is familiar with, he wants to play, or he asks that he be stroked or bathed, and a whole lot of other things. He is fairly aggressive and stubborn; if he does not get what he wants, he first starts to screech nastily, and later starts to tear at his feathers, which worries his masters a lot, because he has hardly any feathers left, and so they basically give him anything he wants. In other words, Alex is a talking tyrant.

The most interesting story is the following: at the same conference, Pepperberg was complaining that she was unable to leave this "beast" for more than three or four days, because if she was absent, sooner or later Alex started calling for her and asking the others where Irene was. No matter how much they tried to calm him, eventually he would start a hunger strike and tear at his already decimated plumage. The others would then have to call to tell her that if she ever wanted to see Alex alive again, she should come home immediately, and she would have no choice but to return, since she had so much invested in him. Two years later, we organized a small conference on cognitive ethology in Budapest. In addition to the many other important scholars, we naturally invited Pepperberg, but I alerted my colleagues that she would probably not be able to attend for the reason cited above. But she came anyway and spent almost a week at the conference. When it was over, my colleagues asked her what had happened that made it possible for her to come. She laughed and explained the situation, but added that this was confidential information because she would not dare to say this in front of a professional forum. What happened was that one of her colleagues discovered a splendid method for letting her take arbitrarily long holidays. The method is the following. When Pepperberg leaves, they show Alex a sheet of paper on which they have drawn as many squares as the number of days that Pepperberg is expected to be absent. The last square on the sheet contains a round smiling face while the others are empty. When Alex is shown the sheet, they explain slowly that Irene has gone away but will return when they reach the square with the smiley face, and then they cross out the first square with a red pencil. This conversation is repeated every day, and each day the next empty square is crossed out in red. Alex always listens carefully to the explanation and mutters that Irene will come back and that he will not make a fuss.

"How do you explain this?" asked my colleagues.

"Leave me alone! Someday I'll write it up, if I dare," she said, and ran off.

Theory, observation, new theory; is this not the way it goes?

There are two classes of theories dealing with the animal mind. The first one explains animal behavior purely on the basis of the simplest genetic and learning mechanisms. The other theories hypothesize very complicated operations of a consciousness that rather resembles the human mind. It seems worthwhile to summarize here an in-between position in order to become familiar with the views of researchers studying various animals.

The Ethology of the Mind

It is commonly accepted today in ethology and in the sciences of the mind that one of the principal functions of the central nervous system is the *modeling* of the environment.[12] The most important theory and belief of cognitive ethology rests on the fact that all animals have senses that transmit to the nervous system the events and phenomena of the external world and environment; that which can be seen, smelled, heard, tasted, or touched. Equally, all animals have a more or less developed memory, which has the function of making it unnecessary for the animal to make decisions on the basis of the immediate state of its environment, but which allows it to recall and use in the decision process its earlier experiences. The importance of environmental factors and memory even applies to insects, whose behavior is decisively affected by genetic rules and takes into account only specific environmental factors. But many insects repeatedly return to the same place and their orientation is guided by their memory in these instances. It can be observed that when a bee leaves the hive, it first makes a scouting trip around it. It has been shown in experiments that during this trip it notes the larger objects around the hive, such as trees, a house, and so on. It seems certain on the basis of the experiments that it records a visual model in its memory and places the hive itself in this model. What it records is not, of course, a photographic image, but an encoded representation in the nervous system about which we know only that it enables the bee to find the hive. This type of environmental representation is a fairly passive structure, not unlike the magnetic blips representing a voice on a magnetic tape. Based on its memory, the insect can carry out in reverse only an action that it has already performed. In general, it is unable to "think up" a new and better course of action.

Mental Maps

It is very important for animals to be able to find the way home, but this ability is not the only benefit they derive from a thorough familiarity with their environment. There may be sources of food there, and the animal may itself have a hoard that it carefully keeps track of. New objects or unknown creatures encountered in its territory may imply danger or unexpected good fortune, and the more familiar the animal becomes with the "structure" of its environment, the better its chances for survival. Many observations and laboratory experiments prove that the various animals can store in their memories, depending on how highly developed their nervous system is, more or less complicated "maps" of their environment, which we refer to as *cognitive maps*. Of course, this statement should not be taken literally; the animal does not store an analog of a human map printed on paper. Rather, what is stored in memory are the spatial relations, the characteristics of certain objects, and, of course, the precise location of some. Hence the justification of the term *map*. Perhaps the most important feature is that this memory map is *specific to the species*; it contains only those objects and relations that are relevant for the survival of the given species.

In laboratory experiments, after a few runs through a maze, rats are able to remember its details, and if they have a good reason, to select the shortest path. When running through a highly complicated maze, they are even able to recognize *en route* minor changes introduced by the experimenter since the previous run and to recognize when a shorter and more rational path has opened up. It has been unambiguously proved that a rat is able to store the entire map of a maze in its memory, and if necessary, it can use this map to think through the course of the possible actions and can select among them the most favorable one.

When experiments of this type were highly fashionable, researchers tested the behavior of many kinds of animals in mazes. It was very disappointing to find that many, such as birds, did not even get started in the maze. Today that is no longer surprising, since it is obvious that in their natural environment birds have no need for solving such problems. Hence, they did not develop genetic talents for mazes and they have no reason to learn a maze. But researchers have also found animals that were well suited to mazes. For example, ants are excellent at navigating labyrinths and are almost as fast as rats, although their nervous system is much more primitive than that of rats. But researchers were able to design a maze problem in which the advantages of the rats' more complicated nervous system became evident. In this particular experiment, rats (and, with minor changes, ants) were taught to navigate a certain maze. Then the problem was reversed in the sense that the starting point became the objective, and the original objective the starting point. It turned out that the ants needed just as much trial and error to learn the maze in reverse as they needed to learn it the first time; in other words, they thought of the maze in reverse as a new maze. In contrast, the rats realized right away, in their very first run in the reverse direction, that it was the same maze, only reversed. This experiment shows that a higher order nervous system prepares a dynamic map of the environment that is an *independent neural system* or *model*, which can be *operated* by the animal for deducing useful conclusions. The ant's nervous system is also able to acquire experience and learn, but the rat's brain is capable of drawing conclusions and thus modifying its behavior on the basis of simple events that took place in its imagination.

There are many animals among the vertebrates that are able to employ three-dimensional maps of the environment in planning their course of action. A precondition for constructing such a map is the ability to accurately estimate the distance between objects. The field of comparative psychology has long dealt with similar problems, which are referred to as problems of invariance. Their study asks the questions whether an animal is able to estimate the size of an object from various distances or how accurately it is able to measure the distance between objects from various locations. Many animals possess the property of size invariance, but many fewer have distance invariance. Those that have both invariance properties are, in effect, "conscious" of the physical dimensions of objects and of the distances separating them.

Higher order animals and humans can construct a three-dimensional cognitive map after a momentary look at a space filled with various objects, which they would then have to navigate blindfolded. The map constructed after such a fleeting look stays in short-term memory for about seven seconds. If the target distance can be covered in seven seconds, they can navigate the obstacle course flawlessly, but as the distance becomes greater, they would increasingly make errors. With appropriate practice, it is of course possible to construct a large and permanent cognitive map. During World War II, the British Secret Service blew up a building in Norway that housed the Germans' heavy-water manufacturing laboratory. In preparation for the attack, an exact duplicate of the building was constructed in England, in which the commandos practiced for weeks. In the duplicate building, the corridors, doors, light switches, and even the placement of items of furniture agreed completely with the original. After suitable practice, the commandos became thoroughly familiar with the German building even in the dark and the commando action was carried out successfully.

We do not yet know well enough how the maps of the environment get stored in the nervous system, or how the brain uses them in the process of orienting oneself. But an examination of our own mind, *introspection*, can provide some helpful hints. If we move around in a familiar place with our eyes closed, mental images of familiar objects will flash before us and will follow each other according to our movements. It is therefore probable that the pictures that we stored about the environment somehow guide our movements, which in turn provide a feedback that changes the images. It is also well known that in a familiar environment our movements are guided more by our *expectations* than by visual stimuli. If we reach for a customary object on a table, we often react with astonishment that it is not in its usual place because somebody happened to move it while cleaning the house.

The Mind Builds Its Models from Neurons

We know about cognitive maps not only from experiments in the fields of ethology and comparative psychology, but also from studies in neurophysiology. By implanting electrodes in the brain, it is possible to map out which neurons respond in the appropriate part of the brain to the stimuli received by the animal and what their structure is. The study of mammalian hearing has shown that there exist specific large neurons in the hearing cortex of the brain that fire only if the animal hears a sound in a very narrow frequency band, and that the entire frequency domain is covered by a range of neurons sensitive to different sounds. Sound-sensitive cells are arrayed in a planar fashion, next to each other according to the frequency bands they represent. The similar placement of receptor neurons is a quite general property of the nervous system of higher-order animals. For example, in the visual center of the brain one finds the exact planar representation of the receptors of the retina, and particular neurons in this representation respond only to stimuli from specific sectors of the visual field. Since the brain processes the two-dimensional picture appearing on the retina in various ways (the direction of movement, the angle subtended by edges, etc.), it seems that the processing is simplest if the spatial placement of neurons in the brain corresponds exactly to the placement of receptor cells in the retina. But this also means that we have identified here the physical realization of the cognitive map. In other words, the brain "builds" or models the various important properties of the environment out of neuron building blocks.

In the preceding examples, the central nervous system was seen to "transcribe" the pattern of stimuli appearing in the sense organs in identical form to the network of neurons in the center. The explanation for this observation may well be that for various developmental reasons this is the simplest method for processing patterns arrayed in a plane. But in recent years, some data have been uncovered that show that the spatial representation of the environment appears in an analog form in the central nervous system even if the sense organs do not present patterns in the plane; in other words, the brain constructs a genuine *model* of the environment.

The hearing of owls is extraordinarily refined and this is their most important sense for the predatory behavior they engage in. Scholars have found a region in the middle brain of owls that contains a precise spatial representation of the direction of sounds, which is similar to the brain representation of visual images seen by mammals, although the ears of owls perceive not planar patterns but series of sounds. In the cognitive map, individual neurons react to sounds emanating from specific spatial areas and the various neurons "listen" to these different areas. Whereas in sight the location of the stimulus is determined by the horizontal and vertical coordinates of the retina, the direction of sound is computed by the brain of owls and mammals on the basis of the *difference* between its arrival times at the two ears. This makes it possible to construct a three-dimensional map of sound sources. In the case of owls, about one-half of the region of the brain involved in constructing the sound map is devoted to representing an auditory cone of about fifteen degrees lying in front of the owl, which is the space in which their hearing is the sharpest. Greater portions of the brain are devoted to coping with the space below than above the bird, presumably because the information coming from below is the most important from the point of view of catching prey.[13]

An equally elegant example of the existence of cognitive maps is provided by the electrophysical study of the auditory brain center of bats.[14] Bats produce a model of their environment through an analysis of the echoes of the ultrasounds that they emit. The brain regions dealing with the analysis of sounds is accordingly much larger than those of other animals. The auditory brain center has several parts with different biological functions and each provides some important information about accessible insect prey. Different subregions represent the distance from the prey, its size, its relative speed, and the speed of its wing-beats (which evidently helps in the identification of the prey). From the elapsed time between the emission of the ultrasound and the arrival of the echo, bats are able to determine with a high degree of precision the distance to the prey. The auditory center contains some neurons that are tuned to the elapsed time between sound emission and its echo. These neurons do not react to the emitted sound if there is no echo, nor to an echo if there is no emitted sound, and they fire only if both members of the pair are present. What is truly fantastic in this mechanism is that the various individual neurons react to different temporal differences, ranging from a fraction of a thousandth of a second up to eighteen thousandths of a second, which implies that bats can perceive and find prey at distances ranging from ten centimeters (four inches) to three meters (ten feet).

Examination of the spatial orientation of mice has revealed that sight, hearing, and touch all play a role in it. (The sense of touch is transmitted to the appropriate receptors by the whiskers.) Accordingly, there are various layers of neurons in the brain, which construct a map of the environment on the basis of the appropriate senses. These neuron layers are positioned in close proximity to each other and are truly faithful models of the mouse's environment.[15]

Inherited Behavioral Rules

The animal's senses and memory play an important role in constructing a cognitive map of the environment, but the map stored in memory is only one of the factors that influence behavior. Observation of many different types of animals shows that they do not use their cognitive maps in arbitrary ways, but that they are constrained in their use by species-specific behavioral rules. The latter, in turn, are determined by genes. It has been noted that the American ovenbird (*Seiurus aurocapillus*) digs for fly maggots in the forest soil. If its search is unsuccessful, it enlarges the area of search. But if it does find something, it stays near the spot and intensively searches around it. Staying with winners is a logical search strategy here. With rats or honeybirds, the search strategy is the opposite: if they find food somewhere, they consume it and try out another location. Even in experimental situations they cannot be taught to seek out within a certain period of time the same spot at which they have had a successful search. Such behavior would offend their common sense. Of course, this is understandable because honeybirds feed on nectar, which is produced slowly by the flower and it takes several hours before it is fully replenished. More highly developed species are able to use both strategies in opportunistic fashion.

C. R. Menzel performed the following experiment with Japanese rhesus monkeys. He placed a ripe fruit that was out of season in a particular forest area on one of the monkeys' trails and a piece of chocolate on another trail.[16] Both pieces of food were found by one or another rhesus monkey, and Menzel observed them for twenty minutes to see what they would do. The one that had found the unexpected ripe fruit ate it and afterward started to search the vines of the plant on which that fruit grows to see if it could find more. It searched for a long time over a wide area. The other monkey that found the chocolate—the new, unknown but very tasty food—stayed in the immediate vicinity of the find and searched and dug around there, and several times returned to the exact spot to see if there might be more of the same. Menzel concluded that one that had found the fruit was behaving logically in checking out other places where it might have found that fruit before, while the one that found the unknown but delectable food item subjected the place where it was discovered to a thorough search, just in case it turned into a new and exploitable source of food.

Thus, the construction of the cognitive map reflects the ecological circumstances of a given species. Some of the permanent conditions of the environment get embodied in the genes, and through their mediation, in the cognitive map, which is otherwise based on experience. Many species carry genetic behavioral instructions that induce the animal innately, without specific experiences, to avoid *deep places*. For example, the animal will stop at the edge of a pit or a rock and will not try to go further. If we cover a hole with a sheet of glass, thus creating purely visual depth, kittens will stop at the edge, even though their sense of touch tells them that they are on solid ground. Depth is not perceived to be dangerous for animals that live in water, which is clearly the reason why sea turtles are unfazed by it, while land turtles react to depth the same way as kittens.

Animals that live in trees move around among the branches, which is much like orienting oneself in a maze, because some portion of the branches may well represent dead ends. As soon as a chameleon emerges from the egg, it is able, looking down from a high vantage point, to "figure out" what the best path is without running into dead ends, and is able to do so without any experience.

Functioning Models of the Environment in the Brain

The study of cognitive maps and of innate behavioral instructions leads to an ethological theory that regards the unified system of inner representations and genetic instructions as a *model*. This model reflects the characteristics of the environment most important for the survival of the animal. The narrower environment of the animal may be understood as an interdependent system obeying certain rules. Something is always happening in this system, but some of the events may be probabilistically predictable. For example, from the point of view of a small predator, the environment is a system that undergoes definite periodic changes, such as the alternation of night and day and the changes of the seasons. There are certain permanent features, such as the presence of water or other characteristics of the terrain. While the availability of food is a permanent feature, the individual habits of predators affect its prevalence, and food will be found in a particular place only with a certain probability. The animate and inanimate environments have numerous additional features that are of no significance for a predator. Cases in point might be the veins in a leaf, the pattern of the clouds, or the types of rocks in the soil. The neurons in the predator's brain construct a representation of the environment that contains only the most essential information. That is why we regard it as a model and not as a photograph or a geographic map; the representation is a *simpler system* in which events occur *analogously* to the much more complicated real system of which the mental representation is a model. If the model provides a reasonable approximation of the events in the environment, the predator will be able to acquire water, food, and shelter when needed, and will be able to escape the larger predators lying in wait for it. The model that the animal builds on the basis of its experiences is thus a dynamic structure that is used by it for predicting events in its environment.[17]

One might think of this phenomenon as a Lego toy composed of identical neurons, except that the final structure is much more complicated and its construction is a very complex operation by the nervous system. Those characteristics of the environment that are, from the evolutionary point of view, unchanging for long periods, such as the alternation of night and day, are genetically represented in every individual of the species, while elements that change rapidly, have temporary validity, and are useful only for an individual animal, get inserted into individual neural memory. The model in the brain contains not only certain traits of the external environment, but also data that pertain to the individual animal that maintains this external representation. It thus also contains *behavioral rules* that, in a given situation, will automatically determine the behavior of the animal. The more highly developed an animal is, the more accurate and detailed is its inner representation. For example, the wolf brain can model not only the places that the wolf should avoid and the dangers that may be lurking there, but also the behavior of its prey and of the individual members of the pack. There is room in the model for the rank order among the wolves, the impact of previous fights, and many other things. The models constructed in the brains of the most highly developed primates probably contain not only their behavioral rules, but they themselves appear in them; in other words *self-consciousness* makes its appearance. The evolution of animals' nervous systems reflects the increasing complexities of model construction.

A very important component of the model of the environment constructed in the brains of social animals is the representation of their species mates. In the course of gathering food, defending oneself, and reproducing, the animal often cooperates with its companions, which may confer significant benefits. Or an animal may be in competition with its companions for some resource, and it is therefore important that they be recognized so that their behavior can be more or less predicted. Researchers have observed that animals can explicitly learn from their companions. The shorebird known as the oystercatcher learns from its parents how to open shellfish, some songbirds learn to sing from their father, and many birds learn from their species mates in the course of mocking behavior what species to regard as a predator.[18] Monkeys, and particularly apes, formulate quite complicated "personality profiles" of others living in their group. They remember quite accurately the rank-order disputes the others have participated in and what consequences the rank order has for themselves. With this knowledge, they can quite accurately predict the activities of various alliances, whether they belong to these or not. These learning processes are normal components of individual development and one can determine reasonable accurately what, when, and how an animal will learn from its species mates.

The Brain as Model Builder and the Mind

The theory of the environment-modeling brain is quite wonderful and has been shown to be very successful in predicting animal behavior. It is not easy to translate the theory of modeling into a description of the mind, but it is not impossible, and I shall take a stab at it.

Let us think of the mind as the workshop of the brain; as the place where behavioral instructions and—surely in the case of humans—thoughts come into being. Many active mechanisms assist decision making in this workshop. This is the place where the sense organs deliver status reports on what is seen, heard, smelled, or touched, and it is also the place where memory representations or images are stored. Since we are unable to recall simultaneously our entire inventory of memories, it is quite clear that this workshop is not a large, well-lit hall in which everything is visible, where we can easily inspect the tools for preparing instructions, the stored representations, and the connections that develop between them as a result of learned or inherited mechanisms. Rather, it is a pitch dark place in which a few spots may be lit up, but only if we happen to be awake and we see, hear, or touch something. Every sensation can be linked to memory and we can determine whether the sensation represents something already known that we have experienced several times or whether it is something brand new.

Of course, the memory stores not only images of objects, but also representations of previous behavior and of its effectiveness or ineffectiveness. As these representations get activated, we get clear signals from the motivational center in the basement of the workshop whether some past action was good or bad and whether we would like to repeat it or rather avoid it. This motivational center also sends signals about pleasant things, such as food, and tells us whether we need some because we might be hungry at that moment. The center contains several motivational systems that are connected to one another in a strict rank order. If several motivations are relevant for the matter at hand, it is easily and automatically decided what is more important: to eat or to flee or to have sex.

These periodically illuminated, active spots also appear in the animal mind. If we could undertake some fantastic voyage into the workshop of an animal's mind, say a fox's, we would see occasional flashes in the pitch dark. On a large screen a rabbit may be running, some memory cells would be blinking, and the instructions to follow and to hunt would begin to appear. If the hunt were successful, small lights would blink where instructions are stored for the behavioral mechanisms connected with feeding. Then it would turn dark again and we would only hear humming from the cellar as the automatic mechanisms of digestion did their work.

I once saw a computer in which hundreds of small blinking lights signaled the operations of the machine. The computer could be slowed down, and then one could follow its inner workings from the more deliberate blinks of the lights, but at its normal speed all one could observe was that the lights were blinking with incredible rapidity. That is the way it is in the mind, too. While we describe what ought to happen as a result of the lightning-fast firing of neurons, the brain has already long completed the corresponding activity.

But one should not assume that there is "somebody" in this dark workshop, a "somebody" who lives there and somehow comprehends and even directs the operations of the mind. We can provide a quite satisfactory explanation of the behavior of most mammals by not assuming the existence of a "somebody" in their brains.[19] On the contrary, what is near miraculous about this workshop is that things in it happen quite automatically. The motivations such as hunger, thirst, and the sex instinct produce the appropriate behavior even without instructions from "somebody" and the learning mechanisms ensure that experience also has a role in making decisions. But the decision maker is the entire workshop and not a tiny, subjective, animate "I" that leads an independent life in the mind.

We know about ourselves that there is a tiny "I" in us, but this human something is unable to have an overview of the workshop of the mind, let alone direct it. However, it is certain that it plays an important role in many decisions and assessments. There exists in humans a system of the highest order for making value judgments: the self. One of the most important questions in the research on the animal mind is whether humans are the only ones who have such a subjective "I"—as many believe even today—or whether we can exhibit the existence of a similar or perhaps somewhat less extensive I-mechanism in the more highly developed animals. And if it exists, what is it like?

The Human Mind

If we compare the operations of the mind in humans and animals, even the most highly developed ones, we can discover surprising similarities as well as remarkable differences. The study of these comparative operations may provide a scientific answer to the question above.

A human may decide to turn off the flow of information from the outside world and may just rummage around in the boxes of memory: how was it yesterday or last week or last year? This rummaging does not need any outside signals to be activated. In other words, humans are able to direct what gets "illuminated" in the workshop of the mind. As far as we know today, animals are unable to do this, and they can reference their memory only if there is an external reason for it. The animal's memory is beholden to the external environment and external stimuli. Animals live perpetually in the present; they are unable to imagine the future or to call up the past at their discretion and cannot accordingly modify their behavior. Humans are not only able to rummage around in their memory, but can imagine in various ways what they might do in the future. For example, a human might realize that he is not hungry yet, but is able to think of dining at a restaurant that evening, where he expects to eat pheasant soup and roast saddle of venison. Animals are able to think about food only when they are hungry, except of course for those that store food; but even those do so on the basis of a rigid genetic program, and it probably never enters their mind that they might be hungry in the future. We, on the other hand, imagine things, such as the many possible variants of an action, we make a plan, and we select in advance the one most favorable to us.

This ability of ours, called most generally *constructional activity*, is based on several natural endowments.[20] The first is the ability to make a copy of the representations made from sensory stimuli, which are technically referred to as *secondary representations*. Humans, just as animals, remember what they have seen or heard and are able to recall this when activated by an external stimulus. The new and special endowment of humans and apes is that they can make a copy of the representation, the activation of which is not controlled by external stimuli. It is perhaps even more important that the copies can be altered, linked with each other, and "annotated." Let us assume that I have seen a lizard and a bird, both of which I remember well. I can blend the copies of these representations without altering the original; the lizard suddenly has wings and from some representation of fire it acquires a flaming tongue, and lo, I have produced a never-before-seen, frightening, fire-belching dragon!

Of course, I can also tell others about the dragon, and if I am sufficiently talented, I could draw or paint it. Thus, humans can create fantasies with the assistance of the copies, certain mental constructs that have a faint relationship to the real world, and that are forged with a great deal of freedom. However, we would not get very far if we could only construct and copy representations, because giving free rein to the imagination would result in confused patterns incomprehensible to others. The ability to construct representations is guided by humans' ability to *follow rules*. We construct representations not only to please ourselves, but to surprise, amaze, or assist our fellow humans. Humans are fundamentally social creatures and their constructions are circumscribed by the accepted rules of their culture. When we tell stories to our children, we couch them in terms that they can understand. When we are playing a game, such as chess, we might be deploying whole armies in our mind, with kings, generals, cavalry, and infantry, but we still obey the rules of chess. If we are passionate about rules, we gladly obey them, although at times we might neglect them in order to give priority to some other rules.

"Well, my son (or "Well, Fido"), the rule is that you get your dinner at exactly 7 p.m., and so stop whining at six-thirty—it doesn't matter that you are hungry and in any case you won't get to eat until seven. That is the rule, get it?"

"Today you are getting your dinner at six, because guests are coming. I didn't say so before, but when guests are coming, the rule is that you have to have your dinner before they arrive. Clear?"

Rules are very often *personal rituals* that appear as stereotypes and express a fixed order for carrying out certain actions.[21] A case in point might be getting up in the morning, after which one might turn on the radio, drink some orange juice, brush one's teeth, take off one's pajamas, take a shower, drink some coffee, have breakfast, and get dressed. Everyone has rituals of this sort in which the order of doing things is scrupulously observed.

Taking a dog for a walk is also a ritual. When the time is right, we first call the dog, then put on our walking shoes, put on an overcoat, take the leash, take the house key, open the door, and so on. It is basically these personal rituals resting on certain rules that have liberated the mind from being enslaved by external stimuli. A personal ritual is really an earlier behavioral rule that the mind executes with reference to the external environment. A great advantage of stereotypes is that we need not think through and put together a very complicated series of actions every single time we repeat it; we just conjure up the secondary representation, which passes *internal* instructions to the mechanism that regulates our behavior.

Humans are capable of carrying out certain actions automatically: for example, driving a car without paying attention to shifting gears, braking, or stepping on the gas pedal, but noting only the car's general progress and the traffic. This ability is very important, but is only partly a stereotype, because only a portion of the aggregate action is automated: the action itself is triggered by stimuli coming from the external environment, such as by the slowing down of the car in front us or by a ball bouncing into the street. However, a personal ritual is independent of the environment, or more accurately, it governs from the inside the succession of activities in the specified environment. And the emphasis is definitely on the word *inside*. It is probably this independence from the environment that formed our peculiar relation to *time*. What this means is that we are able to tie events to a particular moment of time, and that the necessary actions are activated by an inner clock[22] rather than external influences. Hence, the resulting sequence of actions is more or less independent of the external world.

Solitary animals regard the momentary condition of the environment as their most important source of information. Social animals draw their information from a much narrower circle, namely from their companions. The constructional capability of humans has made it possible for them to regard the information stored in the mind as the most important environment, and their actions and decisions always take their starting point from that. An entire new compartment has been created for this in the workshop of the mind, which has enabled us to alter the external world at will on the basis of internal patterns we construct. We can construct a house, a machine, or a book in our mind, and then do it for real. By employing certain rules, we can build the mental constructs out of real materials, and these realizations truly work! I will not discuss here the very important question of how this property developed during the course of human evolution, but I have to emphasize that the existence of tight human groupings played a significant role in it. The continual presence of companions, which characterizes our species, and the continual need to communicate have created the ability to construct and to follow rules. Obedience to the rules and the continual attachment that humans feel toward others and their continual interest in the thoughts, plans, ideas, and mental processes of others are characteristics that are necessary and sufficient conditions for one another. Without rules we could not bear to be with each other, and without attraction we would have no need for rules.

Observation of socially well-developed predators and of apes suggests that in certain cases they, too, are able to make copies of mental representations. But their mental workshop is not equipped for constructional activity; their "toolbox" is rather impoverished, and they do not really know what to do with the copies.

Language Really Helps in Building Models

Could we select a restaurant for an evening meal without using any thoughts expressed in language? This is clearly difficult, but with some practice we might succeed. We could flash pictures or memories of places we have visited before our eyes, but we could not select a restaurant that we have heard has good food or one about which we read something in a newspaper, because all that is information expressed in language. Or consider another task. Suppose we have to travel to Nome, Alaska, where we have never been before. If we can use language, it is very simple to think through this problem and carry it out. We can make an airplane reservation by phone, call a taxi, and we are ready to go. Without language the task is impossible, since we do not have remembrances of this city, no trace of memory. Nome does not appear on our cognitive map of the environment, and without using language we would never find our way there and we could not even imagine the need to go there. The human and animal workshops of the mind differ in that the former has certain upper floors that can easily be illuminated from within. It contains certain tools, namely words, that can be fitted together and with which the most complicated task becomes easy. The human mind uses language as well to do its job of modeling!

This novel modeling ability of humans is so highly developed that it is hard to imagine the inner world of a living being without language ability. The real question is whether such a being possesses at all a modestly humanlike inner world.

Animals are capable of associative learning, which takes the form in the more highly developed ones of learning *signs* or *signals*, but this has little to do with real language. For a fox, it is not only the appearance of a mouse that promises a delightful snack; the rustling of leaves on the ground or a squeak is a signal from which the fox can infer the presence of a mouse. Of course, the connection between the signal and the thing that it denotes can be formulated in ways other than learning. Very important things and the corresponding signals, such as the mouse and its squeak, are not only linked by learning. Laboratory experiments have been done with fox pups that have been brought up in isolation from other foxes and have thus remained inexperienced. If the pup is offered some meat while a musical tone is played, and this is repeated a few times, the connection between the signal and the meat is rapidly established in the fox's mind. But if the tone is played ten or fifteen times without meat being offered, the fox will slowly forget the connection, and afterward will pay no attention to the tone. If the conditioning is done not with a musical tone but with a recording of a genuine mouse squeak, the connection between the signal and the real thing becomes so strong that the fox never forgets it. The experimenters played the recording of the mouse squeak four thousand times without giving the fox the food reward, and the poor fox pricked up its ears at the sound till the bitter end. After four thousand trials, the experimenters gave up because humans are frail.

In other words, a signal is always connected to the thing it denotes and the connection can be established by learning. It is characteristic of this process that one must always rely on reward or punishment, that the connection is built slowly, and if it is not used, it is rapidly erased from the animal's memory.

At first glance we might easily believe that the words in human language are also such signals, since they refer to something. *Meat* means meat, *bread* means bread, and we have to learn that.

But wait a minute! What does meat mean? Surely not only a bite of something to eat—although that, too—but a lot more: animal muscle tissue, leg of venison, short ribs, filet mignon, or even a "meaty proposition," although that really has nothing to do with meat. And if somebody is referred to as a "meaty fellow," that does not mean that it is all right to eat him. "Power and meat to the workers" is just a political slogan. To put it differently, the words are not signals, or hardly so, but *symbols*. What we mean is that words are part of a *system* that contains many other elements that also influence the function of a particular signal. Words have *meaning*. It is the property of symbols that they can be explained and that we can express their inherent sense and their meaning with manifold descriptions, actions, or stories. The meaning refers to the symbol, but is not its property but rather that of the entire explanatory system surrounding it. It is also important to note that the symbols' system does not stand by itself but, at certain points and through the sense organs, it is "anchored" in the external world.[23] It is characteristic of verbal symbols that they can be taught quickly in a single attempt and without rewards or punishments.

A child learning its mother tongue can in practice learn several thousand words in a year, most of which it will have heard only a few times or even just once. The child does not need frequent reinforcement, which is a fundamental property of learning signals by association. Signals are always tied to the signaled item, whereas words relate to one another and are members of a system in which their relationship to each other can change at any time, as in the remark, "Don't eat the flesh of this fruit because it is bitter."

By virtue of this remark, a thing that appeared edible has become something to be avoided, even though the recipient of the warning signal has had no experience with the thing signaled. It also makes a huge difference that once we have learned words in our mother tongue we do not forget them, even if we do not use them for years. We are also able to recall the words without any external stimulus. The usage of the learned words is governed by an internal regulatory mechanism. This is what makes it possible for the human mind to construct with their aid very complicated models that describe the connections between, and the finest details of, the internal and external worlds. Of course, looking at it from the outside, the meaning of words derives from a linguistic community. In this sense, but only in this sense, verbal models are closely attached to the external world and embody the direct link between culture and reality.

I Can Name It, Therefore It Exists

Verbal models start out with *naming things*. This, too, is a novel, genetic property of the human mind. For children, the name of something is often tantamount to an explanation.

"In this picture we see a long-extinct bird, the dodo." This sentence accomplishes the naming of something, and thereby a node has been created in the mind to which we can later tie all kinds of useful information without the dodo having to continually reappear. Having accomplished the act of naming it, we are ready to hear a story. The named animal does something or something happens to it, and even our feelings can get involved in the construct.

"What does the dodo eat?"

"How many eggs does it lay?"

"Why can't it fly?"

"Does its meat taste good?"

"Is it really extinct?"

The animal mind is unable to create such a node and to incorporate stories connected with it. It is not impossible for an animal to build an intelligible connection between an object and its signal, but a signal of something that existed long ago can, by itself, be a point of departure only for the human mind.

The naming of things, the cunning rules for building verbal models, to which we refer in school as grammar, and the previously discussed constructional ability make it possible for us to create constructs removed from the real world—fairy tales, religion, philosophy, or mathematics. These are things that come into being on the upper floors of the workshop of the human mind.

Of course, language does not replace the earlier mental models, but merely complements them and allows us to realize earlier needs on a higher level. The workshop of the human mind is not a very brightly lit room, either, but it is one in which there are more and better-lit spots than in the animal mind. Much of the brain's work in governing our behavior takes place in the dark here, too, and the old, tried and true motivational systems operate in the basement. However, their operations can be influenced to some extent by the tools stored on the upper floors. We are therefore dealing with a genuinely mixed system here, in which the most recent and most ancient methods are inseparably intermingled. It is also certain that humans possess numerous mental properties that are not tied to language and that either cannot be found among animals or can be found only in very primitive form. I mentioned earlier the complicated mechanism of linguistic interpretation, to which we need to add that an *interpretation* is not always linguistic. A story performed by a mime uses no words, but we understand the story perfectly well, because we can interpret his motions, his body language. And the interpretation of spoken language is significantly affected by the tone of voice, or a smile or a frown.

Many scholars believe that under the influence of close human groupings the ability to interpret long preceded the development of language. One of the biggest turning points in human evolution was the development of communication among our ancestors and of the attendant continual interpretation. Modern humans see intentions and complicated stories behind every action and continually try to unravel their threads, even when they are communicating with their spouses or immediate families, and also when they participate in political or other social activities.

The Special Characteristics of Human Thought

The characteristics that rest on the old and new modeling abilities of the human mind constitute a peculiar, mixed bag, and researchers into the mechanism of the animal mind always search for these peculiar traits. They argue a lot about how the existence of this or that ability can be proved. And if a particular ability exists, to what extent do animals have it and how does it agree with or differ from the corresponding human ability? Or to what extent is the ability tied to language or a social environment? And if the ability is absent, can something substitute for it or can it be simulated somehow?

The human mind is not only aware of itself, but is capable of regarding other humans, and in some cases animals or even objects, as having a similar mind and behaving accordingly. In other words, humans assume that their companions think, they try to figure out the thoughts of others, and they attempt to use these assumptions in their social intercourse. In technical terms we would say that humans have a *theory of mind*. The basis of this property is that the human mind is able to make a copy of representations, to alter them with the aid of the constructions discussed earlier, and then to use the new constructions, beliefs, ideas, plans, and thoughts in everyday life. It goes without saying that if we attempt to build a theory of the human mind we must secure adequate proof and make suitable observations about others or even ourselves.

We might, for example, observe the interaction between two humans and note that in the course of some common activity, which could be nothing more than a conversation, their attention acquires a common focus and they follow each other's glances. One might say, "The knife is on the table," and glance at the table. The other follows the glance of the first, because there are three small tables nearby, and finally glimpses the knife. Pointing to something is similar behavior: "I'd like that apple," and while saying this, one would point to it with extended hand and index finger. The grocer would follow the gesture and hand over the desired piece of fruit.

Humans are able to make a distinction between an unpleasantness caused by somebody intentionally or caused inadvertently. If somebody accidentally steps on your toe, he or she would indicate with a brief apology that it was not intentional. We accept and understand that, but might nevertheless keep our eyes open to see whether this is really so. When there is a lot of jostling in a crowd, we are continually paying attention to see whether any of the pushes and shoves might be intentional. If we conclude that a push was intentional, we are likely to become very indignant, while we easily forgive those classified as unintentional, even if they are intrinsically more unpleasant.

Even children quickly understand role switching: "I'll throw the ball, and you try to catch it."

"Now let's do it the other way. You throw and I catch!"

Two persons often engage in intentional communication with each other. They show each other something and talk in such a way that while one is talking, the other listens; then they switch, and the one who talked before now listens and vice versa. They often ask each other for information and give out information.

"You are taller than I, would you look in the window? Is my mom there?"

"I can't see anybody."

The exchange of emotional information is also a common occurrence. If our friend or lover is sad or in high spirits, his or her emotional state communicates itself to us as well. If one is speaking about one's emotional problems, the listener may be able to identify emotionally with the speaker, and the listener's emotional state follows that of the speaker. This ability to feel what the other feels is called empathy and is actually the basis for the experience we have in the theater.

Humans have numerous learning talents related to their companions. We have already mentioned the human trait of following rules; other important ones are imitation, aping, and following patterns, which permit the mind to translate another person's behavior pattern into instructions that guide the behavior of our own body. Teaching is a behavior on a high level in which the teacher not only exhibits a pattern of behavior, but also checks whether the student has appropriately internalized the information conveyed. Other social forms of behavior occurring in interactions with our companions are lying and deceit. We have to consider this a mental process of high order, because in forming this type of behavior the mind has to take into account the beliefs and ideas of another mind. In other words, the mind must build a model of the operations of another mind, which the human mind is able to accomplish successfully.

We have already mentioned that the "I" appears in the human mind. But we can do even better: humans are able to think about the "I"—about themselves—as an object or as an actor. Behind this is the further ability to recognize living creatures as active and independent entities and to model the interactions among inanimate objects.

We may list among the faculties of the human mind the previously discussed penchant for following personal rituals, to which we might add that humans like to divide their days into subperiods and to tie certain actions to particular points of time. This is of great help in arranging the details of one's life. Related to this is the phenomenon, unknown among animals, that humans like to *practice*, that is to acquire skills by manifold repetitions of an action for its own sake. This is a good method for learning certain techniques to perfection. In the course of practice, the mind is able to initiate an activity not only for the sake of a concrete result, but also for the sake of trying out in practice something that has only existed in the mind. All these are properties of the mind that we have already mentioned in connection with the canine mind. It seems worthwhile to list them in the order of their hypothesized type. The list may also be regarded as an enumeration of the most important elements of human intelligence.[24]

The first three items correspond to *physical intelligence*:

- Recognition of causal relations.
- Figuring out the effects of reciprocal influences among objects.
- Recognition of independent, living creatures.

The next eight items belong to *social intelligence*:

- Group membership.
- Intentionality.
- Empathy.
- Joint paying of attention.
- Following glances.
- Pointing.
- Distinguishing between intentional and inadvertent actions.
- Recognition of the self.

The next twelve items could be called part of *cultural intelligence*, which means that humans need these mostly when they live in some organized group or culture:

- Personal rituals, sense of time.
- Following rules.
- Cooperation.
- Social learning: following patterns, imitation, copying, teaching.
- Intentional communication.
- Giving and asking for information.
- Deceit.
- Theory of mind: attributing to another a mind similar to our own.
- Role playing and role switching.
- Interpretation.
- Language ability: naming things, use of symbols, linguistic rules.
- Practice.

Chapter 13

What Do the Relatives Know?

A fundamental question in animal psychology and ethology is whether the targets of study are merely animated objects or whether they are truly subjects: beings with consciousness. My friend István Hernád, an influential personality in the cognitive sciences, formulates this succinctly as "Is there somebody there?" Does a self or a self-conscious mind, perhaps similar to ours here and there, reside in the animal body?

All of us who read know that we are *somebody*. We often say this to one another and demonstrate it almost willy-nilly all our lives. This fact is seemingly the most important thing for us. It is easy to convince somebody that our bodies possess a physical or chemical reality, but it is not so simple to convince others that we are who we are. What would be acceptable proof? The mere assertion that we are?

It is easy to see that such a train of thought will not lead very far. Even beginner computer programmers could write a program that makes such an assertion at will. Every program that asserts that *it exists* tells the truth up to a point, since it truly exists as a program; but this does not allow us to make an essential distinction between it and other programs that say nothing about their existence. The question is really trickier, because we are not only asking whether it exists, but also whether it is a *somebody* beyond mere physical existence. The real issue is what replies to this question can be regarded as true. This is still a fundamental question in philosophy.

The problem is seemingly approachable through classification or categorization. The statement "I am" establishes a fundamental category, and when we examine it, we are really asking whether this peculiar category contains other members in addition to ourselves. What are the criteria by which we might decide that a being belongs to this category? Descartes's statement "I think, therefore I am" just puts off the crux of the problem but does not solve it, because proving the assertion "I think" is no easier than proving "I am."

It might be tempting to think that this is merely an abstract philosophical problem. It is, of course, that, too; but answering the question "Is there somebody there?" is an important, daily task in dealing with animals. Jane Goodall carried out a series of observations of chimpanzee behavior with the following setup. A mechanism was placed in the forest from which the chimpanzees could obtain a banana from time to time, but the experiment was rigged so that each member of the chimpanzee troop living in that area would have to open the mechanism individually at a specific time of the day.[1] The chimpanzees rapidly learned the drill and each one appeared at the appointed time, opened the mechanism, and retrieved its portion of banana. On one occasion, it was the turn of a young male, but an older, dominant male accompanied it. It is easy to predict what was likely to happen. If the younger chimpanzee opened the mechanism and retrieved the banana, the older one would take it away from it, because that is what is customary among chimpanzees. But if "there is somebody there," the younger one should have enough brains to anticipate this. In that case, the appropriate strategy for the young chimpanzee would be to delay, and to open the mechanism only after it has succeeded in somehow getting rid of the older one. This is exactly what happened. The young chimpanzee pretended that it just happened to be there and did not even look at the mechanism. After a while, the older one ambled off, whereupon the younger one leaped at the mechanism and happily retrieved its fruit. It probably had some extra satisfaction from having pulled the wool over the eyes of the old geezer.

But at that point, something unexpected happened. The older chimpanzee suddenly emerged from behind a bush and took the banana away. The observers saw that a few minutes earlier, after it left its younger companion, it circled around and observed the actions of the young one from behind a bush. It calculated correctly: when the unsuspecting young chimpanzee retrieved the banana, the elder one pounced and took it away.

The Theory of Mind about the Intentions of Others

Since our closest relatives are the chimpanzees, and 98 percent of our genes are identical, we have a good basis for assuming that chimpanzees also have a theory of mind; in other words, that they are able to make assumptions about the aims, intentions, plans, and ideas of other chimpanzees, which may lead to certain actions, and that they are able to figure all this out. Of course, a theory of mind does not mean that chimpanzees can necessarily articulate these assumptions, but only that they can somehow use them. Although nobody has tried it, we can be sure that relevant experiments with cockroaches would not be successful. They would probably be unsuccessful with rats, too, but it is almost certain that they would succeed with *dogs*. Anyone who has ever owned a dog knows that dogs can be quite wily and can infer from the tiniest signs whether their master's intentions are favorable for them or not. But lest the reader think that I am too biased in favor of dogs, my next example is about cats. Cats that live in apartments usually select a comfortable resting place in a warm and quiet room, perhaps even a spot from which they can see the television set. To their chagrin, it happens at times that the master preempts the most comfortable spot. Many people have recounted that in such cases, the smarter cats can induce the master to relinquish his place. For example, a cat might go to the door and mew to get out; when the unsuspecting master gets up to open the door, the cat quickly runs back to the comfortable chair and claims it for itself.

What does the cat think while it is doing this?

Higher order animals, particularly those that live in groups, continually face problems of this sort. If two not particularly brilliant chickens simultaneously espy a delicious-looking earthworm and start running toward it, before they reach it, the dominant individual will forcefully peck at the subordinate one, to make sure it understands that the rank order is in effect and the prey belongs to the dominant one. The question is whether this observation entitles us to assume that chickens have a theory of mind. In other words, is it possible that while they were running for the earthworm, the dominant chicken hypothesized that the intentions of the other were similar and found it expedient to rein in the subordinate's enthusiasm?

It is an important part of scientific activity to learn how to reject the theories of others. In daily practice, ethologists emphatically reject the theory of mind. We have found a hundred ways of rejecting the above explanations wholly or at least in part. For example, in the case of chickens, we might argue that intentions have nothing to do with it; the only thing that is going on is that the dominant chicken has a mechanism for aggression that prompts it to chase away other chickens from the vicinity of a tasty morsel.

And the cat? We do not have to assume in the case of the cat that it figured out the events either that would take place or that *potentially might take place*. The only thing going on here is that it has internalized through associative learning that when it mews by the door, the armchair becomes available. But we have to admit that the chimpanzee is different. It is enough to suppose that some dim intention to deceive played a role in its behavior.

If the chimpanzee can have a purpose, an intention, or a plan, however, then this trait is not connected with language and is not wholly owned by humans; it is therefore probable that there are evolutionary antecedents or *gradations*. So we are back to the chicken and the cat!

On similar grounds, the American philosopher D. C. Dennett formulated the possibility of gradations in intentions.[2] A *zero-order intentionality* reflects no mental mechanism, purpose, intention, or plan. Certain butterflies, when startled, spread their folded wings and exhibit two spots on the upper wing surfaces that are reminiscent of eyes. The hapless bird that might have been aggravating the butterfly in the hope of a tasty meal unexpectedly sees a pair of threatening eyes. The bird is taken aback for a second, which is long enough for the butterfly to escape. This is a typical example of zero-order intentionality. The butterfly is what it is, and when something scares it, it spreads its wings. We have no reason to suppose that it does so to engender fear in the predator that is after it or that it has a good laugh once it escapes. The pattern of its wings was shaped by the blind and unconscious forces of evolution in the interest of its survival. We may have to include here the case of the chicken, too; of course, if and only if somebody were to show with some carefully executed experiments that the chicken does have intentions, we would have to reject this theory.

Some *purpose*, which influences the behavior of the animal, is present in what we may call *first-order intentionality*. The cat's behavior may be a case in point, although even this is debatable. Even in the simplest imaginable case, the cat is thinking about the comfortable armchair, and that is why it mews by the door. A more complicated hypothesis is that it thinks through the following: "I will mew a little by the door, the sucker will get up and come here as usual, and presto, I take his seat." But proof of this requires additional observations and experiments.

Second-order intentionality is present, according to Dennett, when the animal does something in order to make someone believe something; that is, in this case the animal attempts to alter someone's beliefs with its behavior. One ethologist was studying baboons in a natural setting and noted that the young regularly undertake a strategy of deceit.[3] In one case, a female had dug up a root especially favored by baboons. A nearby infant baboon was too small to dig for roots, but when the root was almost completely uncovered, the infant started to screech noisily. Its mother, some distance away, heard the infant's screeching and ran to its rescue by pursuing the other female that was of lower rank. Presumably, the mother thought that this female was harming its baby. The pursuer and the pursued were both getting farther from the scene, and the baby took advantage of this by lifting the root out of the hole and eating it. Several similar incidents were also observed, and they all had the common feature that they involved second-order intentionality. The case of the young chimpanzee also belongs to this category: it pretended that it had no reason to be at the food-dispensing mechanism in order to make the older chimpanzee *think* that it had no reason to stay there, either. But the behavior of the older one represents third-order intentionality, because it left in order to make the younger one think that it (the older one) believed that nothing would happen there.

Most of the problems in this area are created by the human propensity to attribute to others good or evil intentions or plans. In social intercourse we continually employ the theory of mind in various gradations and complexity. ("I suspect that you are contemplating whether I have understood how difficult it is for you to get proof of that and whether you have truly understood that I really think that you are capable of recognizing my belief that you want to explain to me that most of us are able to follow intentionalities up to only the fifth or sixth order.")[4] We are willing to attribute intentions not only to animals but also to machines, simple mechanisms, or even objects: "That miserable car key got itself locked in the car *just* when I am in a hurry and don't have the spare key with me." We even attribute intentions to abstractions or abstract concepts. A good example of this is the concept of a deity; as soon as the concept arises, it becomes a "somebody" who gets invested with thoughts and feelings not unlike our own. It is uncertain whether the animal mind also seeks intentions so extensively.

Ethology developed independently of psychology, and initially was not even concerned with the animal mind. The question "Is there somebody there?" did not even arise. Early ethologists dealt mostly with the evolutionary origins of particular observable behaviors and the relationship between behavior and the environment. And then, when they were able to answer the most important questions one way or another, it became clear that the basic question could no longer be avoided and that ethology had to adopt some kind of unified scientific standpoint about the animal mind.

If You Are Intelligent, You Strive to Exist

Ignoring the history of science, one could say that the current ethological point of view rests on a fundamental idea, namely the methodological definition of intelligence: *a system is intelligent if its behavior furthers its uninterrupted existence.* In other words, you are intelligent if you are *striving to exist.* Although this definition originates from outside of ethology, it is important because it is obvious to us that animals live in various environments, and behavior that would be regarded as intelligent in one kind of environment would not be so regarded in another. The only thing that intelligent behaviors have in common is that they promote

the continued existence of the subject. In the preceding chapter we
have already noted the markedly different search strategies of ovenbirds
and rats. Both strategies are intelligent if they are employed by the right
animal in the right environment. If this principle is accepted, then it
makes no sense in practice to compare the behavioral forms of different
species with a view toward ranking their intelligence. After all, what
might be the most intelligent behavior on the part of one species might
well be the dumbest for another. We have to accept that intelligence is a
highly relative characteristic. We could imagine an earthworm that behaves very intelligently and an elephant that appears to be quite dumb,
in spite of the fact that the latter has a huge brain while the former does
not really have one at all. Of course, no problem arises in comparing intelligence in individuals of the same species.

The situation is complicated by the fact that humans are subjective
beings, both as individuals and as a species. But it is probably the case
that anybody who is a "somebody" is a very subjective being, and it is
probably further true that subjectivity is a precondition for being "somebody." Humans are generally inclined to regard behavior as intelligent if it
promotes the maintenance of existence in their own environment. This
naïve view underlies the misery in animal psychology laboratories of tens
of thousands of rats, pigeons, and monkeys that are used in experiments
for comparing their intelligence with ours. For example, the titmouse is
able to recognize the connection between cause and effect as long as it
involves seeds and strings attached to them. To wit: it is able to determine merely on the basis of visual inspection which of a set of strings
protruding from a transparent tube it needs to pull to obtain the otherwise unreachable seed. But the titmouse will fail a simple maze test: it
will not even get started in a maze and will certainly not reach the target.
The reason is obvious: in its natural environment, it never needs to solve
maze problems, whereas searching for seeds and discovering their whereabouts is very important for it. In other words, one of these aptitudes
was not reinforced by evolution, while the other was impressed upon its
genes and became an important trait of the species.

One should also not be surprised by the discovery that *self-consciousness*
has appeared among the more highly developed animals; that is, the animal's inner representation of itself as a "somebody." If the animal's ability to handle information reaches a sufficiently high level, it is able to

recognize that many of its actions provoke an immediate response by its environment. It therefore benefits the animal to gather information pertaining to its *own behavior*. The animal has to observe itself and be able to use the data it collects. We have direct proof of this mental ability from the vertebrates and it does not come only from the behavior of humans or primates.

C. P. Shimp, a researcher who studied pigeons, attempted to determine whether one could pinpoint the knowledge that a bird acquires about its own behavior.[5] That is to say, could pigeons observe their own behavior and use in some fashion the information gained? He designed and carried out some fairly complicated experiments to come to grips with this question. In essence, a pigeon would first face two white discs. It could then peck at either of these for as long as it felt like it; eventually it would spontaneously switch and peck at the other one. After a while, the experimental area would become dark and two new discs would appear: a green one and a red one. If the pigeon had pecked fewer times at its second white disk than at the first, it would now have to peck at the red disc and conversely; if it had pecked at the second disc more times than the first, it was now supposed to peck at the green one. A reward followed if it acted as prescribed. The pigeons learned this lesson very well: they were able to store in their memory for a few seconds the results of their own spontaneous behavior, and if necessary, to use this in acquiring food.

Observations of chimpanzee behavior in front of a mirror led to the unambiguous inference that they recognize themselves in the mirror; that is, a chimpanzee recognizes the individual that dwells in its body, which says that there really "is somebody there." The initial experiments concerning self-recognition in chimpanzees were carried out by G. G. Gallup.[6] Mirrors were placed temporarily in the cages of chimpanzees with varying prior histories and their behavior was observed. On the first few occasions, the chimpanzees exhibited behavioral patterns commonly encountered when meeting other chimpanzees. Only later did they engage in behavior oriented toward their known bodies. They would stick their tongues out and peer at them, and pull their ears, very much like small children when they look into a mirror. Later, they anesthetized a chimpanzee, and while it was asleep, they painted a red dot on its forehead. After it woke up, it was given a mirror, and as soon as it saw itself in it, it touched the spot that had been painted and started to scratch it and pick at it. When such a chimpanzee was not given a mirror, many fewer of its gestures were directed toward its head. Gallup concluded from this experiment that the chimpanzee is able to recognize itself and to realize that the image in the mirror is of itself and not of another similar animal. Many scholars do not accept this experiment as proving the existence of the concept of the self, but rather think it probable that the chimpanzee somehow confounds the primary representation based on the image with its own movements. According to these scholars, this does not prove that chimpanzees have a secondary representation of themselves that is not subordinated to the primary representation, and which would assist them to think about themselves and their own mental states.[7]

We need to emphasize that the appearance of self-consciousness does not necessarily mean that the animal is capable of complex thoughts about itself. The self-consciousness of animals stands in the same relation to ours as a flickering candle to a powerful searchlight. The self-consciousness of humans is enormously enhanced by their constructional abilities.

Animals That Solve Problems

Comparative psychology avoided the problem of self-consciousness and dealt largely with the components of animal intelligence. Self-consciousness is a part of intelligence, but in itself it gives no indication of the kinds of problems that the individual is able to solve. It turns out that animals can solve many problems that are linked with *conceptual thinking* in humans. For example, given a sequence of objects with an odd number of members, monkeys are able to select the *middle* one. In various cunning experiments they have been able to rationally use the concept of the middle or center and they can distinguish sequences with an odd or even number of members. Pigeons quickly learn to recognize certain *classes* and, for example, can select from among various photographs those that depict fish or insects or humans.

A study by D. Premack and A. J. Premack proves that chimpanzees are quite adept at dealing with causal connections, but are much less so when dealing with time. In one experiment they employed four chimpanzees. Each of the chimpanzees was given the opportunity to observe a person who would first place a banana in a nontransparent container and then, some thirty feet away, would place an apple in another non-transparent container. The experimenters then diverted the chimpanzees' attention from these proceedings for about two minutes, and the chimpanzees were then able to observe the first person eating either a banana or an apple. The four experimental subjects were then released. One of the four chimpanzees would consistently go to the container that still had a fruit in it, because it figured out that if the person was eating a banana, the apple still had to be in its container and vice versa. In a variation of the experiment, they employed containers that could be opened only laboriously, and the chimpanzees were given plenty of opportunity to familiarize themselves with these mechanical difficulties. Then the person would hide the fruits in the containers as before, but would immediately start to eat a fruit thereafter. A three- to four-year-old child can figure out immediately in such an experiment that the person could only have been eating a third piece of fruit, because too little time had elapsed between concealing and eating of the fruit. None of the chimpanzees could figure this out, and the one that had been successful in the previous experiment would also always go the container holding the fruit other than what the person was eating.[8]

Many comparative experiments were done on capuchin monkeys and apes (chimpanzees, bonobos, orangutans) in order to study how causal relations between objects and processes are understood. The experimental subjects had to use various tools to acquire a piece of food that had been placed in a transparent tube.[9] In the simplest experiment, they were given a stick of suitable length, and if they pushed it into the tube, the piece of food would drop out at the other end. All species tested were easily able to accomplish this, although the capuchin monkeys fussed with the problem for a long time, sometimes as much as half an hour. More detailed study showed that they did not really think about the problem, but tried a number of different solutions until one worked; in other words, they operated on the basis of *trial and error* rather than mental inferences.

In a more complicated version of the experiment, the animals received one of three different objects: a bundle of rods tied together, a stick with some side branches, and a collection of three shorter sticks, none of which was long enough to push the desired item out of the tube. They had to figure out what kind of operations on these objects would turn them into usable tools. Sooner or later, all subjects solved this harder problem, but in the process they committed a number of characteristic mistakes. The capuchin monkeys first attempted to stuff the bundle of rods into the tube, which was not workable, after which they disassembled the bundle, but then tried to stuff the string with which it had been tied together into the tube, which also proved to be a bad idea. They finally arrived at the correct solution. The chimpanzees and the other apes immediately understood the problem and did not commit the capuchin monkeys' errors. They would disassemble the bundle right away and tried to use only the longest sticks from it. The two groups also acted differently when they were given a stick with branches. In every case, the capuchin monkeys tried to stick this inappropriate tool into the tube, obviously unsuccessfully. Eventually they would break off one of the side branches and made their attempt with the modified stick. Often they would try to use a side branch that they had removed, which was also a bad idea. With considerable difficulty they hit upon the correct solution, which was to remove both side branches and use the resulting long stick. The apes also tried at least once to use the unmodified stick, but soon found the correct solution. The most marked difference was that during the course of many repeated trials, the performance of the capuchin monkeys did not improve at all, whereas the apes, although not all of them, succeeded in solving the problem faster and faster during repetitions of the experiment.

The third task proved to be the most difficult. The correct solution was to stick, one after another, all three of the short sticks into the same end of the tube, which would cause the food item to drop out at the other end. This was very difficult for the capuchin monkeys, which in most cases pushed a short stick into both ends of the tube. But the apes did not excel, either. In some cases they solved the problems, but apparently by accident, because their performance did not improve even after numerous repetitions.[10] Children can easily solve the first two problems by the age of twenty-four months, and the third one by the time they are thirty months old.[11] These and similar experiments led to the conclusion that capuchin monkeys have but a modest understanding of the causal relations among objects, apes have a deeper understanding, but even theirs is fairly limited in comparison with humans.

We have already discussed the concept of the permanence of objects and related experiments, and it seems that monkeys do not develop this concept. Only few experiments were carried out with apes, and the results are somewhat contradictory; but in the case of at least one gorilla, it seemed that it was able to form mental representations of objects.[12] According to our observations and the studies of others, dogs are able to accomplish this task just as well as children.[13]

Numerous experiments have tested for the presence of mental abilities requiring some mathematical-logical intelligence. It has turned out that chimpanzees are able to classify objects on the basis of their properties. Of course, this is not terribly surprising, since all vertebrates need some ability to classify in order to stay alive. But it also turned out that their classificatory abilities are rather modest, since they could not classify a group of objects on the basis of two different properties.

However, they are able to solve problems based on the similarity of objects. In the pertinent experiments, the experimental subjects are usually shown three objects, of which two are identical and the third one is different; the animal is rewarded if it chooses the object that differs from the other two. For example, if one blue and two yellow dice are shown, it has to select the blue one; if the animal is shown two dice and a ball, it has to select the ball. Once animals have learned to solve these particular problems reliably, they are shown objects that they had not seen before, such as two sticks and a ring or two triangles and a square. If the animal is able to make the right choice at once, it is assumed that it can conceptualize identity and difference. Monkeys and apes solve these problems easily.

A separate question is what role is played in the solution by mental representations. The scholars who have interpreted these experiments have opined, not entirely uniformly, that mental representations play a role only in the case of apes. In some experiments, the tube containing the food was in one room, but without any tools. In another, adjacent room, accessible to the experimental animals, were various objects, including some tools appropriate for removing the food from the tube. Only the apes selected appropriate tools. It has been assumed on the basis of this finding that the apes are somehow able to *imagine* the task and the process of accomplishing it.

One might be entitled to object to these experiments and conclusions on the grounds that the task is rather artificial and that in nature these animals do not really have to think about excessively complicated causal relations. For this reason, D. L. Cheney and collaborators used baboons to examine the understanding of causal relations in a different realm of intelligence.[14] The question posed was whether baboons are capable of recognizing causal relations among socially interacting individuals in a situation in which they cannot see them, but only hear them. The researchers recorded the vocalizations of a few females in social intercourse and then played the recordings to the experimental subjects. When the experimental baboons heard a vocalization that did not fit into the social order—when the experimenters played a recording of a cry of fear by a female as a response to a vocalization by another female of lower rank—the experimental baboons became highly excited. When sounds were heard in a socially logical order—when a middle-ranked female's cry of fear was a response to a higher ranked female's vocalization, indicating a possible attack against the lower ranked one—the experimental subjects acknowledged the exchange of vocalizations but continued with their own activities.

Experiments conducted with dolphins are very interesting. It has been shown that they are able to solve complicated problems that require the cooperation of and communication between two animals. One dolphin was placed in each of two tanks arranged in such a manner that they could not see each other, but were able to hear each other through microphones and loudspeakers in each tank. In the first tank, they placed two lamps close together, while in the other tank they placed, again close together, two buttons that could be activated by the dolphin. The task was the following: if in the first tank the right-hand lamp was lit, the dolphin in the other tank had to press the right-hand button, and conversely if the left-hand lamp was lit in the first tank. The dolphins were rewarded if they solved this problem correctly. It turned out that that they solved this problem within seconds, without any particular training, and failed only when the microphones were switched off. In other words, the dolphin in the first tank was able to communicate to the other dolphin the status of the lamps in its tank by voice.

The experimental study of this type of problem-solving behavior has a huge literature. As early as the 1920s, Wolfgang Köhler began his famous experiments with chimpanzees.[15] Köhler suspended a banana from the ceiling, but sufficiently high so that a chimpanzee could not reach it even if it was jumping for it. When there was also a large wooden chest in the room, the chimpanzees sooner or later figured out that they had to push the chest under the banana, and if they climbed up on it, they could easily get to the fruit. Köhler named this behavior insightful learning, and he thought that after the animal has repeatedly tried to reach the banana unsuccessfully, it reached the solution in a flash merely by *thinking*.

The results of the experiments engendered a huge debate. Köhler and many others thought that in the course of this insightful learning, an original, new thought is born in the chimpanzee's brain, and they thought that their observations represented examples of thinking of the highest order. Later studies rather confirmed an alternative explanation, namely that chimpanzees are able to solve a problem from one moment to the next only when they have had the opportunity to practice the component parts of the solution over a long time. The Hungarian Paul Schiller, who did his work in America, showed that numerous genetic factors also play a role in problem-solving behavior.[16] In one of Köhler's experiments, the chimpanzees fitted several suitable sticks together in order to reach an object outside their cage. Schiller showed that these animals have an innate inclination to fit sticks together, and if given the opportunity, will practice this without being shown how to do it, quite independently of whether a problem can or cannot be solved in this fashion. Köhler's experiments were replicated countless times and it was determined quite unambiguously that the results depended on the number of opportunities that the chimpanzees had had to familiarize themselves with wooden chests or sticks.

Animal psychologists have always been interested in the question whether some animals can count, or rather whether it can be proved that they employ some number concept while they count. Of course, most animals cannot count, but there are a few cases that are hard to decide. The many mutually contradictory chimpanzee experiments allow us to infer that those individuals that have been taught to use signs are able to solve problems of counting and addition as long as small numbers are involved.

They can learn the numerals and they can employ the concepts of "greater than" or "less than" with respect to sets of countable objects and even with respect to numerals. They are able to comprehend a notion of regularity; that is, if they are dealing with a set of objects differing in the magnitude of a single attribute, they recognize the ordering of the objects. Imagine that a number of sticks of different lengths are arranged in a row and they have to select the larger or smaller of two adjacent sticks. If they have learned to do this correctly, then they are also able to make the correct choice if the sticks are not arrayed in a row or if they are asked to pick between two sticks that are not adjacent. The corresponding ability of children gets solidified only after they learn to use language, and for this reason, researchers have hypothesized that these abilities are tied to language or at least sign use.[17]

Sarah, the chimpanzee used by Premack and Premack, provided useful examples of analogic thinking as well as indications that the efforts to teach it language had powerfully affected its thinking. Sarah and four chimpanzees that had not had language training were put through the following experiments. First, an apple was cut into several pieces of different size. By comparing the pieces with models they were shown, the chimpanzees had to recognize which apple piece was identical to which model and match the quarter apple and the three-quarter apple pieces to the corresponding models. In the second part of the experiment, they had to solve the corresponding problem with liquids and match from among several pitchers either the quarter-filled or three-quarter filled pitcher to the model pitcher. All of the chimpanzees learned this exercise with ease. But then the two parts of the experiment were combined: from among two pitchers filled one quarter and three quarters respectively, the chimpanzees had to match the right one to the quarter apple. Well, Sarah made her selections quickly and unerringly, while the chimpanzees that had not had language training were unable to solve this problem.[18]

The concept of hypotheses in animals emerges from the study of problem-solving behavior. The Russian American researcher I. Krechevsky studied the problem-solving behavior of rats in mazes in which four choices were to be made. At each decision point, the animal had to decide whether to pass through a gate on the right or the left. The study of numerous individual animals revealed that after ten to fifteen trials most animals learned the task and largely selected the correct option (the one that had a reward at the end), and the *average* performance of the group gradually improved. But the study of the individual performances yielded quite different results. It seemed as if the animals were trying out definite theories or *hypotheses*. For example, at the initial trials they would always select the left-hand (or the right-hand) gate. If the hypothesis proved false, they would switch and try the opposite side. Then suddenly, they would hit upon the correct solution, and stick to it afterwards. It was often the case that they happened to select the correct solution right at the outset; but they would then still try the other potential solutions and return to the correct one only afterward. This shows that it is not exclusively the reward that influences the animal's behavior in the course of learning.[19]

Companions Cause the Most Trouble

We have seen that the intelligence of primates manifests itself not only with respect to the objects of the physical world or the members of other species, but that it reaches its highest levels in the social world through social intercourse. *Social intelligence* far surpasses physical intelligence in its complexity and is obviously a special ability peculiar to a species; in this apes significantly surpass the talents of other social vertebrates.

The first and fundamental problem of social life is that the "other" behaves according to its own circumstances and its own decisions. Accordingly, individuals can garner an advantage when their predictions come true; that is, when they are able to predict what the other will do in the next moment. The members of a group of monkeys know each other as individuals and are able therefore to take into account the others' habits and their relationships to others as well as to themselves. This information is used to create a complex *social space*, which is not a static system, but one that is continually moving and changing. The changes in this system are due partly to the customary events in the monkeys' life—such as feeding, reproduction, growth, and defense—and partly to the fact that individuals continually battle for resources and for success in mating, which in turn continually alters the dominance relations. The complexity of the social sphere is further enhanced by the fact that monkeys characteristically keep track of their relatives and enter into friendships or alliances on a reciprocal basis.

A second fundamental characteristic is that the behavior of species mates cannot be altered like that of a physical object, but only with communication and other complicated social manipulations, such as deception and occasionally with collaboration and appeasement. Primate communication rests on visual and auditory signals and far surpasses in complexity the forms used by other animals. Social manipulation, also called *Machiavellian intelligence*, includes all the particular techniques that an individual in such a complex social medium is able to use to further its own objectives.[20]

Machiavellian manipulation has many gradations. It is difficult to interpret its most cunning forms without assuming that the animal has a mental representation of the mental processes of its species mates. Primate researchers refer to this as the animals' ability to formulate a *theory of mind* concerning their species mates, which then influences their behavior.

The third fundamental factor in the social life of primates is the appearance of social learning among the several mechanisms that aid problem solving. Species mates can be useful for social animals in many ways, and this holds true not only for primates. For example, it is generally true among mammals that the young follow their mother, who defends and cares for them and, when necessary, feeds them. Maternal care and setting an example have a prominent role among primates, and among chimpanzees the latter probably encompasses teaching as well. It is also very important that they be capable of learning from their contemporaries as well as from unrelated adults. This rests on a goal orientation in which the animal is motivated by the results of a companion's behavior rather than by just following its own behavioral pattern.

Of course, the three factors do not operate in isolation from one another. Research in this area is addressing precisely the question whether the imitation of a companion is contingent on a theory of mind and on self-consciousness and whether deception is tantamount to having a theory of mind. Studies that describe the behavior of monkeys or apes often assert that their behavior occasionally permits the inference that they are able to recognize their species mates and other beings as *living creatures*. That is, they see them as objects that have independent and spontaneous movements, which distinguishes them from inanimate physical objects, even if the latter are capable of movement. The monkeys and apes are able to regard other living creatures as *agents with intentions*; in other words, entities that have plans, objectives, and decision mechanisms. Finally, they are able to visualize other living creatures as having *mental* or *psychological* attributes, that is to say as entities with thoughts and beliefs that might agree with or might differ from their own.

Of course, these assertions may be accepted only if they are supported by rigorous proof, and much of the relevant research is devoted to precisely this issue.

Do Chimpanzees Think about the Mind of Others?

Two American psychologists, D. Premack and G. Woodruff, have asked the question whether chimpanzees think about the *mental state* of others. Or as they put it: do chimpanzees make *hypotheses* about the mental states of others?[21] This rather surprising question emerges from the fact that humans employ expressions such as "he or she expects, believes, thinks, associates, plans," and so on, all of which are theories pertaining to another person's momentary mental state. They are theories, because we can only infer that they are true but cannot observe their truth directly. The question is whether chimpanzees employ such theories in their mental processes, albeit not in verbal form.

Researchers attempted to answer this question with the following experiment. The chimpanzees were shown various short videos, each of which showed a person facing an unsolved *problem*. For example, the person was extremely cold and was obviously shivering, and it was clear that the electric heater next to him was not plugged into the wall outlet. Or a person was unable to get out of a cage, although the key was lying next to him on the floor. In still another scene, the person was trying to reach a banana, but his arms were too short. After viewing a video, the chimpanzees were shown several photographs, one of which depicted the correct solution to the problem. For example, the person in the cage was using the key, the one after the banana was employing a stick, and the person who was freezing had plugged in the heater. The chimpanzees made their choices with the experimenter absent and received a small reward if they chose correctly. Of course, the chimpanzees had all participated in various learning situations, watched television, and were quite familiar with the objects shown in the videos and the snapshots.

Correct answers were given in about 80 percent of the cases, which vastly exceeded the fraction that would have been attained if they had been choosing purely at random. The explanation was that chimpanzees are able to put themselves into the position of the person depicted in the videos and are able to recognize what the person is doing wrong, what would be needed, and what the objective is. They are able to conjure up the correct solution, or at least select it from among other, inappropriate solutions.

The researchers' explanation was that the chimpanzees were able to put themselves into the mind of the persons they had watched on the screen and could understand their problems, and remembering all this, they were able to select the correct solution. To put it differently, they had a conception or "theory" of the inner mental state of the person they had seen on the screen.

Chimpanzees and rhesus monkeys were compared in a set of role-reversal experiments.[22] The experiments involved the formation of teams of two, one member of which was an adult human experimenter and the other a chimpanzee or monkey, as the case may be. A delicious morsel of food was then placed in a box, with three other boxes remaining empty, but this was observed by only one member of the team, either the human or the animal. In the next phase of the experiment, the team member who did not know what was in the boxes was allowed to acquire one but only one of them. The other member of the team, who knew which box was worth having, did not have access to the boxes. It soon turned out that if this member of the team signaled the other which box should be picked, they would get the reward. The simplest thing to do was to point to the right box. Both chimpanzees and rhesus monkeys quickly learned to point and all pairs received the reward. After they had learned this task well, the roles were reversed: the team member who earlier provided the information became the one who acquired the box and vice versa. The results were very interesting. The two chimpanzees whose new role was to provide information recognized immediately what they had to do and behaved accordingly. Only one of the two chimpanzees whose new role was to interpret the information and acquire the box realized immediately what it had to do, but the other one also caught on fairly soon. But the rhesus monkeys did not understand what had happened after the role reversal, and had to learn their new task from scratch.

According to the researchers who designed the experiment, the results showed that the chimpanzees had some kind of theory of mind. The chimpanzees whose new role was to provide information recognized that their partners lacked the right information; a matter that they could assist with. The experiments were also repeated with two humans acting as information providers, only one of whom knew which box contained the reward, because the other either left the room while the food was being hidden or if he stayed in the room, he had a large paper bag over his head so he could not see which box was selected for the food. The chimpanzees realized immediately that only a person who was present and was not visually impeded when the food was being hidden could provide accurate information, and they responded to the signals of such persons, while ignoring those of the uninformed one. The rhesus monkeys were unable to cope with this situation.

Experiments with children revealed that three-year-olds performed exactly like the rhesus monkeys: they did not recognize that one person had accurate information while the other one did not. But four-year-old children did as well as the chimpanzees. Many scientists have disagreed with the interpretation of the experiments and have attempted to prove that a successful response in the experiments does not require that chimpanzees necessarily think about the mental state of the information giver, but that it is sufficient to posit lower-order mechanisms, such as associative learning and conditioning. While it may be difficult to resolve the dispute, the difference between the chimpanzees and rhesus monkeys does rather argue in favor of a theory of mind. It is quite improbable that the difference between the chimpanzees and rhesus monkeys is simply their propensity for conditioning, because both species learn tasks that can be accomplished through conditioning rapidly and reliably.

Animals Tell Lies

Subsequently, observations were made in nature that made the presence of a theory of mind quite plausible. Seyfarth and Cheney describe a case in which a green vervet monkey was being aggressively attacked by some of its species mates, whereupon it escaped from its desperate straits by emitting an alarm cry reminiscent of those heard during leopard attacks.[23] This type of behavior was named *intentional or tactical deception*, and has been frequently observed, among not only primates, but other mammals and even birds.[24]

Much deceptive behavior can be observed among apes, in both natural and laboratory environments. I have already described the cases of baboons and chimpanzees. Four chimpanzees were taught in Premack's laboratory. In the first part of the experiment, three boxes were placed in the chimpanzees' exercise area, and the animal selected for the experiment was able to observe that some desirable food item was placed in one of these. The boxes were so placed that the chimpanzees had no physical access to them. At that point another person, who did not know which box contained the food, would enter and wait for the animal to start communicating with him. Communication started fairly quickly and without prompting: the chimpanzee in question started to *point* to the box that contained the food. If the person found the food as a result of the chimpanzee's signals, he would share it with the animal. In time, an effective collaboration grew up between the humans and the chimpanzees.[25]

In the second part of the experiment, a "selfish" type of person entered, and if he found the food, he did not share it with the chimpanzee and ate it himself. Another rule was also in effect: each person was allowed to open only one box; if he found no food in the box (whether it was the "selfish" person or the "unselfish" one), he would simply leave. In this part of the experiment, the chimpanzee's behavior slowly changed. It would still point to the right box when the "unselfish" experimenter entered, but it was reluctant to show the location of the food to the person who did not share it. The experimenter would open a box anyway, and frequently did hit upon the food. After about 120 trials, the chimpanzee consistently pointed to an *empty box*, that is, provided information with the *intent to deceive*.

Since these questions have been raised, more and more animals have been found to take advantage of deceitful behavior even in their natural environment. A. P. Moller has observed that some great tits (*Parus major*) employ alarm calls to chase off sparrows or other great tits from the location of a plentiful food source.[26] It was always the weaker tits that employed this cunning strategy; dominant ones did not resort to it and would simply chase off subordinate individuals.

These experiments are considered to be very important, because through such deceit the animal communicates something that does not exist in reality; in other words, instead of formulating in its brain a representation of reality, it is capable of formulating the *representation of a nonexistent thing*. This testifies to the extraordinary flexibility of the animal mind.

Readers who have accompanied us in this line of reasoning have probably recognized that in their study of higher order animals, ethologists no longer ask, "Is there somebody there?" because we are already certain of that. But they do ask who that somebody is, how it thinks, what its intentions are, what plans it hatches, or rather *how much* of a somebody this is compared to us, who basically do the same kinds of things. We need to stress that there are many ways of being *somebody*. If this somebody is a very simple organism, its tiny mind may barely flicker; it may have some objectives, and may even remember them, but it cannot cogitate over the affairs of the world. But to take the other tack—and it does not hurt to leave some doubt in the reader's mind—let me note that bees, with a brain weighing one milligram, are frightfully smart at times. In some experiments, the researchers manipulated the behavior of scout bees and thus sent the members of the bee family artificially altered information concerning plentiful food supplies. In one experiment, the scout bees reported that food was present at the shore of a lake not far from the hive, and indeed the experimenters had placed a plate of honey in a boat tied up there. After receiving this intelligence, the members of the hive started out for the indicated place and began to carry the honey back to the hive. In the next experiment, the scout bees were manipulated to report to the hive that the honey was in the middle of the lake, and for the sake of verisimilitude, the boat with the plate of honey was anchored there. To the researchers' astonishment, the bees receiving this information *did not even start out* toward the indicated place.[27] In other words, the bees are able to comprehend that there can be no flowers in the middle of a lake. Their one-milligram brains understand this and they behave accordingly.

Which means they can think!

Chapter 14

The Minds of Children

Psychologists have long studied how the various abilities of the human mind are formed in the development of a child. The study of the minds of children who do not yet speak poses the same problems as, say, the study of the monkey or ape mind. We cannot ask them questions, and we can make inferences about their mental processes only from their behavior. When children begin to speak, the psychologist's task becomes somewhat easier. Animal psychologists dealing with apes and monkeys, and child psychologists have discovered that they have many common problems, and it is very fashionable nowadays to compare the behavior and problem-solving abilities of children and various types of animals. Far-reaching research[1] and common ideas have benefited both areas of research. Here we shall discuss only those few that are important for what follows.

Children Are Not Small Mewling Animals

Early child psychologists' interpretation of their observations was that human children become familiar with the world in a gradual way. After birth, they are just some kind of mechanism based on reflexes, helpless little animals that respond only to environmental stimuli and repeat motions only if they provide pleasure. Then, slowly, they begin to sense the physical processes in the world around them and learn that it is possible to move objects. Even later, they learn more complicated activities in order to achieve some desired effect. They start to experiment, and before they reach the age of two, they begin to use the symbols of language. However, the more recent studies have exhibited some characteristics that imply a much more complicated mind and one that exists only in humans.

These characteristics are all related to the human attribute that the connection between the individual and the group is quite different and much more intimate in our species than among animals, bar none. Two reactions manifest themselves in the first phase of a child's life that markedly differentiate it from monkeys and apes. The first of these could be called preconversation, in which both the child and the parent concentrate on the *attention* paid to it by the other. In face-to-face contacts, the touch, caress, look, vocalization, speech, or cooing are all directed toward creating a common emotional state. The first sign of this is the smile, which appears soon after birth and is the most important form of communication for maintaining contact.

This behavior is characterized by a cyclic mechanism through which the two parties continually switch back and forth. Either the parent communicates feelings to the baby and then the baby is watchful, or the reverse. While preconversation can have many individual manifestations in various cultures, it can be shown that it is a general and characteristic attribute of our species.[2]

The other typical reaction to early social contacts is the imitative ability of neonates, which is again a human characteristic. A. N. Meltzoff at the University of Washington and M. K. Moore discovered that soon after birth a baby is able to imitate certain facial expressions or head movements of the adults leaning over it.[3] According to scholars, this is an expression of a profound tendency by babies to identify themselves with their species mates.[4] According to Hungarian researchers, some neonates not only imitate, but in the expectation of an imitative response, they initiate gestures.[5]

Acquiring Culture May Derive from Childhood Bonding

The innate abilities to initiate contacts and to respond to them are fundamental human attributes. Scholars believe that these two abilities are the basis of the great breakthrough that appears roughly at age one and that unambiguously distinguishes us from apes. This innovation is a clear-cut tendency of nine-to-twelve-month-olds to get in tune with the interests and behavior of adults and to induce the adults to get in tune with their interests and behavior. This process has numerous submechanisms: the baby follows the glances of adults, attempts to do what they do, checks on and assumes the emotional state of the adults, and attempts to participate with them, briefly or at length, in activities dealing with objects. The child tries, with vocalizations, glances, or pointing, to direct the attention of adults toward the object or activity that it is interested in.

I have already mentioned that the color pattern of the human eye differs appreciably from that of animals, and even of chimpanzees. The whites of the human eye are instrumental in our figuring out where a person *is looking*. This enables both children and adults to link their attention. It is much more difficult to identify the object of an animal's glance, which has the evolutionary consequence of protecting the individual animal by disguising from its companions what it is looking at; hence its intentions concerning some object, say a piece of food, remain hidden from them.

According to Michael Tomasello, at the Max Planck Institute for Evolutionary Anthropology in Leipzig, the fact that children call our attention to things indicates unambiguously that they are beginning to understand that another person has intentions.[6] In other words, they not only discover that another person moves and undertakes activities, but they also understand that the reactions of others reflect the structure of their environment.[7] A consequence of this kind of understanding is that the child is capable of learning about culture: that there is a distinction between observed actions and intended actions. In a very interesting experiment, Meltzoff found that if a child eighteen months old observes an adult in an activity in which the latter is unsuccessful, the child is able to carry out the intended activity itself (in the experiment, the adult attempted to take an object apart, unsuccessfully).[8] This kind of behavior can occur only if the child is able to distinguish the observed action from the intended action, able to put itself in the place of the other person, and willing, in the interests of achieving the objective, to identify itself with the other. It is quite certain that this ability is the basis of learning language or other systems of symbols, and it is further certain that it is related to the brain's ability to form secondary representations. We need to emphasize that the child acquires this ability through exceptionally strong social attraction. It is not overly bold to claim that our ability to learn the human culture we live in rests on social bonding.

Humans are able to accomplish many things because of their exceptional sociability and the strong bonds they have to each other, to a degree not seen in the animal kingdom. In the general configuration of social attraction one can distinguish certain constituent parts. The attraction in the relationship between the child and its mother or caretaker does not require special explanation, since it is present for shorter or longer periods among all mammals. Human ethologists believe that this ancient characteristic was modified during evolution and became adapted to the creation of bonds among adults.[9]

The work of British psychologist John Bowlby on bonding between mother and child is well known in psychology and was motivated precisely by ethological considerations.[10] It is well known among ethologists that in species in which the young require nurturing at the beginning of their lives, a strong bond is formed between the mother and the young. The biological advantage of this bonding is that the mother and the young continually seek each other's proximity, which guarantees food and protection for the young that are not otherwise able to care for themselves. Humans are also born helpless, and Bowlby infers from this fact that similar mechanisms have to come into being among humans as well. All neonates and all young children considered normal, irrespective of culture, do their utmost to be in the presence of their mother or caretaker. If the mother, for whatever reason, disappears for a relatively long period of time, the child's behavior exhibits three phases. The first reaction is *protest*, namely loud crying and calling for the mother. If this is unsuccessful in producing the mother, *passive phases* ensue: for a few days the child will be sad, quiet, and withdrawn. In the third phase, *separation*, the bond that has been formed begins to dissolve and the child attempts to bond with others.

Children who grow up without a mother or regular caretaker are unable to bond normally and get stuck in the initial phase of bonding. They are nice and accommodating with everybody, but they are afraid of strangers. If their urge to bond remains unsatisfied, their entire life is affected: they can easily form transitory bonds, but even as adults they are unable to form lasting and deep bonds. Physical contact, such as embraces and caresses, is an important mechanism for forming and maintaining bonds.

We have mentioned earlier that the behavioral reactions of children in strange places allow us to determine their type of bonding very reliably, and these results can be well replicated. The type of bonding is a reasonably permanent personality characteristic.[11]

Children's initial reaction to strangers is a human characteristic. In the first few months, they will smile at anybody who approaches them. Babies begin to exhibit the signs of fear of strangers at the age of five to six months. In this critical period, they will smile only at relatives or close acquaintances, and strangers elicit an avoidance reaction in them. If the child is with its mother, it will first smile at the stranger briefly, then avert its eyes and turn toward the mother, then seek another contact with the stranger, and this cycle may repeat itself a few times. If the stranger is mindful of this reaction cycle and approaches the child slowly and in a friendly manner, the child will make friends with the newcomer; but if this person approaches abruptly, and particularly if the person picks up the child, it will react with fear and even panic and begin to cry. The cyclic alternation between approaching and avoiding the stranger shows that the child is under the influence of two different motivations. It would like to approach the stranger, but it is also afraid. Of course, fear can have different degrees, and if the mother is absent, the child may seek security with a stranger. In other words, the child has a strong attraction to other humans, but is well able to distinguish acquaintances, and will turn to strangers only as a last resort. In a later stage of development, children learn their community's cultural rituals that are appropriate for accepting the approach of a stranger.

The special attraction of children to other members of their group, or rather their early ability to get in tune with others, leads to behavioral forms not known among animals. Even a nine- to twelve-month-old baby is able to call adults' attention to something with its eyes. Equally well, it understands situations in which the behavior of adults reveals some intention; for example, when the adult attempts to retrieve a ball from behind a piece of furniture. After a child is one year old, it becomes better and better at watching and understanding the movement and behavior of objects and living creatures and also becomes better at predicting the future course of events from the currently prevailing situation. It is generally believed that by the time a child is two years old, its mind is about as well equipped to understand the physical world as that of an adult ape, such as a gorilla or a chimpanzee.

Children's Games and Theories of Mind

Around the age of two, many attributes manifest themselves in children that are not known among animals. The first of these is obedience to rules or norms, which develops when the child recognizes the customs that adults around it observe and attempts to comply with them. The child begins to accept that things have a customary place, complies with various rituals and develops an ability to imitate. One can also observe a second attribute, namely that in the course of learning to speak, also around the age of two, the child begins to use words that suggest the existence of self-consciousness. A new and very interesting group of attributes appears in connection with the use of language: the first element of this group is the *theory of mind* and the second, *pretend games*.

Research psychologists believe that all three attributes rest on the ability of the human mind to form representational copies of its experiences;[12] the property of the mind that enables it, independently of the senses, to represent objects, events, and connections and to mentally manipulate these representations. We have mentioned the theory of mind several times before, and we need to add only that it manifests itself in children in two stages. In the first stage, it seems that the child uses such a theory only to attempt to explain the actions of its companion. The components of this theory can be grouped into the categories of belief, desire, intention, and feeling. Children younger than four can really construct a theory of mind only in relation to themselves. But in the second stage, children aged four or older are able to completely fathom a situation in which somebody has an erroneous idea. They are able to distinguish the mental model that describes a companion's actions from its symbolic, linguistic meaning. They will know precisely what a belief or an intention is, and these notions are not only components of an explanatory theory, but they also have an independent symbolic meaning.

Many scholars have studied the formation of a theory of mind in children. Relevant observations can be derived from the "Sarah and Ann game." Sarah and Ann are two dolls, and during the game, Sarah hides a glass ball in a box and leaves the room. While she is gone, Ann transfers the ball from the box to a small basket. Sarah then returns, and the child watching the game is then asked, "Where will Sarah look for the ball?" Well, three-year-old children, who do not yet understand that the answer should not pinpoint the position of the ball but speak to Sarah's beliefs, invariably say that she will look for it in the basket. A four-year-old child understands precisely what a belief is, and that Sarah *believes* that the ball is still in the box, and they will designate the box as the object of Sarah's search. In this situation, the mind has to construct and handle two contradictory representations. One of these represents reality, namely that the ball is in the basket, while the other represents Sarah's belief that the ball is still in the box. The two representations can coexist peacefully if the mind can apply the concept of a belief appropriately; if it is able to comprehend that the beliefs and opinions in one's own head may differ from those in somebody else's.

Pretend games and the child's early stage theory of mind appear roughly at the same age. In one of the examples cited by Alan M. Leslie of Rutgers University, a child at play uses a banana as a telephone. It is clear that when the banana plays the role of a telephone handset and the child talks into it as it would into a telephone, it simultaneously sees and perceives it as a banana. If it did not, something would have to be wrong with its vision. But that is not the case; beside the primary representation of the perceived banana, there appears a *secondary* representation, in which the banana acts as a telephone handset, and the child's mind is able to handle these two side-by-side representations together.

During the development of a child, the pretend game becomes increasingly complicated. Even a fourteen-month-old baby is able to play the simplest form, in which it is the actor. For example, it may pretend to take a bite from a spoonful of food, but not actually do so. In the next stage, the principal actor may be another, passive person, such as a doll, that is being fed by the child. In the third phase of pretend games, the passive actor is replaced by a substitute; the child may replace a sleeping doll by putting a building block on a pillow. In the most complicated version of the game, the actor is active and the child plays with the doll as if it were spoon-feeding itself.

Andrew Whiten and Richard W. Byrne of the University of St. Andrews have pointed out that the connection between the theory of mind and pretend games noted among children is also supported by data obtained from observing apes.[13] For example, Kanzi, a bonobo, once imitated the act of eating, as if it were consuming a nonexistent fruit, and while doing so, it was spitting out nonexistent seeds, and even indicated that they were "bad."[14] Koko, a gorilla, once pressed a rubber tube to its nose and indicated with sign language, "Koko is an elephant."[15] Captive apes often play with dolls, and this is a pretend game, but such symbolic play has not been observed among monkeys.

According to Whiten, in addition to theory of mind and pretend games, the third related component of this mental faculty is imitation.[16] These three attributes always occur together, and only among the same few species. One might think that this is stretching the point, since the imitator merely copies the behavior of its model. Why would it have to know the mental state of its model? If merely copying the behavior were all that is involved in imitation, it would not be too difficult, but in practice it is impossible to get monkeys to engage in genuine imitation. The reason is that secondary representations are prerequisites of successful imitation. The primary representation governs the imitator's actual behavioral program, the secondary representation reflects the behavior of the model, and the imitation is expressed through the synchronization of these two representations.

Unfortunately, there is no generally accepted, precise definition of imitation. In animal experiments, imitation is generally understood to refer to conscious copying, when for some reason an individual copies the behavior of a companion down to the last detail. As far as human imitation is concerned—except for literal copying, which belongs in another category—we do not absolutely require consciousness, precision, or even the presence of a reason for it. Many believe that the mechanism of *self-recognition* also belongs to the trio of imitation, pretend games, and theory of mind.

Are Animals Also Able to Imitate?

The theoretical discourse of scholars was accompanied by the study of animal imitation and many interesting observations were made. It turned out that many behavioral phenomena that had been cited as examples of imitation represented an entirely different mechanism. It is frequently the case that an animal's inherited behavioral pattern is elicited when a species mate makes a related movement that triggers it. This phenomenon, for example, plays an important role in synchronizing the activities within a flock of birds, but this is not genuine imitation. There are even more complex cases: monkeys that observe their companions in some complicated food-gathering activity are able to do likewise. But more detailed analysis has revealed that this behavior is not genuine imitation in which the monkey would imitate the model's behavior down to the last detail, but rather what may be called *stimulus enhancement*. The activities of the model call the companion's attention to certain characteristics of the environment, which act as a stimulus that guides the individual toward the proper solution, but a solution that differs in various details from that of the model.

As early as the 1950s, English researchers showed that titmice had a propensity to remove the caps from milk bottles placed by the front door and to drink the cream accumulated at the top. It seemed to be the case that imitation played a role in the spread of this custom, because the radius of the area in which this behavior was occurring was growing by approximately thirty kilometers (19 miles) per year. But laboratory experiments revealed that this was not a case of imitation. A number of titmice were placed in a large aviary, among them one smart and experienced titmouse that knew how to open a milk bottle. A full bottle was also placed in the aviary, and the smart titmouse promptly addressed itself to the task and obtained the cream. Of course, the others became aware of this accomplishment and joined the experienced one in the meal. After a few days of feasting in this fashion, the smart titmouse was removed from the aviary, while the supply of milk bottles continued. The remaining titmice surrounded the bottle and were waiting for the one that could open it, without addressing the problem themselves. After a while, one of the more impatient ones started to fuss with the cap and hit on a method for opening the bottle, but, and this is important, it arrived at the same outcome with a completely different technique than that of the bird they had observed before. This kind of behavioral imitation is called emulation—it is the functional but not formal copying of behavior.

Monkeys react to such tasks in similar fashion. The behavior of the imitators of the famous rhesus monkey inventor, Imo, revealed that they learned the technique of cleaning grain not by imitation but by the mechanism of emulation. Even simpler animals are able to posit a general cause-and-effect relationship between an activity and a reward, and monkeys are particularly good at that. But this ability does not extend in most species to enabling them to mentally decompose the solution method into small, imitable details and to carrying out the individual behavioral components in the right order. To do that truly requires the tools of secondary representations.

In the past few years and under very strict conditions, some researchers succeeded in finding convincing proof of humanlike imitation in the case of chimpanzees and one orangutan. D. M. Custance of Goldsmith College, University of London, and her collaborators worked out a fairly complicated training system in which, on the command "Do this!", the animal had to imitate the activity that it was observing. The animal was rewarded only if it faithfully imitated the action down to the last detail. Once the animal had learned this lesson well, it was shown an activity not seen before, and its behavior was accepted as genuine imitation only if it successfully copied this new activity as well.[17] Needless to say, human children learn this lesson very rapidly and are able to imitate quite complicated series of movements. Chimpanzees learn it more slowly and are able to imitate only simpler movements, but are ultimately up to it. One orangutan succeeded in imitating a fairly complicated pattern of movements.[18] Many people believe that apes imitate only if they are taught to do so by humans, because no one has yet observed them doing so in nature.

Mental Representations Become More Complicated

The assessment of imitation by apes needs to be amplified by noting that they are never observed to *practice*, an activity that is common among children over a certain age. It is obvious that the mind of a practicing individual contains a secondary representation, and the imagined patterns of movement in the representation provide the objective, which has to be coordinated with the self's sensory inputs and the movements of the body. In more complicated cases, this result can be achieved only through practice.

In the case of humans, representations have three levels.[19] The *primary representation* relies substantially on the sense organs, and its task is to provide the mind with a picture of the world around us that is true to reality. This is the only representation that children are able to muster until about the age of one. Later, *secondary representations* appear gradually and have the task of letting us see what the world could be like. They are always connected to some primary representation, for example the representation of the banana itself in the case of the child using it for a telephone; but there also appears a hypothetical new element that allows the child to imagine a different world. The third level of representation, called *metarepresentation* by the Austrian psychologist Josef Perner, appears around the age of five. In this stage, the child understands clearly the nature of representations, it knows that it can have ideas or beliefs about the world that are independent of reality, and it understands that others can have ideas and beliefs about the world that differ from its own. In other words, the child understands that the mind can construct representations. In this stage, the mind consciously employs modeling in order to understand and influence phenomena in the world.

Of course, as discussed before, these forms of representation have to be complemented by linguistic, symbolic representations, which is the most important representational mechanism in the world of humans.

The mind of the ape probably transcends the phase of primary representation and is capable, in simple cases, of secondary representations, but—at least on the basis of proofs adduced to date—does not reach the third level, the metarepresentation, by which humans can even form representations of representations. There is a great deal of overlap between the intelligence of monkeys and apes, although the latter, it seems, have mechanisms such as secondary representations, which in certain cases make them more intelligent than monkeys. But even in the most exceptional cases they do not reach, though may approach, the level of intelligence of an average four-year-old human child.

Chapter 15

The Functioning of the Canine Mind

We began the ethological analysis of canine behavior in the hope that familiarity with the behavioral similarities between humans and dogs would aid our understanding of how and why those exceptional attributes developed that characterize humans. Let us take stock of those similarities that may be regarded as firmly established, those that may become so with further experiments, and those that are not genuine.

Similar Components in Human and Canine Intelligence

It may be useful to list the various components of human intelligence.

Physical Intelligence
- Recognition of causal relations.
- Ability to calculate the results of interaction among objects.
- Recognition of independent, living creatures.

Social Intelligence
- Group membership.

- Intentionality.
- Empathy.
- Joint or linked attention.
- Following glances.
- Pointing.
- Ability to distinguish between intentional and inadvertent actions.
- Recognition of the self.

Cultural Intelligence
- Personal rituals, sense of time.
- Following rules.
- Cooperation.
- Social learning: following patterns, imitation, copying, teaching.
- Intentional communication.
- Giving or asking for information.
- Deception.
- Theory of mind: attributing to another being a mind similar to our own.
- Recognition of role playing, role reversal.
- Interpretation.
- Linguistic ability: naming things, using symbols, obedience to linguistic rules.

It is clear from the enumeration of the various types and components of intelligence that the behavior of dogs, observed either passively or in experiments, unambiguously demonstrates their *physical intelligence*. They are able to follow the movement of an object, and they can determine, for example, that an object that they have moved might cause another object to come near enough to be reached. It is equally obvious that they recognize other living creatures, something that even simpler beings are able to do.

It is also quite certain that they do not have a technical intelligence, which we omitted from the above list. This ability is particularly well developed among humans and is the reason for our predilection to make, and generally fuss with mechanical devices. Humans are unique in that among all living creatures and there is not much sense in comparisons of technical intelligence.

elligence characterizes animals living in groups, and the extent has developed depends on the extent of the cooperation present in the species, which can range from minor to extremely high. Wolves were already social animals, and the social capabilities of the dogs that evolved from them developed still further, so that they could establish groupings not only with other dogs but with humans as well. All dogs want to belong to some human group, even if that group consists of only a single human. It is characteristic of dogs that they like joint group actions; they accept the internal rules of the group and are capable of self-sacrificial behavior for its sake. The social attributes of humans could be characterized the same way, with the most important addendum that humans have a capacity for culture, for a common language and common ideas. But of course, that is where humans part company with dogs.

We have failed to mention so far the very important human attributes that the *level of aggression within the group is low, the hierarchy is not strict, and the bonding among the group members is strong*; all three statements hold for dogs as well, in contrast to wolves or the majority of monkeys. Close cooperation could never develop without these three attributes.

As far as the intentional behavior or the empathy of dogs is concerned, we have to rely on our real-life experiences and on the stories from the diary, but I think we can say without exaggeration that these attributes are present in dogs. In their ability to experience the feelings of others, dogs probably even surpass the apes and resemble only humans.

In linking their attention to that of another, in pointing and in following glances as well as in *distinguishing between intentional and inadvertent actions* they are surely on a par with the highly developed chimpanzees.

There is one question about which we know nothing, and that is the question of self-recognition. The well-known mirror experiments with chimpanzees and orangutans[1] make it plausible that they have self-consciousness similar to that of humans, but not all scholars accept this. The experience with dogs is that only very young, inexperienced pups are interested in mirror images, but even they are not interested for long. For example, Flip was afraid of his mirror image when he was tiny and made a point of giving the mirror a wide berth in the front hall, although he later got used to it. We also found that small dogs quickly figure out the reversal of the physical world in a mirror image. To wit, if they are looking in a mirror, and somebody hands them something behind their backs, they do not run toward the mirror, but turn around quickly, which is another proof of good physical intelligence. Negative outcomes in mirror experiments say nothing about self-consciousness, since only those who care about their external appearance will primp in a mirror—as humans and chimpanzees do; that is, those who have a mental image of themselves that they approve of, and who want to know why this image has changed. It is quite probable that dogs do not have this trait. A dog can be scraggly, muddy, or dirty, and it will not make an effort to clean itself until it starts to itch; it cares not a whit about what is on its fur.[2] It is probable that we shall not be able to exhibit self-consciousness in dogs with mirror experiments. Unfortunately, we know of no other method for proving self-consciousness, although researchers are hard at work on this.

It is a very exciting development that numerous elements of human cultural intelligence—although perhaps not the most important ones—can be identified in dogs to a greater or lesser degree. Cases in point are personal rituals and a sense of time, as well as the experimentally oft-confirmed obedience to rules.

Personal rituals play an important role in human life. If we analyze this peculiar behavioral form from the point of view of understanding the mind, we might think that rituals were used in ancient times as a tool to galvanize the mind and activate the memory. As a matter of fact, as many anthropological studies have argued, rituals aided the comprehension of the notion of time.[3] It is generally believed that if an animal is safe and its stomach is full, it will be in a state of rest, or at least it will give no sign that its mind is active, with the exception of the not very demanding task of staying alert for potential danger. In contrast, the human mind—at least in its present state—is almost continually active in the waking state. The mind is much assisted in this by personal rituals and well-earned rules. I believe that it is a characteristic of the mind of dogs that v can think only about something that we activate in their minds: a ˈ leash, a few words, and the dog's mind goes to work full steam. If ˈdy is busy with something else, the dog lies down, snoozes, and ˈast flickers at its lowest setting. I believe that dogs have taken ˈp toward a more enduring wakefulness, and this is under- ˈ fact that they easily learn rituals, because the elements of ˈ the activation of the mind. They have also developed a keen sense of time and it is easy to teach them a ritual that has to be carried out at a particular time.

It is quite certain that apes, precisely because of their aggressiveness, have only very limited ability to obey rules, and predominantly only when young. In contrast, dogs formulate rules easily and obey them throughout their lives. This is supported by numerous types of experimental proof as well as by our daily experience.

The most interesting result of the analysis of human-dog *collaboration* is that all essential properties that characterize humans are present in dogs, too. Examples are bonding; the recognition of a problem and the preparation of an action plan; the decomposition of an action into complementary subparts; obedience to rules; the frequent and mutual alternation of dominance roles; and the exchange of information. It is probably no accident that these types of human attributes grew strong in dogs in the course of evolution, because these were the ones of greatest interest to humans.

We have shown that dogs are capable of the type of social learning that depends on *imitation* and they are rather like chimpanzees in this respect. Because of their lack of hands, it will be difficult to analyze their potential ability to imitate exactly, but a whole lot of interesting findings are probably just around the corner. Only isolated observations confirm the presence of *teaching behavior* among dogs, which occurs when older dogs induce their younger companions to observe the rules. But it is quite certain that dogs are unable to play the role of teacher in the kind of teacher-pupil relationship that characterizes humans, because this behavior is probably linked to human language.

Dog owners require no proof that dogs are capable of *intentional communication*; those who do not have dogs may be convinced by the stories taken from the diary of Flip and Jerry.[4]

I believe it is also easy to prove, with the aid of the experiments and data in chapter 1, that dogs give and request information. The most important and perhaps least well-known fact is that dogs *ask questions* and accept answers. This attribute is quite exceptional in the animal world and it is evident that it developed only as a result of artificial evolution and domestication.

Many researchers have studied and confirmed the existence of deceptive behavior among monkeys and apes; it remains to be seen whether dogs ever tell lies.

In a very important experiment, we have determined that dogs have a theory of mind; they are able to think about the *beliefs* of their companions, namely humans. Dogs think about what humans may or may not have information about: if the master's cane is hidden by somebody, a dog will help find it, while if it remembers that the master himself placed the cane somewhere, it will passively wait for the master to retrieve it himself. This seems plausible, but it is a sufficiently important finding that it needs further study.

The ability to *recognize roles* and to *engage in role reversal* requires similar mental abilities, such as a theory of mind and an ability to imitate. Flip's episodes of imitating children sledding or riding in a toy car[5] are sufficient proof for me that dogs possess this ability, and the experiments in which dogs simulate aggressiveness in defending a backpack provide solid underpinning for this. But it is clear that the importance of the findings compels us to seek further experimental proof. The crucial question about the canine mind is whether this mind is capable of constructing secondary representations, and if so, to what extent it is capable of modifying them.

The ability to *interpret* was already present in wolves to a certain extent. I have already indicated that interpretation plays a prominent role among humans, who continually interpret the actions and the speech of others. I have described numerous instances in which dogs are also sometimes capable of high-level interpretation. A case in point is when Flip was able to interpret the hand signal for "No!" in the social context of a particular situation and understood that the signal was not meant for him but for a person, and that the intention in giving the signal to the person was to enable this person to ultimately give him instructions.[6] No matter how hard I have tried, I have not been able to find a simpler explanation for that incident, and it is by no means the only complicated one awaiting an explanation.

It is also typical that very elaborate, complicated solutions do not occur to dogs. The exceptions occur only if all circumstances are favorable: the motivation is right, the mind is well honed and "on the job," and external circumstances are favorable. It is easiest to characterize the mind of a dog by saying that its knowledge is *sporadic* or at times *scattered*. It is capable of great accomplishments, but only infrequently. We saw in our discussion of the human mind that representations of the environment are constructed on various organizational levels, and thanks to humans' good memory, they can alternate between representations; they can try them out in the mind and then use the most suitable one in their behavior. We do not know as yet just how the human brain does this. For example, what kind of memory is required? It is possible that the short-term memory of the dog is not suitable for storing the individual representations side by side and for comparing them with each other. In general, it is easy to fool dogs (and small children); we can divert their attention from something, and this is probably because of memory problems. It is possible that someday a new dog breed will come into being that has a good short-term memory, in which case we could expect that its abilities to deal with secondary representations will also improve. This conjecture is underscored by examples in which strongly motivated dogs are capable of high-level accomplishments.

Equally complex from the point of view of interpretation are the four observations concerning keys, which actually address the use of signs and symbols.[7]

Dogs do not have humanlike linguistic abilities. Naming things, which is especially important for humans, means nothing to dogs. If one says a strange word to a child, as in the sentence, "Tomorrow I will tell you about *thingiboops*," one can be sure that next day the child will come and say, "You promised that you would tell me about thingiboops."

Why is the child interested in thingiboops, about which it knows nothing, except that there is *something* that we have called thingiboop? It is, of course, possible that it is of no interest to the child; after all, one could have said "interest rate" or "gross national product" instead, and if one were telling the child about these, it would soon become bored.

"There was a large and dense forest, and in it lived a thingiboop" is how we might begin the tale, but we still do not know what the thingiboop is, although the dense forest is a well-known locale and is sufficient for maintaining the child's interest.

"It was very lonely, the poor thing," we continue, and we know that this plays very effectively to the child's emotions and raises its feelings of empathy: anybody who is alone and lonely will engender feelings of social attraction in the child through empathy, even if it does not know anything about this creature.

"The thingiboop cried a lot because its mommy went away," continues the story. This makes things very clear to the child; the thingiboop is obviously a "somebody" who deserves our compassion, because it has a mommy, and such a person is definitely all right. On top of all that, its mommy went away, so it is understandable that it cries a lot. We need not continue the story here, but it is clear that the act of naming "it" opened up a "page" in the child's mind, which was filled up with various things, particularly with a story. The more things that appear on this page that have some interpretation in the child's mind, the sooner the child is able to create a story or a construction with the assistance of the speaker, and the child actually enjoys this process. This ability is lacking in dogs, and a sign or a name in itself means nothing. It can become something only if it is interesting or important, or if it can be chased or grabbed, and if the dog is able to experience these possibilities.

The child fills its mind with symbols, and the *thingiboop* is a named but empty symbol that has only a sign; it acquires its relationships, meaning, and attributes only in the course of the story, and since it is only a story, it does not matter that this sign, *thingiboop*, is not connected to any concrete, visible, touchable thing in the real word. Other symbols maintain some connection with reality, such as the symbol *key*. This could be a concrete key, an object, or it could be a logical operation, such as the key to the solution, or the key to a cipher with which we can decipher a text.

I recounted four stories from the diary of Flip that featured keys, and what they have in common is that the dog understood the function of the object, and what is more, interpreted correctly the *verbal* sign of the object. He was able to understand in a complicated situation the function of the key I was holding (on the occasion of our visit to Aunt Gizi);[8] in other words, he was able to generalize. In the most complicated story, he was able to analyze an entire series of events on the basis of the object he saw. We should add to the story about Zsuzsika's summer house that it is visible from our garden, and so Flip would always know when there were people there. Of course, there were also other times when people appeared at her summer house, but he never evinced the least desire to go there except on the one occasion when the key was being taken back and forth; hence the key must have triggered his request to go there. This is not a straightforward usage of a sign, nor the result of a simple conditioning process. Nor can I assert that it is an unconditional and complete proof that he used symbols. But I firmly believe that the use of signs and symbols is not an all-or-nothing proposition. Dogs learn signs easily and are perhaps able to endow some of them with the properties of symbols. Exactly the same (a much more complicated mechanism than the simple use of signs) is indicated by the ability to interpret the expression "if . . . then . . ." I think of this as a sort of *delayed present time* and believe it to be a step from signs toward symbols.

Symbols constitute a whole system in the human mind. We do not have one or two symbols, but hundreds of thousands, and they refer not only to our environment, but they also are connected and refer to each other as well. It is an interesting question whether it might be possible to build inside the canine mind a system consisting of a few symbols that actually refer to one another. If it were possible and if we could prove that we had done so, we would have brought about the simplest and most ancient system of language use and cultural evolution. It seems worthwhile to invest some effort in this experiment.

A few words about understanding language: I think that dogs understand language as signals for action. Nouns do not mean much to them. A cat is not a thing about which one might have a conversation, but it denotes a concrete and immediate action, such as play or chase. If we, too, were able to think only in terms of actions, we would understand a great deal, but we would use only verbs, without nouns, adverbs, or other subtleties of language. Did we start out like that ourselves? Did we name objects right at the beginning? It is not impossible, because monkeys have been used to look for and manipulate passive objects for millions of years, such as fruits, branches, and leaves, because they have *hands*. Dogs are predators, and their ancestors acquired food by the action of chasing their prey. Can we exhibit this difference in the realm of thoughts? It would be enormously exciting to compare the speech of a creature that thinks exclusively in terms of actions with the speech of one that thinks in terms of both actions and objects, and to study the ways in which the two understand each other. Can this dream be realized someday?

A Well-Brought-Up, Human-Loving Chimpanzee in Our Home?

The comparison of the mental abilities of dogs and our closest relatives, for which we unfortunately do not have a great deal of good data, yields a peculiar picture. Most of the components of human intelligence are present in both species. The mass of the dog's brain is only about a quarter to a third of that of the chimpanzee; is it nevertheless possible that the intellectual level of dogs is the same as that of apes? It might be. In the appropriate environment of evolutionary selection, certain species acquire quite special abilities. A case in point is the dance of the bees, which mammals could be proud of, even though the mass of the bee's brain is only one thousandth of a gram. Chimpanzees can be experimented with only in their childhood, when they are pleasant and tame and can become fond of their caretakers. One problem with them is that they cannot be housebroken. Grown chimpanzees are very strong and have a morose temperament, and males in particular are unpredictable and subject to fits of rage in which they rampage and smash things. They will never be our companions. Grown chimpanzees are predominantly locked in a sturdy cage during experiments. But even so, there is no doubt that their thinking is well advanced, and because of our common origins, they resemble us humans in many respects.

Dogs are housebroken, love us, obey us, and *are our best friends*. The foregoing has perhaps convinced the reader that the mind of dogs is not inferior to that of our relatives. Perhaps someday we shall be able to converse with them. I am convinced that a dog is a "somebody," and to reply to the question of István Hernád,[9] the little soul of a dog may not be all that tiny after all.

Humans created dogs in a cheerful spirit and in their own likeness.

Part
Five

Humans and Dogs

It might have been better to start the book with the question "Why should we have a dog?" But I also think that a person who is serious about this question should probably not have a dog. Having a family dog has many delightful aspects—dogs are loving and intelligent companions, they are great partners on a walk or a hike, they are reliable playmates for our children, and often the only solace for older people—but taking care of them also imposes obligations. Depending on the breed, they need to be walked one to two hours a day, we have to spend time with them, and our emotional bond with them can become quite a burden. People who cannot or do not want to bear this responsibility had better live without a dog. Dogs are very emotional animals, and we have seen that they bond with their masters just as much as a human child with its mother. To neglect or to cruelly abandon a dog that has bonded with humans causes spiritual pain and suffering in these unfortunate animals that is comparable to what humans would feel in similar circumstances.

Chapter 16

How to Be a Dog Owner

L et us deal with how to be a dog owner. The first item on the agenda is to pick a dog. The key is to get the right breed for the right personality. There is plenty of good advice about this choice in dog books and I cannot add much. Everybody should try to pick a breed that suits his or her personality. People who are active and always on the move should pick from among the more active breeds, but there are plenty of dogs for those who prefer a more restful way of life. Those who only want a dog to love them and wait for them when they come home and have no other requirements should pick a lapdog bred explicitly for that. Others who desire an intellectually more active partner need to select a dog from among the more intelligent breeds,[1] but they should not forget that these dogs need a lot of mental stimulation. An intelligent dog will occupy its master's attention for several hours a day, and only then will it be able to fully unfold its intellectual capacities. In any event, such a dog needs to be occupied; otherwise it becomes bored and often turns into a wild and unmanageable creature that spends its time thinking up mischief.

The American psychologist Stanley Coren wrote a book about matching breeds to human personalities.[2] He classifies dogs into seven groups according to their basic psychological makeup.

1. *Friendly* dogs: the bearded collie, collie, spaniel, English setter, retriever, vizsla.

2. *Protective* dogs: komondor, rottweiler, schnauzer, boxer, Briard.

3. *Independent* dogs: Airdale terrier, greyhound, Shar-Pei, Dalmatian, Irish setter, samoyed, husky.

4. *Self-confident* dogs: Irish terrier, basenji, miniature schnauzer, Scottish terrier, Shih Tzu, Welsh terrier, wire fox terrier, Yorkshire terrier, smooth fox terrier.

5. *Steadfast* dogs: French bulldog, Lhasa Apso, Pekingese, Chihuahua, dachshund, Boston terrier, Skye terrier, Tibetan terrier, pug.

6. Dogs with a *strong character*: bulldog, basset, beagle, Great Dane, Pyrenean mountain dog, mastiff, Newfoundland, St. Bernard.

7. *Intelligent* dogs: Australian shepherd, Belgian shepherd, puli, border collie, Doberman, German shepherd, poodle, sheltie.

This is Coren's classification, and if I were to set up my own, my categories and descriptions might well be different. He set up his classification after consulting a number of U.S. veterinarians.

He worked out a canine intelligence test for selecting "smart" dogs, and the interested reader may wish to consult Coren's book for the details. My view is that we know too little about the canine mind to set up a good intelligence test. It is, for example, very difficult to distinguish between innate and acquired elements of intelligence. Dogs that have a lot to occupy them and are made to solve all kinds of problems usually do much better on intelligence tests. Another unsolved problem in evaluating tests is the role of motivation. There are merry and active dogs that are always ready for some test, while others are calmer and react more slowly; however, that does not mean that they are less intelligent, because with appropriate motivation they can produce the same results as the more active types. In a word, there is still a lot to be done.

Of course, Coren takes into account the potential owners' personalities as well, which he places into several categories on the basis of complicated psychological tests according to several criteria. On the basis of certain attributes, he classifies personalities into contrasting categories.

Extroverts versus introverts. Extroverts are cheerful, friendly, like to connect with people, and like to be the focus of a group's attention. Introverts are not particularly fond of being in the center of a group's attention and are rather retiring in social contacts.

Dominant versus timid people. Dominant people like to lead or direct others, are ambitious, like and make efforts to gain recognition, and are able to make decisions quickly. Timid people do not share these attributes to any great extent and are sometimes characterized by the very opposite traits.

Trusting versus distrustful people. Trusting people are easy to persuade, they believe what other people say, and they do not harbor suspicions toward other people. Distrustful people are the exact opposite.

Compassionate versus indifferent people. A compassionate person is good-humored, nice, good-hearted, adaptable, and can easily be appealed to on an emotional level. An indifferent, cold person is like a lone wolf; such a person relies more on rational considerations than on emotions, considers himself to be more independent than others, and is not much interested in their opinion.

Potential owners could try to locate their personality traits among these attribute pairs, although most people will not fall near the extremes of the various attributes but somewhere in the middle.

Coren then recommends particular canine types to persons who fall into one or the other of the above personality groups. A few examples follow.

He recommends the *friendly* dogs to people who are roughly in the middle of the scale according to the above personality types; they are not excessively trusting, but are also not too distrustful; are not very dominant but are also not very submissive, and so on.

Protective dogs are appropriate for reasonably trusting and good-natured women and for timid men with a cold personality.

Independent dogs are good for extroverted, nondominant, good-natured women and for introverted, nondominant, distrustful, and indifferent men.

Self-confident dogs are suitable for introverted, distrustful, and indifferent women and for dominant, distrustful men with a medium degree of extrovertedness.

Steadfast dogs should be owned by distrustful women with a medium degree of extrovertedness and by extroverted men.

Dogs with a *strong character* should belong to introverted and distrustful women and to introverted, dominant, distrustful, and cold men.

Finally, *intelligent dogs* are well suited to trusting and compassionate women with a moderately extroverted character and to introverted, moderately dominant, trusting, and compassionate men.

All that is needed is for the reader to know his or her own personality type, and the rest is easy.

It is fashionable to own expensive breeds. The advantage of this is that one can know ahead of time what one may expect, because the various breeds have characteristic attributes. I am very fond of mixed breeds because they sometimes exhibit unexpected and special attributes, although not always favorable ones.

And what kind of breed should one not own? Please, no dangerous breeds in the family! Many breeds have been created for tasks requiring strength and aggressiveness. The training of such dogs requires expert knowledge and I do not recommend these as family dogs. These breeds carry aggressiveness in their genes and they have a low threshold for attack. Neither child nor adult is safe in the presence of a gentle-appearing pit bull if some mistaken gesture or movement should awaken the breed's uncontrollable aggressiveness. And finally, please do not buy a dog from one of the many puppy mills that breed dogs in large numbers without regard to genetic consequences, just so they can maximize their profit!

The Socialization of Dogs

If we want to get a puppy, it is very important that its early socialization take place under the right circumstances. It is useful for the puppy to have contact with many humans, because this will help it become a friendly dog later on. It is also very important that we be consistent in its upbringing. Consistency is the foundation of the canine character, but this does not imply that we need to be rough. The biggest punishment we can mete out to a misbehaving dog is to express our disapproval, and if this does not do it, we can always shake the dog by grabbing the skin at its neck.

The employment of consistency has to be breed-specific. One must never hit a golden retriever; a tap or a shake is enough to make it understand. But a rottweiler or Caucasian shepherd needs stronger discipline and sometimes even physical punishment. Of course, this does not mean that one may beat the dog for just any old reason. A thorough thrashing is no more effective than a single smack at the right time. The important thing is that the dog know and accept what we are commanding it to do. If we attain that, the dog will be quite manageable. We have discussed earlier the development of *inhibited biting*, which regulates the extent of playful aggression that a dog may engage in toward its companion.[3] The principle of inhibited biting can be extended to a dog's entire behavior: every dog eventually learns what kind of behavior is permitted toward its master and other family members. Anyone who does not teach his dog these rules at the outset, perhaps because he or she feels sorry for the dog or thinks of a correction as cruelty, might well pay a heavy price for the omission. The result may well be an ill-mannered, undisciplined dog, which could even pose a danger for others. Such a dog may be impossible to restrain when it sees a person running or riding a bicycle. The two extreme environments that must be avoided are total permissiveness on the one hand and a totally inflexible discipline that breaks the dog's spirit. The appropriate middle ground differs among the various breeds, but there are a lot of good books around that help one find it.

It is very important for a dog to fit into its group, even if the group consists only of the master and the dog itself. The dog should know what is permitted and what is not. Dogs are group-oriented creatures and feel really happy when they can often take part in some joint activity with the members of their group. It is very useful for the dog to *have something to do*, like bringing the slippers or the newspaper, its dog dish, or even the TV remote. Dogs are extremely happy if they can participate in something. In the discussion of cooperation, I showed that except for not having hands, dogs have almost all the attributes that are necessary for collaboration with humans. These attributes have to be developed further with common games and tasks. We have seen how well developed the canine mind is and how advanced is its social intelligence and its ability to understand. This mind needs to be exercised! The only people who should own dogs are those who like to talk to their dogs, pay attention to them, and jointly solve problems with them. The true joy of owning a dog is that it permits us to develop and deepen mutual social understanding.

Equally important for every breed is love, the guiding light of a dog's life. To withhold one's love is as serious a punishment for dogs as it is for children, and they need the frequent manifestation of the master's love. Putting one's arms around them, caressing them, and giving them occasional presents of delicious tidbits or objects are always important events.

The general rule is that we should treat dogs as we treat three- to four-year-old children. In other words, we should love them a lot, without letting them get the upper hand.

One often hears that a dog's "pack leader" should be a hard taskmaster. This belief originates in the study of wolf behavior, but except for the rougher working-dog breeds, it really does not hold for most dogs. Dogs love their "pack" and reciprocate the love they receive. Because of this trait, it is entirely sensible to adopt a dog from a shelter, because if we love it enough, it will become as faithful a companion as if we had brought it up ourselves. In choosing a shelter dog, we should ask that four or five dogs be allowed to roam freely in a play area and then pick the one that seems most eager to be with us, since dogs, too, have ideas about what kind of person they want to be with.

It is also said that a potential dog owner should consider the physical environment: the size of an apartment or house, what floor the apartment is on, and so on. But except for unusually large dogs, or those that are much more active than the average, this is not an important consideration. Dogs are social creatures and what is important for them is the functioning and the joint activities of the group and the love they receive.

Genetically Manipulated Dogs

Dog owners have been *manipulating the genes* of dogs for tens of thousands of years by breeding them selectively according to various criteria. For a long time, after the alliance between humans and dogs came into being, dogs probably looked like wolves on the whole and were real dogs only in their *behavior*. In other words, the general characteristics of dogs, their attraction toward humans, their ability to collaborate, their social understanding, and the well-developed canine mind probably came into being and solidified in this period. This is the reason these attributes are present in every decent dog breed that developed since that time. The breeding of dogs for various specialized tasks began, more or less, in the Neolithic period, when humans finally established permanent settlements and discovered agriculture. Herding dogs, guard dogs, and even lapdogs appeared around that time. But initially there were not many breeds. The innumerable breeds we encounter nowadays are a few decades or at most one or two centuries old. Originally, they were bred for special purposes; a case in point is the large variety of hunting dogs that came into being when the hunt became a sport rather than a food-gathering activity. In more recent times, the most pronounced factor is the breeding of dogs for their external appearance. Many sporting or working breeds are now bred for their shape or color, without regard to the behavioral characteristics required for their original tasks. Even professional breeders debate whether this trend is desirable or not. Some people believe that the selection exercised in breeding should be based on the behavioral characteristics of the original breeds; that is, herding dogs should be able to herd, and hunting dogs should have a keenly refined hunting instinct. Both points of view are defensible, but there is a third one, namely that it might be worthwhile to breed *family dogs*, which could be of different sizes and shapes, but would be adapted for living with a family in tight quarters. These dogs would be tame and gentle, but very intelligent, with a highly developed social intelligence.

I can accept the use of appearance in the breeding of dogs, but I consider it a grave error, indeed reprehensible negligence, that many breeders do not seem to care about analyzing the *behavior* of the various breeds, controlling for behavioral factors, and using expert knowledge to breed on this basis. This leads to the deterioration of the good qualities of the original breeds and to the appearance of neurotic, hysterical, or seriously psychotic dogs in many breeding kennels. These dogs often play a prominent role in some horror story. It is high time for breeders and their organizations to introduce, in their own self-interest, breeding criteria based on behavior. This is particularly important because the selectivity criteria are not exercised by those who ultimately own and use the dogs, since breeding and use have become increasingly separated.

Those of us who are interested in genetics hope that dog breeders will eventually realize the advantages of producing hybrids. But dog breeders strive for the *purebreds* and give pedigrees only to individual dogs, generally on the basis of external characteristics. The purity of breeds is not a genetic concept, however, and the markings of such dogs are not necessarily derived from identical gene pools. The concept of an *inbred stock* is used in scientific and agricultural breeding, and the animals in such a stock are also purebreds. Such a stock may be regarded as a variety and is homogenous with respect to a large proportion of genes, which may have numerous advantages and disadvantages. Dogs, like other higher-order creatures, carry two sets of genes in their cells, one of which comes from the father and the other from the mother. If corresponding genes in the two sets are identical, the zygote formed by the sperm cell and the ovum is called homozygous for this gene, and if they differ, it is called heterozygous. If the majority of the genes are in a homozygotic state, the stock may be referred to as homozygous. Such a stock of animals can be created by inbreeding, for example, by mating siblings, in about twenty generations. In this process, harmful genes may make an appearance and breeders may prevent these from being passed on to subsequent generations by careful selection of the animals to be bred to one another.

Homozygous stocks pay a stiff price for genetic order. Whatever the species, its viability, resistance, and performance are generally below that of heterozygous stocks. But the efforts of dog breeders to safeguard the various breeds increase the extent of inbreeding and thus reduce their viability and other desirable attributes. This process appears to be unstoppable. It is hardly possible to create a homozygous dog breed without damaging side effects. But the hybrids created by crossbreeding inbred stocks may have excellent attributes. The population of hybrids created by crossbreeding two inbred stocks is quite uniform and can always be reproduced with identical quality. The genes of the two stocks used to create hybrids sort of complement each other and the descendants have better attributes than either parent.

Hence there is only one scientifically based solution, namely the creation of uniform hybrids. This would represent a brand-new approach in dog breeding, although in agriculture, in livestock breeding, and in plant growing, this has been accepted practice for a long time. Such a breeding program operates on two levels. The first is the creation and maintenance of the parent stocks. The parent stocks are largely homozygous, obviously purebred, but are not well adapted to being used, because they are too fragile. For this reason, it is expensive to maintain them, because they have to receive special treatment, and the individual animals themselves are expensive. But by crossing them one can produce two or four parent hybrids that are uniform in appearance and behavior, and are strong, handsome, and viable. This is the second level of the breeding program.

If dog breeders produced several inbred stocks of a particular breed and then crossed them to produce hybrid breeds, they would create superbly "marketable" dogs that would satisfy all consumer demands with their uniformity and excellent attributes. Just to mention a few Hungarian breeds, one could generate outstanding pumis, pulis, and vizslas.

My friends among professional breeders rather sneer at this and argue that too many economic interests are involved for such a system to be adopted. But I think that real-life circumstances will force the adoption of such a system because its introduction will not damage economic interests in the long run, since the inbred stocks themselves will represent a new asset and the hybrids will become trustworthy and useful animals. Even if they cost more, they will be well worth the extra expenditure, particularly because current breeding practices are primitive from the genetic point of view and will unavoidably lead to the deterioration of breeds and the disappearance of many. The legitimate defense is that mixed breeds are increasingly widespread, which is not in the interests of professional breeders. If breeders were to recognize that they and owners have common interests, and were to institute the system advocated above, with appropriate genetic expertise and organization, they would create a win-win situation.

It would also be possible to employ an alternative genetic approach, which would not even require that we wait for the creation of inbred stocks. One could create hybrids by *crossbreeding different existing breeds*, and this would create tremendous diversity. One could create fantastic dogs with new attributes practically on demand and always with identical qualities.[4] If we were to do this with just four-hundred-plus well-known breeds, we could try over one hundred thousand combinations. Undoubtedly, there would be unpleasant, useless, and ugly beasts among the offspring, but we would also generate tens of thousands of new dogs in which the desirable attributes of the parents would be joined. The breeding activities in the past few centuries have established or strengthened many special traits in the various breeds. It is quite certain that bringing together favorable traits, as in hybrids that have the characteristics of four different breeds, could lead to quite extraordinary attributes. It would be a pity to forgo this possibility. If we take care to maintain the parent breeds, which is not difficult since they have been around for a long time, we can always produce good hybrids, and the desirable characteristics will reliably appear in the descendants. But the hybrids produced from different breeds should not be bred further, because their descendants would become inferior mongrels of dubious genetic condition.

Let's Create a "Talking" Dog

Once we are in the realm of genetics, it is irresistibly tempting to persuade the most enthusiastic and interested owners to try an exciting experiment. Let us breed a talking dog!

Anyone who has read this book carefully may accept the notion that domestication over tens of thousands of years and selective breeding (often done subconsciously) have produced dogs that resemble humans here and there. But by no means is this partial resemblance the final possibility. The canine mind occasionally exhibits such high-level abilities that it seems plausible to argue that a well-planned program of selective breeding might produce much more intelligent and better communicating dogs than those of today: practically "talking" dogs. If we succeeded in breeding dogs that were smarter, understood human speech better, and could express themselves more effectively, everybody would be delighted, since they would be even more lovable and would take even more pleasure in being our friends. A Seeing Eye dog would become ever so much more valuable if it not only stopped at a street crossing, but could say to us the word "car," or, for example, if its owner were looking for a telephone booth, the dog would not only guide the person to one but would verbally indicate that he or she had arrived there. Dogs that assist the disabled would also become more efficient if canine intelligence, comprehension, and expression developed further. We would take more joy in family dogs if our canine companions were smarter and talked and understood more.

If owners were truly assiduous in occupying themselves with their dogs and attempted in all possible ways to develop their ability to understand speech, their problem-solving methods, and their collaborative behavior, we would find that quite extraordinary abilities would unfold in certain individuals. All we would need then would be to mate individuals of striking ability, if such individuals could be found, and the merging of genes determining intelligence would lead to offspring of even greater achievement. I am sure it will be considered very bold to claim that there might be dogs among these that could vocalize as many as perhaps ten different voice signals and that would understand many, many more words. Yet I do not think that this is impossible. But of course, only if we brought up and taught these dogs and monitored their abilities in the appropriate fashion.

Perhaps there are foundations or other organizations that specialize in dogs and that could provide some financial support for such purposes. Perhaps we could even organize a movement for the creation of a new and more intelligent family dog. The Department of Ethology at the Eötvös Lóránd University would gladly provide technical assistance. Anybody who has a dog and is willing to spend the time and energy would be welcome to join the Program for Talking Dogs. We could organize annual contests for "talking" dogs at which their abilities could be compared through various trials, and this might help provide further direction to breeding programs.

A Request to the Reader

I mentioned at the beginning of this book that individual dog stories or anecdotes must be handled with considerable care when we want scientific proof. But as we have seen, the stories help to design appropriate scientific experiments and can contribute to enhancing our understanding of the abilities of the canine mind. I would like therefore to ask every reader whose dog exhibits some unusual talent or does something from time to time that appears to be the action of an intelligent mind to write us and describe the details of the dog's achievement.[5] We would like to know the breed, gender, and age of the dog and would be most appreciative if contributors could provide a dispassionate but detailed description. We would like to collect these stories and use them in our further work. As soon as we can, we propose to publish the stories on the Internet and request our contributors to give us permission to publish the stories in one form or another (with the name of the contributor included or omitted, as desired).

Dogs and Human Morality

Human morality generally characterizes those societies and cultures in which moral principles are formulated, but the morality in question always deals with *humans*. Good and evil are always embodied in human relations. In the past few decades, however, the concept of moral behavior has been extended to matters that are linked to humans more remotely. Nowadays we consider it evil or immoral to exterminate an animal or plant species, or to irresponsibly damage the environment or those few corners of nature that are more or less intact. Enthusiastic environmentalists have saved many an old tree from being felled. Many international organizations do battle to secure special protection for intelligent animals such as apes, dolphins, whales, and elephants, over and above the obligatory protection of the environment, and the special justification for this is the higher intelligence of these animals. I think that there are communities beyond the ones we have created with other humans; for example, the community of intelligent beings. Our moral principles may be extended to these as well if the majority of our society agrees and deems it important.

Although the study of canine behavior is in its infancy, it nevertheless provides scientific support for the view that we have created dogs in the course of living with them for tens of thousands of years. We created them in our own image. Dogs are truly our most devoted servants, companions, and friends. In this long process, dogs lost many of the abilities of their wolf ancestors, and gained in their place the ability to love, a well-developed social intelligence, the human tools of collaboration, and the ability to understand human behavior up to a certain point. This slow but very successful process of identification with humans imposes certain obligations on us. We have to consider the extension of our moral principles to dogs, or at least a modest proportion of these principles. I believe that dogs deserve humane treatment.

The experimental sciences have sacrificed millions of dogs in the course of biological, biochemical, and pharmaceutical experiments. The results of these experiments are of dubious value, because from the biological point of view the human organism resembles much more the organism of apes than that of dogs. Unfortunately, many dogs that have been abandoned by families are still suffering in experimental laboratories. Often they become the subjects of very painful and long-term experiments, but even if the experiments were of shorter duration, they would have to live through and emotionally suffer the horrors of confinement, preparation for the experiments, and the carrying out of the experiments. Dogs are also often stolen, and some of the experimental animals claimed to have been strays are the result of theft. Some unfortunate dog that may have spent eight to ten years with its loving master may suddenly find itself in a torture chamber.

Irrespective of the justifications of my learned colleagues, I believe that this kind of scientific animal torture is incompatible with morality.

Notes

Translator's Note

1. Pitcher, George, *The Dogs Who Came to Stay*, Plume, reprint ed., 1996.

Part 1: The Alliance of Two Minds

1. Ethology may be defined as the scientific study of animal behavior.
2. No dog owner should therefore be surprised if he or she has not observed in his or her own dog the particular examples of behavior that will be discussed in the subsequent chapters. Like every owner, every dog is an individual.

1. The Wolf

1. The source of most of the information about wolves is Mech, D., *The Wolf: The Ecology and Behavior of an Endangered Species*, Minneapolis: University of Minnesota Press, 1970.
2. Peters, R., "Mental Maps in Wolf Territoriality," in Klinghammer, E. (ed.), *The Behavior and Ecology of Wolves*, New York: Garland STPM Press, 1979.
3. For the properties of cognitive maps, see chapter 12.
4. A very interesting comparative analysis of play by dogs, wolves, and coyotes is Bekoff, M., "Social Communication in Canids: Evidence for the Evolution of Stereotyped Mammalian Display," *Science*, 197 (1997), 1097–99.
5. This is particularly relevant when strange wolves approach, but in the case of captive wolves, it also applies to strange humans.
6. Zimen, E., *The Wolf: His Place in the Natural World*, New York: Souvenir Press, 1981.
7. Lawrence, R. D., "Pretense and Representation in Infancy: The Origins of the 'Theory of Mind,'" *Psychological Review*, 94 (1987).
8. This probably derives from the similar behavior of the young when they beg for food.
9. Mech, D., op. cit.

10. Mech, D., op. cit., p. 89.
11. This is observed most frequently among captive wolves; for these animals, accustomed to vast spaces, even an amount of space that may appear ample to us is nevertheless too tight. This might be the explanation why captive wolves often kill the weak members of the pack. These have no place to flee, are always "in the face" of the others, and this provokes continual aggression. Under natural circumstances, these weaker wolves would probably just flee and thus save their lives.
12. Frank, H., "Evolution of Canine Information Processing under Conditions of Natural and Artificial Selection," *Zeitschrift für Tierpsychologie*, 53 (1980), 389–99.
13. Peters, R., "Mental Maps in Wolf Territoriality," in Klinghammer, E. (ed.), *The Behavior and Ecology of Wolves*, New York: Garland STPM Press, 1979; and Zimen, E., op. cit.
14. Zimen, E., op. cit., p. 74.
15. Mech, D., op. cit.
16. An excellent account of the gentler northern wolves is provided by the outstanding wolf ethologist F. Mowat in *Ne féljünk a farkastól* (*Let Us Not Fear Wolves*), Budapest: Gondolat, 1976.
17. Zimen, E., op. cit., p. 96.
18. Masson, J. Moussaieff, *Dogs Never Lie About Love*, New York: Three Rivers Press, 1997.
19. See Mech, D. , op. cit., p. 298.

2. Humans

1. Details of man's own story can be found in another book of mine, namely in Csányi, V., *Az emberi természet. Humánetológia* (*Human Nature, Human Ethology*), Budapest: Vince Kiadó, 1999. But for English-speaking readers I would recommend Mithen, S., *The Prehistory of the Modern Mind*, London: Phoenix, 1996.
2. Csányi, V., "Ethology and the Rise of Conceptual Thoughts," in Deely, J. (ed.), *Symbolicity*, Lanham, Md.: University Press of America, 1992, pp. 479–84; Csányi, V., "The Brain's Models and Communication," in Sebeok, Thomas A., and Jean Umiker-Sebeok (eds.), *The Semiotic Web*, Berlin: Moyton de Gruyter, 1992, pp. 27–43; Csányi, V., "The 'Human Behavior Complex' and the Compulsion of Communication: Key Factors of Human Evolution," *Semiotica*, 128 (3/4) (2000), 45–60; Csányi, V., "An Ethological Reconstruction of the Emergence of Culture and Language during Human Evolution," in Győri, G. (ed.), *Language Evolution*, Frankfurt am Main: Peter Lang, 2001, pp. 43–55.

3. The Alliance

1. For a discussion of various types of intelligence, see Mithen, S., *The Prehistory of the Modern Mind*, London: Phoenix, 1996. Ecological intelligence manifests itself in the fact that the animal rapidly learns the most important properties of the animal and plant life occurring in its habitat and is able to use this knowledge to further its own interests.
2. According to the theory of Coppinger and Coppinger, at the time that villages came into being, the accumulation of human garbage attracted wolves and they gradually started to adapt to this new resource, primarily through the strengthening of their ability to withstand stress. They slowly started to get used to and to tolerate the proximity of humans, which was the precondition of the subsequent changes. See Coppinger, R., and L. Coppinger, *Dogs*, New York: Scribner, 2001. In

my opinion, the development of villages is not absolutely necessary for such a process, since humans have lived for hundreds of thousands of years in camplike cultures. These camps existed for a few weeks or months and, like villages or perhaps even more so, led to the accumulation of consumable garbage.

3. Jolicoeur, P., "Multivariate Geographical Variation in the Wolf, *Canis Lupus L.*," *Evolution*, 13 (1959), pp. 283–89.

4. Gould, R. A., "Journey to Pulyakara," *Natural History*, 79 (1970).

5. Ungváry, K., *Budapest Ostroma (The Siege of Budapest)*, Budapest: Corvina, 1998.

6. Nobis describes a canine puppy skeleton found in Israel in the burial place of a child belonging to the Natufian culture. See Nobis, G., "Der älteste Haushund lebte vor 14.000 Jahren," *UMSHAU*, 19 (1979), pp. 215–25.

7. Olsen, S. J. and J. W. Olsen, "The Chinese Wolf, Ancestor of New World Dogs," *Science*, 197 (1977).

8. Serpell, J., *The Domestic Dog*, Cambridge: Cambridge University Press, 1995, p. 8.

9. Vilá, C., P. Savolainen, J. E. Maldonado, I. R. Amorim, J. E. Rice, R. L. Honeycutt, K. A. Crandall, J. Ludenberg, and R. K. Wayne, "Multiple and Ancient Origins of the Domestic Dog," *Science*, 276 (1997), pp. 1687–89.

10. Mitochondria are cellular organelles that are the power source of the cell and contain DNA rings independent of the nucleus.

11. Lorenz publicly withdrew his theory in his foreword to Fox, M. W. (ed.), *The Wild Canids: Their Systematics, Behavioral Ecology and Evolution*, New York: Van Nostrand Reinhold Co., 1975.

12. Savolainen, P., Y. Zhang, J. Ling, J. Lundberg, and T. Leitner, "Genetic Evidence for an East Asian Origin of Domestic Dogs," *Science*, 298 (2002), pp. 610-13.

13. According to Mech, there are at least four hundred dog breeds, but it is possible that the true number is double that.

14. See Mech, D., *The Wolf: The Ecology and Behavior of an Endangered Species*, Minneapolis: University of Minnesota Press, 1970.

15. Scott, J. P., and J. L. Fuller, *Genetics and the Social Behavior of the Dog*, Chicago: University of Chicago Press, 1965.

16. Situated in Göd, a small town north of Budapest.

17. Belyaev, D. K., and L. N. Trut, "Some Genetic and Endocrine Effects of Selection for Domestication of Silver Foxes," in Fox, M. E. (ed.), *The Wild Canids*, New York: Van Nostrand, 1975.

18. Wild foxes will emit a yip here and there, but these bark a lot and just like dogs.

19. See Serpell, J., op. cit. It has been shown that the teachability of puppies exhibits breed-specific differences, but in general, dogs are very teachable and they are able to generalize their obedience by obeying commands given by humans other than their teachers.

20. Army dogs were widely used in World War I. *Vasárnapi Könyv*, 1916, no. 24, reports that apart from carrying messages and materials, the most important tasks were performed by dogs serving in the medical corps. During lulls in the battle, they would search for wounded, guard them, or run back to the medics to indicate that they had found somebody, often taking with them an object or article of clothing belonging to the wounded. Dogs were particularly successful in locating soldiers covered by snow in the battles fought in the Carpathian Mountains. According to the report, they were used not only in the Hungarian armed forces, and there were days on the French battlefields when they located some one thousand wounded.

Thurston, M. E., *The Lost History of the Canine Race*, Kansas City, Mo.: Andrews and MacEel, 1996, a recent book on canine history, contains a detailed account of U.S. Army dogs in Vietnam. The army employed several hundred dogs, mostly German shepherds that contributed greatly to locating Vietcong fighters and their booby traps and were also helpful in many other respects. They saved the lives of many thousands of American soldiers. After the U.S. Army left in defeat, the dogs were either left behind or euthanized on army orders. Many veterans whose lives were saved by these dogs, in some cases several times, could never come to terms with this.

21. Davis, K. D., *Therapy Dogs*, New York: Howell Bookhouse, 1992.
22. Csányi, V., and Á. Miklósi, "A kutya mint a korai evolúció modellje" (Dogs as Models for Early Evolution), *Magyar Tudomány*, 63 (1998).
23. The wheels of evolution turn slowly, and it is not necessary for the appearance of such changes that dogs be continually talked to in every generation. It would have been sufficient for humans to talk to dogs every once in a while, but keep only the offspring of dogs that were more sensible in obeying orders. Through a hundred thousand generations, even tiny selective advantages can lead to significant genetic changes.

Part 2: Similiarites between Human and Canine Behavior

4. Bonding

1. I am speaking here specifically of monkeys and not apes, such as chimpanzees, bonobos, gorillas, orangutans, or gibbons.
2. Durkheim, É., *The Elementary Forms of Religious Life*, translated by Joseph Ward Swain, New York: Collier, 1961; and Wallace, R. A., and S. F. Hartley, "Religious Elements in Friendship: Durkheimian Theory in an Empirical Context," in Alexander, J. C. (ed.), *Durkheimian Sociology: Cultural Studies*, Cambridge: Cambridge University Press, 1988.
3. In my book on human nature (Csányi, V., op. cit.), I showed that the four factors may be considered, with some additions, as a unified principle for organizing social systems. Their role is clearly demonstrable in explaining the origins and functioning of human social and group structures, irrespective of whether we are looking at friendship or pairwise relations, a workplace, or an entire state or society.
4. Also referred to as a "conspecific."
5. Pfaffenberg, C. J., J. P. Scott, J. L. Fuller, B. E. Ginsburg, and S. W. Bielfeldt, *Guide Dogs for the Blind: Their Selection, Development and Training*, Amsterdam: Elsevier, 1976.
6. Dog experts distinguish *single-master* and *multiple-master* dogs according to whether they obey only one or more persons in a family.
7. Freedman, D. G., J. A. King, and O. Elliot, "Critical Period in the Social Development of Dogs," *Science*, 133 (1961).
8. Cairns, R. B., and J. Werboff, "Behavior Development in the Dog: An Interspecific Analysis," *Science*, 158 (1967).
9. Gácsi, M., J. Topál, A. Dóka, and V. Csányi, "Attachment Behavior of Adult Dogs (*Canis familiaris*) Living at Rescue Center: Forming New Bonds," *Journal of Comparative Psychology*, 115 (2001), pp. 423–31.
10. Scott, J. P., and M. V. Martson, "Critical Periods Affecting Normal and Maladjustive Social Behavior in Puppies," *Journal of Genetic Psychology*, 77 (1950).

11. Pettijohn, T. F., T. W. Wong, P. D. Ebert, and P. J. Scott, "Alleviation of Separation Distress in 3 Breeds of Young Dogs, *Developmental Psychobiology*, 10 (1977), pp. 373–81.

12. Ainsworth, M. D. S., M. C. Blehar, E. Walters, and S. Wall, *Patterns of Attachment: A Psychological Study of the Strange Situation*, Hillsdale, N.J.: Erlbaum, 1978.

13. Topál, J., Á. Miklósi, V. Csányi, and A. Dóka, "Attachment Behavior in Dogs (*Canis familiaris*): A New Application of Ainsworth's (1969) Strange Situation Test," *Journal of Comparative Psychology*, 112 (1998), pp. 1–11.

14. Scott, J. P., J. M. Stewart, and V. J. Ghett, "Separation of Infant Dogs," in Senay, E., and J. P. Scott (eds.), *Separation and Depression: Clinical and Research Aspects*, Washington, D.C.: American Association for the Advancement of Science, 1973.

5. The Emotions of Dogs

1. The influential and scientifically thorough book by Jeffrey Moussaieff Masson and Susan McCarthy on the problems of studying the emotions of animals was based on recognizing the existence of animal emotions and counts as a breakthrough in the behavioral sciences. Masson, J. Moussaieff, and S. McCarthy, *When Elephants Weep: The Emotional Life of Animals*, New York: Delacorte Press, 1995. If not stated otherwise, my examples are taken from that book.

2. Op. cit., p. 29.

3. Masson, J. Moussaieff, *Dogs Never Lie About Love*, New York: Three Rivers Press, 1997.

4. Of course, dogs are not all equally thoughtful. For example, while Jerry was also worried at the time of the accident, by next winter he had completely forgotten about it.

5. Masson, J. Moussaieff, op. cit., pp. 160–61.

6. Polcz, A., *Asszony a fronton* (*Women on the Front*), Budapest: Szépirodalmi Kiadó, 1991.

7. See Masson, J. Moussaieff, op. cit., p. 176.

8. Op. cit., pp. 119–20.

9. Morris, D., *Dogwatching*, New York: Three Rivers Press, 1993.

10. De La Malle, D., "Mémoire sur le développement des facultés intellectuelles des animaux sauvages et domestiques," *Annales des Sciences Naturelles*, Ser. 1, 22 (1831).

11. Masson, J. Moussaieff, op. cit., pp. 170–71.

12. Darwin, C., *The Origin of Species*, New York: Oxford University Press, 1996.

13. Talking dogs have appeared in many great literary works. Among my favorites are Jack London's *Jerry of the Islands* and Franz Werfel's *Star of the Unborn* (*Stern der Ungeborenen*).

6. Obeying the Rules

1. Tomasello, M., and J. Call, *Primate Cognition*, Oxford: Oxford University Press, 1997.

2. Tomasello refers to this phenomenon as ontogenic ritualization in order to differentiate it from the ethologists' well-known, genetically based evolutionary ritualization. Ontogenic ritualization is always based on mutual learning while evolutionary ritualization, such as the development of threat or courtship postures, is the result of genetic changes.

3. See chapter 15.

4. Sebeok, T. A., and J. Umiker-Sebeok, op. cit.

5. A summary from a philosophical point of view is in Schauer, F., *Playing by the Rules*, Oxford: Clarendon Press, 1991.
6. De Waal, F., *Good Natured*, Cambridge, Mass.: Harvard University Press, 1996. This outstanding book deals principally with the behavior that develops in groups of monkeys and apes and with the kind of animal behavior that might correspond to the human recognition of right and wrong. The next section of this chapter contains examples of dogs and wolves that illustrate the simple form of obeying the rules.
7. See chapter 9.
8. Freedman, D. G., "Constitutional and Environmental Interactions in Rearing Four Breeds of Dogs," *Science*, 133 (1961), pp. 585–86.
9. Similar experiments were conducted with other species as well, such as with rats: Davis, H., "Theoretical Note on the Moral Development of Rats (*Rattus norvegicus*)," *Journal of Comparative Psychology*, 101 (1989), pp. 88–90. Rats were taught to consume only a predetermined number of pieces of food in the presence of the experimenter or they were subject to some mild punishment. It was found that they rapidly learned this, but if the experimenter left the room, the rat would stand on its hind legs, sniff around, and quickly eat the prohibited food.
10. Watson, J. S., J. Gergely, G. Topál, M. Gácsi, Z. Sárközi, and V. Csányi, "Distinguishing Logic Versus Association in the Solution of an Invisible Displacement Task by Children and Dogs: Using Negation of Disjunction," *Journal of Comparative Psychology*, 115 (2001), pp. 219–26.
11. See chapter 14.
12. The alternative command, "csüccs" in Hungarian, might most closely be rendered in English as "sit ya down."
13. Owners frequently complain that their dog is unable to learn something that is routinely done by other dogs. Apart from the fact that the various breeds differ in their ability to learn and their capacity to absorb teaching, it may often be the case that successful teaching is impeded by emotional factors. The master may have spoiled the learning process by an incorrectly issued command, by being in a bad mood, or other reasons. Good trainers stress that apart from consistency and discipline, the emotional stability of the dog has a significant role in training and that listless dogs are unable to learn anything. Exactly the same problems arise in bringing up children; one child happily acquires new knowledge, reads, is interested, learns, and performs, while the parents have continual problems with another. These problems most often have an emotional basis.

7. Cooperation

1. Dugatkin, L. A., *Cooperation Among Animals*, Oxford: Oxford University Press, 1997.
2. For more details see my book on human nature, cited earlier; Csányi, V., op.cit., 1999.
3. A few examples follow: Fox, M. W., *Superdog*, New York: Howell Bookhouse, 1990; about herders, Templeton, J., and M. Mundello, *Working Sheep Dogs*, Ramsbury, U.K.: The Crowood Press, 1988; about gun dogs, Irving, J., *Gundogs—Their Learning Chain*, Dumfries: Loreburn Publ., 1983; about police dogs, *Police Dogs, Training and Care*, London: Home Office, HMSO, undated, an outstanding publication of the Home Office of the United Kingdom; Davis, Kathy D., *Therapy Dogs*, New York: Howell Bookhouse, 1992; about guide dogs, an outstanding volume is Johnston, B., *Harnessing Thought*, Harpenden: Lennard Publishing, 1995.

4. For example, Frank, H., "Evolution of Canine Information Processing under Condition of Natural and Artificial Selection," *Zeitschrift der Tierpsychologie*, 53 (1980), pp. 389–99; and Frank, H., and M. G. Frank, "Comparative Manipulation-test Performance in Ten-Week-Old Wolves (*Canis lupus*) and Alaskan Malamutes (*Canis familiaris*)," *Journal of Comparative Psychology*, 99 (1985), pp. 266–74.

5. Topál, J., Á. Miklósi, and V. Csányi, "Dog-Human Relationship Affects Problem Solving Behavior in the Dog," *Anthozoös*, 10 (1997).

6. For a scientific analysis of the difference between dogs and wolves, see Miklósi, Á., E. Kubinyi, J. Topál, M. Gácsi, Z. Virányi and V. Csányi, "A Simple Reason for a Big Difference: Wolves Do Not Look Back at Humans but Dogs Do," *Current Biology*, 13 (2003), pp. 763–66. This article is critical of a similar and earlier but less careful study; see Hare, B., B. Brown, C. Williamson and M. Tomasello, "The Domestication of Cognition in Dogs," *Science*, 298 (2002), pp. 1634–36.

7. Topál, J., Á. Miklósi, and V. Csányi, op. cit.

8. Pfaffenberg, C. J., J. P. Scott, J. L. Fuller, B. E. Ginsburg, and S. W. Bielfeldt, *Guide Dogs for the Blind: Their Selection, Development and Training*, Amsterdam: Elsevier, 1976.

9. Ireson, P. (ed.), *Guiding Stars*, Harpenden: Lennard Publishing, 1993.

10. Hoken, S., *Emma és én* (*Emma and I*), Budapest: Magyar Könyvklub, 2000.

11. This last group participated with the kind permission of my friend Frigyes Janza, the director of the Police Dog Training School of Dunakeszi.

12. Naderi, S., Á. Miklósi, A. Dóka, and V. Csányi, "Cooperative Interactions between Blind Persons and Their Dogs," *Applied Animal Behaviour Sciences*, 74 (2001), pp. 59–80; Naderi, S., Á. Miklási, A. Dóka and V. Csányi, "Does Dog-Human Attachment Affect Their Inter-specific Cooperation?" *Acta Biologica Hungarica*, 53 (2002), 537–50.

13. For such a story, see Ireson, P., op. cit., p. 93.

14. Tomasello, M., and J. Call, *Primate Cognition*, Oxford: Oxford University Press, 1997. The authors describe numerous relevant experiments in chapter 8.

15. Anderson, J. R., P. Sallaberry, and H. Barbier, "Use of Experimenter-Given Cues During Object Choice Tasks by Capuchin Monkeys," *Animal Behavior*, 49 (1995), pp. 201–8; and Anderson, J., M. Montant, and D. Schmidt, "Rhesus Monkeys Fail to Use Gaze Direction as an Experimenter-Given Cue in an Object Choice Task," *Behavioral Proceedings*, 37 (1996), pp. 47–55.

16. Itakaura, S., and M. Tanaka, "The Use of Experimenter-Given Cues During Object Choice Tasks by Chimpanzee (*Pan troglodytes*), and Orangutan (*Pongo pygmaeus*) and Human Infants (*Homo sapiens*)," *Journal of Comparative Psychology*, 112 (1998).

17. Emery, N. J., E. N. Lorincz, D. I. Perrett, M. W. Oram, and C. I. Baker, "Gaze Following and Joint Attention in Rhesus Monkeys (*Macaca mulatta*)," *Journal of Comparative Psychology*, 111 (1997).

18. The bright yellow eyes of wolves, which do not have a white ring, probably fulfill a social function, too. They probably help to maintain contact during the hunt.

19. Miklósi, Á., R. Polgárdi, J. Topál, and V. Csányi, "Intentional Behavior in Dog-Human Communication: Experimental Analysis of 'Showing' Behavior in the Dog," *Animal Cognition*, 3 (1998), pp. 159–66; Soproni, K., Á. Miklósi, J. Topál, and V. Csányi, "Comprehension of Human Communicative Signs in Pet Dogs," *Journal of Comparative Psychology*, 115 (2001), pp. 122–26; Soproni, K., Á. Miklósi, J. Topál, and V. Csányi, "Dogs' Responsiveness to Human Pointing Gestures," *Journal of Comparative Psychology*, 116 (2002), pp. 27–34.

20. This was important for excluding a peculiar form of learning based on signals that differentiate the objects. If we had not been sensitive to the problem caused by the continuation of the signal after the dog started toward the container, it could have been the signal that guided the animal all the way to the appropriate spot.

21. Miklósi, Á., R. Polgárdi, J. Topál, and V. Csányi, "Intentional Behavior in Dog-Human Communication: An Experimental Analysis of 'Showing' Behavior," *Animal Cognition*, 3 (2000), pp. 159–66.

22. Other scientists have confirmed these findings; see Hare, B., and M. Tomasello, "Domestic Dogs (*Canis familiaris*) Use Human and Conspecific Social Cues to Locate Hidden Food," *Journal of Comparative Psychology*, 113 (1999).

23. The data pertaining to chimpanzees were taken from Itakaura, S., B. Agnetta, B. Hare and M. Tomasello, "Chimpanzee use of Human and Conspecific Social Cues to Locate Hidden Food," *Development Science*, 2 (1999), pp. 448–456.

24. Povinelli, D. J., K. E. Nelson, and S. T. Boysen, "Inferences about Guessing and Knowing by Chimpanzees," *Journal of Comparative Psychology*, 104 (1992), pp. 203–10.

25. I gladly admit that we need further experiments, already under way, to answer questions of such importance.

Part 3: The Diary of Flip and Jerry

1. At this moment, Flip is lying by the front door, and the cheeky Jerry is on my bed.

2. The pumi is a well-known Hungarian breed; for a description see http://home.swipnet.se/-w-59012/pumi4.html.

8. Dogs Understand a Lot

1. In his old age he was cared for by our assistant, Andrea.

2. Menzel, C. R., "Cognitive Aspects of Foraging in Japanese Monkeys," *Animal Behaviour*, 41 (1991).

3. Tomasello, M., and J. Call, op. cit., pp. 300–2.

4. Dodó himself did something odd, which I would not like to advertise, but after all, my colleagues will not read the footnotes. As mentioned above, Dodó lived with us and was eating well, but unfortunately he was unable to fly. Every morning we would have flying lessons in a long and narrow room, but when I tried to launch him, he could only flutter. After about three weeks, he began to exhibit a curious behavior. Until then, he was sitting quietly on a peg in the cage, which he would leave only to eat or drink; but after three weeks he started to flutter at the side of the cage, seemingly wanting to get out. I got mad at him after a couple of days; after all, he could not fly and maybe never would. In my anger I placed the cage outside our front door and opened the door of the cage. Dodó quickly found the exit, stepped out, looked around, and tried two or three times to fly to the railing along the corridor, but fell to the ground each time. I was watching this from behind the front door, and to my immense surprise, Dodó nicely reentered the cage and perched on his peg. I took pity on him and brought the cage back to its usual place, and during the next three weeks he *never* behaved as if he wanted to get out. In a further three weeks there was some definite improvement in the flying lessons and he seemed to be getting better. He was able to start to fly and more or less successfully land on pieces of furniture. One day he resumed the attempt to get out of the cage, and we decided to release him where we had found him. We took him up on Castle Hill and I released him. At first he alit on the

ground, but after a few seconds he rose to an enormous altitude and made a great circle toward the Danube. Eve was sniffling while Dodó soared in the distance. I had never seen before such an expression of animal joy. And I am unwilling to say anything at all about the behavior of this bird in my capacity as a researcher. Anecdotes are just anecdotes, anyone can tell any story he wants.

9. Dogs Imitate but Have No Hands

1. De La Malle, D. op. cit., pp. 388–419.
2. Ireson, P. (ed.), op. cit.
3. Kubinyi, E., Á. Miklósi, J. Topál, and V. Csányi, "Social Anticipation in Dogs: A New Form of Social Influence," *Animal Cognition*, 6 (2002), pp. 57–64.
4. Pongrácz, P., Á. Miklósi, E. Kubinyi, K. Gurobi, J. Topál, and V. Csányi, "Social Learning in Dogs I. The Effect of a Human Demonstrator on the Performance of Dogs (*Canis familiaris*) in a Detour Task," *Animal Behaviour*, 62 (2001), pp. 1109–17. Readers who are interested in the imitative abilities of various animals will find it worthwhile to consult a relevant paper by my colleague Á. Miklósi, "The Ethological Analysis of Imitation," *Biological Review*, 74 (1999), pp. 347–74; and Pongrácz, P., Á. Miklósi, E. Kubinyi, J. Topál, and V. Csányi, "Interaction between Individual Experience and Social Learning in Dogs," *Animal Behaviour*, 65 (2003), pp. 595–603.
5. They probably could smell the balls and realize that they were inside the equipment.
6. Hayes, K. J., and C. Hayes, "Imitation in a Home Raised Chimpanzee," *Journal of Comparative Psychology*, 45 (1952), 450–59; Custance, T. N., A. Whiten, and K. A. Bard, "Can Young Chimpanzees (*Pan Troglodytes*) Imitate Arbitrary Actions? Hates and Hayes (1952) Revisited," *Behaviour*, 132 (1995), 837–59.

10. Can Dogs "Speak"?

1. Seyfarth, R. M., D. L. Cheney, and P. Marler, "Monkey Responses to Three Different Alarm Calls: Evidence of Predator Classification and Semantic Communication," *Science*, 210 (1980).
2. Hayes, K. J., and C. H. Hayes, "The Intellectual Development of a Home-Raised Chimpanzee," *Proceedings of the American Philosophical Society*, 95 (1951).
3. Gardner, B. T., and R. A. Gardner, "Teaching Sign Language to a Chimpanzee," *Science*, 165 (1969).
4. Premack, D., *Intelligence in Ape and Man*, Hillsdale, N.J.: Lawrence Erlbaum, 1976.
5. Rambaugh, D. M. (ed.), *Language Learning by a Chimpanzee: The Lana Project*, New York: Academic Press, 1977.
6. Patterson, F., and E. Linden, *The Education of Koko*, New York: Owl Books, 1981.
7. Sebeok, T. A., and J. Umiker-Sebeok, *Speaking of Apes*, New York: Plenum Press, 1980.
8. Wallman, J., *Aping Language*, Cambridge: Cambride University Press, 1992. Bonobos opened a new chapter in this story. They pay attention to English words and these can be used as symbols. Rumor has it that they can learn many more signs, perhaps in the thousands. If this is true, it may be possible for bonobos to learn a relatively primitive language. Everybody is excitedly awaiting developments.
9. See chapter 12.
10. Schusterman, R. J., and K. Krieger, "California Sea Lions are Capable of Semantic Comprehension," *Psychol. Rec.*, 34 (1984).

11. Hermann, L. M., *Cognition and Language Competencies of Bottlenosed Dolphins*, Hillsdale, N.J.: Lawrence Erlbaum Assoc., 1986.

12. Savage-Rumbaugh, S., K. McDonald, R. A. Sevcik, W. D. Hopkins, and E. Rupert, "Spontaneous Symbol Acquisition and Communicative Use by Pygmy Chimpanzees," *Journal of Experimental Psychology, General*, 115 (1986), pp. 211–35.

13. Warden, C. J., and L. H. Warner, "The Sensory Capacities and Intelligence of Dogs, With a Report on the Ability of the Noted Dog 'Fellow' to Respond to Verbal Stimuli," *The Quarterly Review of Biology*, 3 (1928).

14. Coren, S., *The Intelligence of Dogs*, New York: The Free Press, 1998.

15. Pongrácz, P., Á. Miklósi and V. Csányi, "Owners' Belief in the Ability of Their Pet Dogs to Understand Human Verbal Communication. A Case of Social Understanding" *Current Cognitive Psychology*, 20 (1002), pp. 87–107.

16. Jerry also understood his nickname, Jerke.

17. Diósgyőr is a small town some sixty miles from Budapest.

18. See http://www.akc.org/breeds/recbreeds/puli.cfm.

19. It is possible that for him this means "I am here."

20. Királyrét is a small village, about thirty-five miles from Budapest, and is the starting point for excursions to the Börzsöny Mountains.

Part 4: Scientific Study of the Animal Mind

11. Observation, Theory, and Proof

1. The details can be found in the original report. See Lubbock, J., *Report of the British Association for the Advancement of Science*, 1885, p. 1089.

2. For those interested in the scientific method, I recommend Arthur Koestler's outstanding book, *The Sleepwalkers: A History of Man's Changing Vision of the Universe*, New York: Macmillan, 1959.

12. The Clever Hans and Alex, the Parrot That Understands Words

1. Pfungst, O., *Clever Hans, the Horse of Mr. von Osten*, New York: Holt, 1911.

2. Oskar Heinroth was a teacher of Konrad Lorenz, and his studies greatly assisted Lorenz in his subsequent establishment of the field of ethology.

3. Darwin, C., op. cit.

4. Darwin, C., *The Expression of the Emotions in Man and Animals*, Oxford: Oxford University Press, 1996.

5. Darwin, C., *The Descent of Man and Selection in Relation to Sex*, London: J. Murray, 1913.

6. Romanes, G. J., *Animal Intelligence*, London: Kegan Paul, 1882; Romanes, G. J., *Mental Evolution in Animals*, London: Kegan Paul, Trench and Co., 1883; Romanes, G. J., *Mental Evolution in Man: Origin of Human Faculty*, Kegan Paul, Trench and Co., 1888.

7. Griffin, D. R., *The Question of Animal Awareness: Evolutionary Continuity of Mental Experience*, New York: Rockefeller University Press, 1976. For a more recent and detailed work on this subject, see Griffin, D. R., *Animal Minds*, Chicago: University of Chicago Press, 1992.

8. Both extremist views as well as those of the new anthropomorphists are discussed in the excellent book by Mitchell, R. W., N. S. Thompson, and H. L. Miles (eds.), *Anthropomorphism, Anecdotes and Animals*, New York: State University of New York Press, 1997.

9. Whiten, A., and R. W. Byrne, "The St. Andrews Catalog of Tactical Deception in Primates," *St. Andrews Psychological Reports*, No. 10, 1986, pp. 1–47. For their use of anecdotes and the reaction of numerous researchers see Whiten, A., and R. W. Byrne, "Tactical Deception in Primates," *Behavioral and Brain Sciences*, 11 (1998).

10. Pepperberg, I. M., "Functional Vocalization by an African Grey Parrot (*Psittacus erithacus*)," *Zeitschrift für Tierpsychologie*, 55 (1981), pp. 139–60; Pepperberg, I. M., "Evidence for Conceptual Quantitative Abilities in the African Grey Parrot: Labeling of Cardinal Sets," *Ethology*, 75 (1987), pp. 37–61; Pepperberg, I. M., "Some Cognitive Capacities of the African Grey Parrot (*Psittacus erithacus*)," *Advances in the Study of Behavior*, 19 (1992), pp. 357–409; Pepperberg, I. M., *The Alex Studies*, Cambridge, Mass.: Harvard University Press, 1999.

11. It is noteworthy that scientific freedom really begins only *after* funding has been obtained.

12. Craik, K. J. W., *The Nature of Explanation*, Cambridge: Cambridge University Press, 1943; McKay, D. M., "Mindlike Behavior of Artefacts," *British Journal of The Philosophy of Science*, 2 (1951–52), pp. 105–21; Collett, T. S., "Sensory Guidance of Motor Behaviour," in Halliday, T. R., and P. J. B. Slater, *Animal Behaviour*, vol. 1, *Causes and Effects*, Oxford: Blackwell, 1983.

13. Knudsen, E. I., "The Hearing of the Barn Owl," *Scientific American*, 245/6 (1981), pp. 82–91.

14. Suga, N., K. Kuzirai, and W. E. O'Neill, "How Biosonar Information Is Represented in the Bat Cerebral Cortex," in Syka, J., and L. Aitkin (eds.), *Neural Mechanisms of Hearing*, New York: Plenum Press, 1981, pp. 197–219.

15. Dräger, U. C., and D. H. Hubel, "Responses to Visual Stimulation and Relationship between Visual, Auditory and Somatosensory Inputs in Mouse Superior Colliculus," *Journal of Neurophysiology*, 38 (1975), pp. 690–713.

16. Menzel, C. R., op. cit., pp. 397–402.

17. Csányi, V., "Contribution of the Genetical and Neural Memory to Animal Intelligence," in Jerison, H., and Irene Jerison (eds.), *Intelligence and Evolutionary Biology*, Berlin: Springer-Verlag, 1988.

18. Csányi, V., *Etológia*, Budapest: Nemzeti Tankönyvkiadó, 1994.

19. On the other hand, there could be a little somebody there, but more of this later.

20. For a more detailed discussion of constructional activity, see Csányi, V., *Az emberi természet. Humánetológia (Human Nature, Human Ethology)*, Budapest: Vince Kiadó, 1999.

21. We are not speaking here of other social rituals such as being knighted, or a graduation ceremony or religious rites that carry complex symbolic meanings.

22. All animals have groups of nerves the activation of which follows a regular rhythm and that act as an inner clock. Some of these are related to the diurnal cycle.

23. Harnad, S., *Categorical Perception: The Groundwork of Cognition*, Cambridge: Cambridge University Press, 1987.

24. Csányi, V., op. cit. In this book, there is a more detailed discussion of human intelligence and much supplementary material. Here we have discussed only those matters that are important for understanding the canine mind.

13. What Do the Relatives Know?

1. Byrne, R., *The Thinking Ape*, Oxford: Oxford University Press, 1995.

2. Dennett, D. C., "Intentional Systems in Cognitive Ethology: the 'Panglossian Paradigm' Defended," *Behavioral Brain Science*, 6 (1983).

3. Byrne, R., op. cit.

4. See Dennett, D. C., op. cit.

5. Shimp, C. P., "On Metaknowledge in the Pigeon: An Organism's Knowledge About Its Own Behavior," *Animal Learning Behavior*, 10 (1982), pp. 358–64.

6. Gallup, G. G., Jr., "Chimpanzees: Self-recognition," *Science*, 167 (1970).

7. Heyes, C. M., "Reflection on Self-recognition in Primates," *Behavioral and Brain Sciences*, 16 (1994), pp. 524–25.

8. Premack, D., and A. J. Premack, "Does the Chimpanzee Have a Theory of Mind?" *Behavioral Brain Science*, 1 (1978), pp. 347—62.

9. Visalberghi, E., and L. Trinca, "Tool Use in Capuchin Monkeys: Distinguishing between Performing and Understanding," *Primates,* 30 (1989), pp. 511–21.

10. Bard, K. A., D. M. Faragaszy, and E. Visalberghi, "Acquisition and Comprehension of Tool-using Behavior by Young Chimpanzees (*Pan troglodytes*): Effects of Age and Modelling," *International Journal of Comparative Psychology*, 8 (1995), pp. 47–68.

11. Visalberghi, E., D. M. Faragaszy, and E. S. Savage-Rumbaugh, "Performance in a Tool-using Task by Common Chimpanzees (*Pan troglodytes*), bonobos (*Pan paniscus*), and an orangutan (*Pongo pygmaeus*), and capuchin monkeys (*Cebus paella*)," *Journal of Comparative Psychology*, 109 (1995), pp. 52–60.

12. Natale, F., F. Antonucci, G. Spinozzi, and P. Poti, "Stage 6 Object Concept in Nonhuman Primate Cognition: A Comparison between Gorilla (*Gorilla gorilla*) and Japanese Macaque (*Macata fuscata*)," *Journal of Comparative Psychology*, 100 (1986), pp. 335–39.

13. Triana, E., and R. Pasnak, "Object Permanence in Cats and Dogs," *Animal Learning and Behavior*, 9 (1981), pp. 135–39; Gagon, S., and F. Doré, "Search Behavior in Various Breeds of Adult Dogs (*Canis familiaris*): Object Permanence and Olfactory Cues," *Journal of Comparative Psychology*, 106 (1992), pp. 58—68.

14. Cheney, D. L., R. M. Seyfarth, and J. B. Silk, The Response of Female Baboons (*Papio cynocephalus ursinus*) to Anomalous Social Interactions: Evidence for Causal Reasoning?" *Journal of Comparative Psychology*, 109 (1995), pp. 131–41.

15. Köhler, W., *The Mentality of Apes*, New York: Harcourt Brace, 1925.

16. Schiller, P., "Innate Constituents of Complex Responses in Primates," *Psychological Review*, 59 (1952), pp. 177–91.

17. Tomasello, M., and J. Call, op. cit.

18. Woodruff, G., and D. Premack, "Primitive Mathematical Concepts in the Chimpanzee: Proportionality and Numerosity," *Nature*, 293 (1981), pp. 568–70.

19. Krechevsky, I., "Hereditary Nature of 'Hypotheses,'" *Journal of Comparative Psychology*, 16 (1933), pp. 99–116.

20. Byrne, R., and A. Whiten, *Machiavellian Intelligence*, Oxford: Clarendon Press, 1998.

21. Premack, D., and G. Woodruff, "Does the Chimpanzee Have a Theory of Mind?" *Behavioral Brain Science*, 1 (1978), pp. 515–26.

22. Povinelli, D.J., K. E. Nelson, and S. T. Boysen, "Comprehension of Role Reversal in Chimpanzees: Evidence of Empathy?" *Animal Behavior*, 43 (1992), pp. 633–40.

23. Seyfarth, R. M., and D. L. Cheney, "The Assessment by Vervet Monkeys of Their Own and Other Species' Alarm Calls," *Animal Behavior*, 40 (1990), pp. 754–64.

24. Byrne, R., and A. Whiten, op. cit., pp. 669–73.

25. Tomasello, M., and J. Call, op. cit.

6. Moller, A. P., "False Alarm Calls as a Means of Resource Usurpation in the Great Tit (*Parus Major*)," *Ethology*, 79 (1988), pp. 25–30.

27. Gould, I., and C. G. Gould, *The Honey Bee*, New York: Freeman Press, 1988.

14. The Minds of Children

1. Cole, M., and S. R. Cole, *The Development of Children*, 3rd ed.; New York: W. H. Freeman and Co., 1996.

2. Trevarthen, C., "The Functions of Emotions in Early Communication and Development," in Nadel, J., and L. Camaioni (eds.), *New Perspectives in Early Communicative Development*, New York, Routledge, 1993.

3. Meltzoff, A. N., and M. K. Moore, "Imitation of Facial Expression and Manual Gestures by Human Neonates," *Science*, 198 (1977), pp. 75–78.

4. Tomasello, M., and J. Call, op. cit.

5. Nagy, E., and P. Molnár, "Az első dialogus: útban a szoptatás interdiszciplináris szemlélete felé" (The First Dialog: Toward an Interdisciplinary View of Nursing), *Lege Artis Medicinae*, 6 (1996), pp. 314–22.

6. Tomasello, M., "Joint Attention as Social Cognition," in Moore, C., and O. Dunham (eds.), *Joint Attention: Its Origins and Role in Development*, Hillsdale, N.J.: Lawrence Erlbaum Assoc., 1955.

7. Gergely, G., Z. Nádasdy, G. Csibra, and S. Bíró, "Taking the Intentional Stance at 12 Months of Age," *Cognition*, 56 (1995), pp. 165–93.

8. Meltzoff, A., "Understanding the Intentions of Others: Re-enactment of Intended Acts by 18-month Old Children," *Developmental Psychology*, 31 (1995), pp. 838–50.

9. Eibl-Eibesfeld, I., *Human Ethology*, New York: Aldine de Gruyter, 1989.

10. Bowlby, J., *Attachment and Loss, Attachment*, vol. 1, London: The Hogarth Press and The Institute of Psycho-Analysis, 1969; Bowlby, J., *Attachment and Loss, Separation*, vol. 2, London: The Hogarth Press and The Institute of Psycho-Analysis, 1973; Bowlby, J., *Attachment and Loss, Loss*, vol. 3, London: The Hogarth Press and The Institute of Psycho-Analysis, 1980.

11. Ainsworth, M. D. S., M. C. Blehar, E. Waters, and S. Wall, op. cit.

12. Leslie, A. M., "Pretense and Representation in Infancy: The Origins of the 'Theory of Mind,'" *Psychological Review*, 94 (1987), pp. 84–106.

13. Whiten, A., and R. W. Byrne, "The Emergence of Metarepresentation in Human Ontogeny and Primate Phylogeny," in Whiten, A. (ed.), *Natural Theories of the Mind: Evolution, Development and Simulation in Everyday Mindreading*, Oxford: Basil Blackwell, Ltd., 1991, pp. 276–81.

14. Savage-Rumbaugh, E. S., and K. McDonald, "Deception and Social Manipulation in Symbol Using Apes," in Byrne, R. W. and A. Whiten (eds.), *Machiavellian Intelligence*, Oxford: Clarendon Press, 1988, pp. 224–37.

15. Patterson, F., and E. Linden, op. cit.

16. Whiten, A., "Imitation, Pretence and Mindreading: Secondary Representation in Comparative Primatology and Developmental Psychology?" in Russon, A. E., K. A. Bard, and S. T. Parker (eds.), *Reaching into Thought: The Minds of the Great Apes*, Cambridge: Cambridge University Press, 1996, pp. 300–24.

17. Custance, D. M., A. Whiten, and K. A. Bard, "Can Young Chimpanzees Imitate Arbitrary Actions? Hayes and Hayes (1952) Revisited," *Behaviour*, 132 (1995), pp. 839–58.

18. Russon, A., and B. M. F. Galdikas, "Imitation in Free-ranging Rehabilitant Orangutans (*Pongo pygmeus*)," *Journal of Comparative Psychology*, 107 (1993), pp. 146–61.

19. Perner, J., *Understanding the Representational Mind*, Cambridge, Mass.: MIT Press, 1991.

15. The Functioning of the Canine Mind

1. Gallup, G. G., Jr., op. cit., pp. 417—21.
2. This is entirely consistent with the results of a series of experiments with tamarin monkeys. It was shown that, like chimpanzees, they react to their mirror image and are probably able to recognize themselves in the mirror. Their brains are much less developed than those of the chimpanzees, but as was pointed out by researchers, certain white tufts in their pelt play an important part in their lives. In the experiments, these tufts were painted a different color by the researchers, and these animals were able to recognize themselves because their image is important to them. Hauser, M. D., J. Kralik, C. Botto-Mahan, M. Garrett, and J. Oser, "Self-recognition in Primates: Phylogeny and Salience in Species-typical Features," *Proceedings of the National Academy of Sciences*, 92 (1995), pp. 10811–14.
3. Gell, A., *The Anthropology of Time*, Oxford: Berg, 1992.
4. See chapters 8–10.
5. See chapter 9.
6. See chapter 8.
7. See chapter 8.
8. See chapter 8.
9. See chapter 13.

Part 5: Humans and Dogs

16. How to Be a Dog Owner

1. Coren, S., *The Intelligence of Dogs*, New York: The Free Press, 1998. Coren worked out special tests for measuring the intelligence of dogs.
2. Coren, S., *Why We Love the Dogs We Do*, New York: The Free Press, 1998.
3. See chapter 5.
4. An outstanding article dealing with the deterioration of breeds and with the genetic methods for arresting the decline is McGreevy, P. D., and F. W. Nichols, "Some Practical Solutions to Welfare Problems in Dog Breeding," *Animal Welfare*, 8 (1999), pp. 329–41.
5. Department of Ethology, Eötvös Lóránd University, Jávorka Sándor u. 14, 2131 Göd, Hungary. Please write on the outside of the envelope the words "Beszélőkutya" (Talking Dog).

Bibliography

Ainsworth, M.D.S., M. C. Blehar, E. Walters, and S. Wall, *Patterns of Attachment: A Psychological Study of the Strange Situation*, Hillsdale, N.J.: Lawrence Erlbaum, 1978.

Anderson, J., M. Montant, and D. Schmidt, "Rhesus Monkeys Fail to Use Gaze Direction as an Experimenter-Given Cue in an Object Choice Task," *Behavioral Proceedings*, 37 (1996), pp. 47–55.

Anderson, J. R., P. Sallaberry, and H. Barbier, "Use of Experimenter-Given Cues During Object Choice Tasks by Capuchin Monkeys," *Animal Behavior*, 49 (1995), pp. 201–208.

Bard, K. A., D. M. Faragaszy, and E. Visalberghi, "Acquisition and Comprehension of Tool-Using Behavior by Young Chimpanzees (*Pan troglodytes*): Effects of Age and Modelling," *International Journal of Comparative Psychology*, 8 (1995), pp. 47–68.

Bekoff, M., "Social Communication in Canids: Evidence for the Evolution of Stereotyped Mammalian Display," *Science*, 197 (1997), pp. 1097–99.

Belyaev, D. K., and L. N. Trut, "Some Genetic and Endocrine Effects of Selection for Domestication of Silver Foxes," in Fox, M. E. (ed.), *The Wild Canids*, New York: Van Nostrand, 1975.

Bowlby, J., *Attachment and Loss, Attachment*, vol. 1, London: The Hogarth Press and The Institute of Psycho-Analysis, 1969.

——, *Attachment and Loss, Separation*, vol. 2, London: The Hogarth Press and The Institute of Psycho-Analysis, 1973.

——, *Attachment and Loss, Loss*, vol. 3, London: The Hogarth Press and The Institute of Psycho-Analysis, 1980.

Byrne, R., *The Thinking Ape*, Oxford: Oxford University Press, 1995.

Byrne, R., and A. Whiten, *Machiavellian Intelligence*, Oxford: Clarendon Press, 1998.

Cairns, R. B., and J. Werboff, "Behavior Development in the Dog: An Interspecific Analysis," *Science*, 158 (1967).

Cheney, D. L., R. M. Seyfarth, and J. B. Silk, "The Response of Female Baboons (*Papio cynocephalus ursinus*) to Anomalous Social Interactions: Evidence for Causal Reasoning?" *Journal of Comparative Psychology*, 109 (1995), pp. 131–41.

Cole, M., and S. R. Cole, *The Development of Children*, 3rd ed., New York: W. H. Freeman & Co., 1996.

Collett, T. S., "Sensory Guidance of Motor Behaviour," in Halliday, T. R., and P. J. B. Slater, *Animal Behaviour*, vol. 1, *Causes and Effects*, Oxford: Blackwell, 1983.

Coppinger, R., and L. Coppinger, *Dogs*, New York: Scribner, 2001.

Coren, S., *The Intelligence of Dogs*, New York: The Free Press, 1998.

——, *Why We Love the Dogs We Do*, New York: The Free Press, 1998.

Craik, K.J.W., *The Nature of Explanation*, Cambridge: Cambridge University Press, 1943.

Csányi, V., "Contribution of the Genetical and Neural Memory to Animal Intelligence," in Jerison, H., and Irene Jerison (eds.), *Intelligence and Evolutionary Biology*, Berlin: Springer-Verlag, 1988.

——, "Ethology and the Rise of Conceptual Thoughts," in Deely, J. (ed.), *Symbolicity*, Lanham, MD: University Press of America, 1992, pp. 479–84.

——, "The Brain's Models and Communication," in Sebeok, Thomas A., and Jean Umiker-Sebeok (eds.), *The Semiotic Web*, Berlin: Moyton de Gruyter, 1992, pp. 27–43.

——, *Etológia*, Budapest: Nemzeti Tankönyvkiadó, 1994.

———, *Az emberi természet. Humánetológia* (*Human Nature, Human Ethology*), Budapest: Vince Kiadó, 1999.

———, "The 'Human Behavior Complex' and the Compulsion of Communication: Key Factors of Human Evolution," *Semiotica*, 128 (3/4) (2000), pp. 45–60.

———, "An Ethological Reconstruction of the Emergence of Culture and Language during Human Evolution," in Győri, G. (ed.), *Language Evolution*, Frankfurt am Main: Peter Lang, 2001, pp. 43–55.

Csányi, V., and Á. Miklósi, "A kutya mint a korai evolúció modellje" (Dogs as models for early evolution), *Magyar Tudomány*, 63 (1998).

Custance, D. M., A. Whiten, and K. A. Bard, "Can Young Chimpanzees Imitate Arbitrary Actions? Hayes and Hayes (1952) Revisited," *Behaviour*, 132 (1995), pp. 839–58.

Darwin, C., *The Descent of Man and Selection in Relation to Sex*, London: J. Murray, 1913.

———, *The Expression of the Emotions in Man and Animals,* Oxford and New York: Oxford University Press, 1996.

———, *The Origin of Species*, New York: Oxford University Press, 1996.

Davis, H., "Theoretical Note on the Moral Development of Rats (*Rattus norvegicus*)," *Journal of Comparative Psychology*, 101 (1989).

Davis, K. D., *Therapy Dogs*, New York: Howell Bookhouse, 1992.

De Waal, F., *Good Natured*, Cambridge: Harvard University Press, 1996.

De La Malle, D., "Mémoire sur le développement des facultés intellectuelles des animaux sauvages et domestiques" ("Notes on the Development of the Intellectual Faculties of Wild and Domestic Animals"), *Annales des Sciences Naturelles*, Ser. 1,22 (1831).

Dennett, D. C., "Intentional Systems in Cognitive Ethology: the 'Panglossian Paradigm' Defended," *Behavioral Brain Science*, 6 (1983).

Diezel, M., *Vadászebek* (*Hunting Dogs*), Szeged: Szukits Könyvkiadó reprint, 1899.

Dräger, U. C., and D. H. Hubel, "Responses to Visual Stimulation and Relationship between Visual, Auditory and Somatosensory Inputs in Mouse Superior Colliculus," *Journal of Neurophysiology*, 38 (1975), pp. 690–713.

Dugatkin, L. A., *Cooperation Among Animals*, Oxford: Oxford University Press, 1997.

Durkheim, E., *The Elementary Forms of Religious Life*, transl. by Joseph Ward Swain, New York: Collier, 1961.

Eibl-Eibesfeld, I., *Human Ethology*, New York: Aldine de Gruyter, 1989.

Emery, N. J., E. N. Lorincz, D. I. Perrett, M. W. Oram, and C. I. Baker, "Gaze Following and Joint Attention in Rhesus Monkeys (*Macaca mulatta*)," *Journal of Comparative Psychology*, 111 (1997).

Fox, M. W. (ed.), *The Wild Canids: Their Systematics, Behavioral Ecology and Evolution*, New York: Van Nostrand Reinhold Co., 1975.

Fox, M. W., *Superdog*, New York: Howell Bookhouse, 1990.

Frank, H., "Evolution of Canine Information Processing under Condition of Natural and Artificial Selection," *Zeitschrift für Tierpsychologie*, 53 (1980), pp. 389–99.

Frank, H., and M. G. Frank, "Comparative Manipulation-Test Performance in Ten-Week-Old Wolves (*Canis lupus*) and Alaskan Malamutes (*Canis familiaris*)," *Journal of Comparative Psychology*, 99 (1985), pp. 266–74.

Freedman, D. G., "Constitutional and Environmental Interactions in Rearing Four Breeds of Dogs," *Science*, 133 (1961).

Freedman, D. G., J. A. King, and O. Elliot, "Critical Period in the Social Development of Dogs," *Science*, 133 (1961).

Gácsi, M., and T. Ferenczy, *Kutyaiskola* (*Dog School*), Budapest: privately published, 1998.

Gácsi, M., J. Topál, Á. Dóka, and V. Csányi, "Attachment Behavior of Adult Dogs (*Canis familiaris*) Living at Rescue Center: Forming New Bonds," *Journal of Comparative Psychology*, 115 (2001), pp. 423–31.

Gagon, S., and F. Doré, "Search Behavior in Various Breeds of Adult Dogs (*Canis familiaris*): Object Permanence and Olfactory Cues," *Journal of Comparative Psychology*, 106 (1992), pp. 58–68.

Gallup, G. G., Jr., "Chimpanzees: Self-Recognition," *Science*, 167 (1970).

Gardner, B. T., and R. A. Gardner, "Teaching Sign Language to a Chimpanzee," *Science*, 165 (1969).

Gell, A., *The Anthropology of Time*, Oxford: Berg, 1992.

Gergely, G., Z. Nádasdy, G. Csibra, and S. Bíró, "Taking the Intentional Stance at 12 Months of Age," *Cognition*, 56 (1995), pp. 65–93.

Gould, R. A., "Journey to Pulyakara," *Natural History*, 79 (1970).

Gould, I., and C. G. Gould, *The Honey Bee*, New York: Freeman Press, 1988.

Griffin, D. R., *The Question of Animal Awareness: Evolutionary Continuity of Mental Experience*, New York: Rockefeller University Press, 1976.

———, *Animal Minds*, Chicago: University of Chicago Press, 1992.

Hans-Günther, H., *Játsszunk a kutyánkkal! Agility (Let Us Play with Our Dog! Agility)*, Budapest: Holló és Társa, 1998.

Hare, B., B. Brown, C. Williamson, and M. Tomasello, "The Domestication of Cognition in Dogs," *Science*, 298 (2002), pp. 1634–36.

Hare, B., and M. Tomasello, "Domestic Dogs (*Canis familiaris*) Use Human and Conspecific Social Cues to Locate Hidden Food," *Journal of Comparative Psychology*, 113 (1999).

Harnad, S., *Categorical Perception: The Groundwork of Cognition*, Cambridge: Cambridge University Press, 1987.

Hauser, M. D., J. Kralik, C. Botto-Mahan, M. Garrett, and J. Oser, "Self-Recognition in Primates: Phylogeny and Salience in Species-Typical Features," *Proceedings of the National Academy of Sciences*, 92 (1995), pp. 10811–14.

Hayes, K. J., and C. H. Hayes, "The Intellectual Development of a Home-Raised Chimpanzee," *Proceedings of the American Philosophical Society*, 95 (1951).

———, "Imitation in a Home-Raised Chimpanzee," *Journal of Comparative Psychology*, 45 (1952), pp. 450–59.

Hermann, L. M., *Cognition and Language Competencies of Bottlenosed Dolphins*, Hillsdale, N.J.: Lawrence Erlbaum, 1986.

Heyes, C. M., "Reflection on Self-Recognition in Primates," *Behavioral and Brain Sciences*, 16 (1994), pp. 524–25.

Hoken, S., *Emma és én (Emma and I)*, Budapest: Magyar Könyvklub, 2000.

Ireson, P. (ed.), *Guiding Stars*, Harpenden: Lennard Publishing, 1993.

Irving, J., *Gundogs—Their Learning Chain*, Dumfries: Loreburn Publishing, 1983.

Itakaura, S., and M. Tanaka, "The Use of Experimenter-Given Cues During Object Choice Tasks by Chimpanzee (*Pan troglodytes*), and Orangutan (*Pongo pygmaeus*) and Human Infants (*Homo sapiens*)," *Journal of Comparative Psychology*, 112 (1998).

Itakaura, S., B. Agnetta, B. Hare, and M. Tomasello, "Chimpanzee Use of Human and Conspecific Social Cues to Locate Hidden Food," *Development Science*, 2 (1999), pp. 448–56.

Johnston, B., *Harnessing Thought*, Harpenden: Lennard Publishing, 1995.

Jolicoeur, P., "Multivariate Geographical Variation in the Wolf, *Canis Lupus L.*," *Evolution*, 13 (1959), pp. 283–89.

Knudsen, E. I., "The Hearing of the Barn Owl," *Scientific American*, 245/6 (1981), pp. 82–91.

Koestler, Arthur, *The Sleepwalkers: A History of Man's Changing Vision of the Universe*, New York: Macmillan, 1959.

Köhler, W., *The Mentality of Apes*, New York: Harcourt Brace, 1925.

Kováts, Zs., and M. Zaharovics, *A vakvezető kutya (The Seeing-Eye Dog)*, Budapest: Vakok és Gyöngelátók Szövetsége, undated.

Krechevsky, I., "Hereditary Nature of 'Hypotheses,'" *Journal of Comparative Psychology*, 16 (1933), pp. 99–116.

Kubinyi, E., Á. Miklósi, J. Topál, and V. Csányi, "Social Anticipation in Dogs: A New Form of Social Influence," *Animal Cognition*, 6 (2002), pp. 57–64.

Lawrence, R. D., *In Praise of Wolves*, New York: Ballantine Books, 1986.

Leslie, A. M., "Pretense and Representation in Infancy: The Origins of the 'Theory of Mind,'" *Psychological Review*, 94 (1987), pp. 84–106.

Lubbock, J., *Report of the British Association for the Advancement of Science*, 1885, p. 1089.

Masson, J. Moussaieff, *Dogs Never Lie About Love*, New York: Three Rivers Press, 1997.

Masson, J. Moussaieff, and S. McCarthy, *When Elephants Weep: The Emotional Lives of Animals*, New York: Delacorte Press, 1995.

McGreevy, P. D., and F. W. Nichols, "Some Practical Solutions to Welfare Problems in Dog Breeding," *Animal Welfare*, 8 (1999), pp. 329–41.

McKay, D. M., "Mindlike Behavior of Artefacts," *British Journal of the Philosophy of Science*, 2 (1951–52), pp. 105–21.

Mech, D., *The Wolf: The Ecology and Behavior of an Endangered Species*, Minneapolis: University of Minnesota Press, 1970.

Meltzoff, A., "Understanding the Intentions of Others: Re-enactment of Intended Acts by 18-Month-Old Children," *Developmental Psychology*, 31 (1995), pp. 838–50.

Meltzoff, A. N., and M. K. Moore, "Imitation of Facial Expression and Manual Gestures by Human Neonates," *Science*, 198 (1977), pp. 75–78.

Menzel, C. R., "Cognitive Aspects of Foraging in Japanese Monkeys," *Animal Behaviour*, 41 (1991).

Miklósi, Á., "The Ethological Analysis of Imitation," *Biological Review*, 74 (1999), pp. 347–74.

Miklósi, Á., E. Kubinyi, J. Topál, M. Gácsi, Z. Virányi, and V. Csányi, "A Simple Reason for a Big Difference: Wolves Do Not Look Back at Humans but Dogs Do," *Current Biology*, 13 (2003), pp. 763–66.

Miklósi, Á., R. Polgárdi, J. Topál, and V. Csányi, "Intentional Behavior in Dog-Human Communication: Experimental Analysis of 'Showing' Behavior in the Dog," *Animal Cognition*, 3 (1998) pp. 159–66.

Mitchell, R. W., N. S. Thompson, and H. L. Miles (eds.), *Anthropomorphism, Anecdotes and Animals*, New York: State University of New York Press, 1997.

Mithen, S., *The Prehistory of the Mind*, London: Phoenix, 1996.

Moller, A. P., "False Alarm Calls as a Means of Resource Usurpation in the Great Tit (*Parus Major*)," *Ethology*, 79 (1988), pp. 25–30.

Morris, D., *Dogwatching*, New York: Three Rivers Press, 1993.

Mowat, F., *Ne féljünk a farkastól* (*Let Us Not Fear Wolves*), Budapest: Gondolat, 1976.

Naderi, S., Á. Miklósi, A. Dóka, and V. Csányi, "Cooperative Interactions between Blind Persons and Their Dogs," *Applied Animal Behaviour Sciences*, 74 (2001), pp. 59–80.

——, "Does Dog-Human Attachment Affect Their Inter-Specific Cooperation?" *Acta Biologica Hungarica*, 53 (2002), pp. 537–50.

Nagy, E., and P. Molnár, "Az első dialogus: útban a szoptatás interdiszciplináris szemlélete felé" (The first dialog: toward an interdisciplinary view of nursing), *Lege Artis Medicinae*, 6 (1996), pp. 314–22.

Natale, F., F. Antonucci, G. Spinozzi, and P. Poti, "Stage 6 Object Concept in Nonhuman Primate Cognition: A Comparison between Gorilla (*Gorilla gorilla*) and Japanese Macaque (*Macata fuscata*)," *Journal of Comparative Psychology*, 100 (1986), pp. 335–39.

Nobis, G., "Der älteste Haushund lebte vor 14.000 Jahren" ("The Oldest Domestic Dog Lived 14,000 Years Ago"), *Umschau*, 19 (1979), pp. 215–25.

Olsen, S. J., and J. W. Olsen, "The Chinese Wolf, Ancestor of New World Dogs," *Science*, 197 (1977).

Patterson, F., and E. Linden, *The Education of Koko*, New York: Owl Books, 1981.

Pepperberg, I. M., "Functional Vocalization by an African Grey Parrot (*Psittacus erithacus*)," *Zeitschrift für Tierpsychologie*, 55 (1981), pp. 139–60.

——, "Evidence for Conceptual Quantitative Abilities in the African Grey Parrot: Labeling of Cardinal Sets," *Ethology*, 75 (1987), pp. 37–61.

——, "Some Cognitive Capacities of the African Grey Parrot (*Psittacus erithacus*)," *Advances in the Study of Behavior*, 19 (1992), pp. 357–409.

——, *The Alex Studies*, Cambridge, Mass.: Harvard University Press, 1999.

Perner, J., *Understanding the Representational Mind*, Cambridge, Mass.: Bradford, MIT Press, 1991.

Peters, R., "Mental Maps in Wolf Territoriality," in Klinghammer, E. (ed.), *The Behavior and Ecology of Wolves*, New York: Garland STPM Press, 1979.

Pettijohn, T. F., T. W. Wong, P. D. Ebert, and P. J. Scott, "Alleviation of Separation Distress in 3 Breeds of Young Dogs," *Developmental Psychobiology*, 10 (1977), pp. 373–81.

Pfaffenberg, C. J., J. P. Scott, J. L. Fuller, B. E. Ginsburg, and S. W. Bielfeldt, *Guide Dogs for the Blind: Their Selection, Development and Training*, Amsterdam: Elsevier, 1976.

Pfungst, O., *Clever Hans, the Horse of Mr. von Osten*, New York: Holt, 1911.

Police Dogs, Training and Care, London: Home Office, HMSO, undated.

Pongrácz, P., Á. Miklósi, and V. Csányi, "Owners' Belief on the Ability of Their Pet Dogs to Understand Human Verbal Communication. A Case of Social Understanding," *Current Cognitive Psychology*, 20 (2001), pp. 87–107.

Pongrácz, P., Á. Miklósi, E. Kubinyi, K. Gurobi, J. Topál, and V. Csányi, "Social Learning in Dogs I. The Effect of a Human Demonstrator on the Performance of Dogs (*Canis familiaris*) in a Detour Task," *Animal Behaviour*, 62 (2001), pp. 1109–17.

Pongrácz, P., Á. Miklósi, E. Kubinyi, J. Topál, and V. Csányi, "Interaction between Individual Experience and Social Learning in Dogs," *Animal Behaviour*, 65 (2003), pp. 595–603.

Povinelli, D. J., K. E. Nelson, and S. T. Boysen, "Inferences about Guessing and Knowing by Chimpanzees," *Journal of Comparative Psychology*, 104 (1990), pp. 203–10.

——, "Comprehension of Role Reversal in Chimpanzees: Evidence of Empathy?" *Animal Behaviour*, 43 (1992), pp. 633–40.

Premack, D., *Intelligence in Ape and Man*, Hillsdale, N.J.: Lawrence Erlbaum, 1976.

Premack, D., and A. J. Premack, "Levels of Causal Understanding in Chimpanzees and Children," *Cognition*, 50 (1994), pp. 347–62.

Premack, D., and G. Woodruff, "Does the Chimpanzee Have a Theory of Mind?" *Behavioral Brain Science*, 4 (1978), pp. 515–26.

Rambaugh, D. M. (ed.), *Language Learning by a Chimpanzee: The Lana Project*, New York: Academic Press, 1977.

Rithnovszky, J., *A fény túlsó oldalán (On the Other Side of Light)*, Budapest: Gondolat, 1991.

Romanes, G. J., *Animal Intelligence*, London: Kegan Paul, Trench and Co., 1882.

——, *Mental Evolution in Animals*, London: Kegan Paul, Trench and Co., 1883.

——, *Mental Evolution in Man: Origin of Human Faculty*, London: Kegan Paul, Trench and Co., 1888.

Russon, A., and B.M.F. Galdikas, "Imitation in Free-Ranging Rehabilitant Orangutans (*Pongo pygmeus*)," *Journal of Comparative Psychology*, 107 (1993), pp. 146–61.

Savage-Rumbaugh, E. S., and K. McDonald, "Deception and Social Manipulation in Symbol Using Apes," in Byrne, R. W., and A. Whiten (eds.), *Machiavellian Intelligence*, Oxford: Clarendon Press, 1988, pp. 224–37.

Savage-Rumbaugh, E. S., K. McDonald, R. A. Sevcik, W. D. Hopkins, and E. Rupert, "Spontaneous Symbol Acquisition and Communicative Use by Pygmy Chimpanzees," *Journal of Experimental Psychology, General*, 115 (1986), pp. 211–35.

Savolainen, P., Y. Zhang, J. Ling, J. Lundberg, and T. Leitner, "Genetic Evidence for an East Asian Origin of Domestic Dogs," *Science*, 298 (2002), pp. 610–13.

Schauer, F., *Playing by the Rules*, Oxford: Clarendon Press, 1991.

Schiller, P., "Innate Constituents of Complex Responses in Primates," *Psychological Review*, 59 (1952), pp. 177–91.

Schusterman, R. J., and K. Krieger, "California Sea Lions are Capable of Semantic Comprehension," *Psychol. Rec.*, 34 (1984).

Scott, J. P., and J. L. Fuller, *Genetics and the Social Behavior of the Dog*, Chicago: University of Chicago Press, 1965.

Scott, J. P., and M. V. Martson, "Critical Periods Affecting Normal and Maladjustive Social Behavior in Puppies," *Journal of Genetic Psychology*, 77 (1950).

Scott, J. P., J. M. Stewart, and V. J. Ghett, "Separation of Infant Dogs," in Senay, E., and J. P. Scott (eds.), *Separation and Depression: Clinical and Research Aspects*, Washington, D.C.: American Association for the Advancement of Science, 1973.

Sebeok, T. A., and J. Umiker-Sebeok, *Speaking of Apes*, New York: Plenum Press, 1980.

Serpell, J., *The Domestic Dog*, Cambridge: Cambridge University Press, 1995.

Seyfarth, R. M., and D. L. Cheney, "The Assessment by Vervet Monkeys of Their Own and Other Species' Alarm Calls," *Animal Behaviour*, 40 (1990), pp. 754–64.

Seyfarth, R. M., D. L. Cheney, and P. Marler, "Monkey Responses to Three Different Alarm Calls: Evidence of Predator Classification and Semantic Communication," *Science*, 210 (1980).

Shimp, C. P., "On Metaknowledge in the Pigeon: An Organism's Knowledge about Its Own Behavior," *Animal Learning Behavior*, 10 (1982), pp. 358–64.

Soproni, K., Á. Miklósi, J. Topál, and V. Csányi, "Comprehension of Human Communicative Signs in Pet Dogs," *Journal of Comparative Psychology*, 115 (2001), pp. 122–26.

——, "Dogs' Responsiveness to Human Pointing Gestures," *Journal of Comparative Psychology*, 116 (2002), pp. 27–34.

Suga, N., K. Kuzirai, and W. E. O'Neill, "How Biosonar Information Is Represented in the Bat Cerebral Cortex," in Syka, J., and L. Aitkin (eds.), *Neural Mechanisms of Hearing*, New York: Plenum Press, 1981, pp. 197–219.

Szinák, J., and I. Veress, *Harci kutyák: Őrző-védő ebek (Fighting Dogs: Dogs for Protection)*, Budapest: Dunakanyar 2000, 1996.

Templeton, J., and M. Mundello, *Working Sheep Dogs*, Ramsbury: The Crowood Press, 1988.

Thurston, M. E., *The Lost History of the Canine Race*, Kansas City, MO: Andrews and MacEel, 1996.

Tomasello, M., "Joint Attention as Social Cognition," in Moore, C., and O. Dunham (eds.), *Joint Attention: Its Origins and Role in Development*, Hillsdale, N.J.: Lawrence Erlbaum, 1955.

Tomasello, M., and J. Call, *Primate Cognition*, Oxford: Oxford University Press, 1997.

Topál, J., Á. Miklósi, and V. Csányi, "Dog-Human Relationship Affects Problem Solving Behavior in the Dog," *Anthozoös*, 10 (1997), pp. 219–29.

Topál, J., Á. Miklósi, V. Csányi, and A. Dóka, "Attachment Behavior in Dogs (*Canis familiaris*): A New Application of Ainsworth's (1969) Strange Situation Test," *Journal of Comparative Psychology*, 112 (1998), pp. 1–11.

Trevarthen, C., "The Functions of Emotions in Early Communication and Development," in Nadel, J., and L. Camaioni (eds.), *New Perspectives in Early Communicative Development*, New York: Routledge, 1993.

Triana, E., and R. Pasnak, "Object Permanence in Cats and Dogs," *Animal Learning and Behavior*, 9 (1981), pp. 135–39.

Ungváry, K., *Budapest Ostroma (The Siege of Budapest)*, Budapest: Corvina, 1998.

Vilá, C., P. Savolainen, J. E. Maldonado, I. R. Amorim, J. E. Rice, R. L. Honeycutt, K. A. Crandall, J. Ludenberg, and R. K. Wayne, "Multiple and Ancient Origins of the Domestic Dog," *Science*, 276 (1997), pp. 1687–89.

Visalberghi, E., D. M. Faragaszy, and E. S. Savage-Rumbaugh, "Performance in a Tool-Using Task by Common Chimpanzees (*Pan troglodytes*), bonobos (*Pan paniscus*), and an orangutan (*Pongo pygmaeus*), and capuchin monkeys (*Cebus paella*)," *Journal of Comparative Psychology*, 109 (1995), pp. 52–60.

Visalberghi, E., and L. Trinca, "Tool Use in Capuchin Monkeys: Distinguishing between Performing and Understanding," *Primates,* 30 (1989), pp. 511–21.

Wallace, R. A., and S. F. Hartley, "Religious Elements in Friendship: Durkheimian Theory in an Empirical Context," in Alexander, J. C. (ed.), *Durkheimian Sociology: Cultural Studies*, Cambridge: Cambridge University Press, 1988.

Wallman, J., *Aping Language*, Cambridge: Cambridge University Press, 1992.

Warden, C. J., and L. H. Warner, "The Sensory Capacities and Intelligence of Dogs, with a Report on the Ability of the Noted Dog 'Fellow' to Respond to Verbal Stimuli," *The Quarterly Review of Biology*, 3 (1928).

Watson, J. S., G. Gergely, G. Topál, J. Gácsi, Z. Sárközi, and V. Csányi, "Distinguishing Logic Versus Association in the Solution of an Invisible Displacement Task by Children and Dogs: Using Negation of Disjunction," *Journal of Comparative Psychology*, 115 (2001), pp. 219–26.

Whiten, A., "Imitation, Pretence and Mindreading: Secondary Representation in Comparative Primatology and Developmental Psychology?" in Russon, A. E., K. A. Bard, and S. T. Parker (eds.), *Reaching into Thought: The Minds of the Great Apes*, Cambridge: Cambridge University Press, 1996, pp. 300–24.

Whiten, A., and R. W. Byrne, "The St. Andrews Catalogue of Tactical Deception in Primates," *St. Andrews Psychological Reports*, no. 10, 1986.

——, "Tactical Deception in Primates," *Behavioral and Brain Sciences*, 11 (1988).

——, "The Emergence of Metarepresentation in Human Ontogeny and Primate Phylogeny," in Whiten, A. (ed.), *Natural Theories of the Mind: Evolution, Development and Simulation in Everyday Mindreading*, Oxford: Basil Blackwell, Ltd., 1991, pp. 276–81.

Woodruff, G., and D. Premack, "Primitive Mathematical Concepts in the Chimpanzee: Proportionality and Numerosity," *Nature*, 293 (1981), pp. 568–70.

Zimen, E., *The Wolf: His Place in the Natural World*, New York: Souvenir Press, 1981.

Acknowledgments

Since we have begun the scientific study of canine behavior in the Department of Ethology at the Eötvös Lóránd University in Budapest and reported some of our results, many people have expressed unusual interest in our work. Television, radio, and newspaper reporters often seek us out with the request that we explain what we have done, and it is an almost daily occurrence that some unknown person stops me on the street—often while I am walking with our dogs—just to tell me that he has heard of us and is interested in our work. To my enormous surprise, my professional colleagues, with whom we are in fierce competition for research funds and professional recognition, have also exhibited sincere interest in our scientific agenda for dogs.

For a while now, I have had a hunch about what this all means. A few years ago, at an international ethological conference in Hawaii, my colleague Szima Naderi and I were standing near a poster that we had prepared. The poster was a fairly standard one, of the type that describes some results of one's scientific work; it may have contained a few graphs, or pictures and some text. Interested colleagues could come and look at it, ask questions, and engage in debates. The motif of our poster was an observation we made while studying Seeing Eye dogs, namely that the cooperation between such a dog and its master was like that observed only among humans, but never among animals. We were gratified to see that lots of participants seemed interested in the details, but our happiness rapidly evaporated when a young man walked by and said rather pointedly, "You are light-years away from being able to prove that!" At that point an older participant turned to us and said simply, "I have a Labrador and I believe everything you say."

In this book, I have explained in an easily understandable way what we do with dogs, how we work, and what we have discovered. I would be pleased to have among my readers persons who are not particularly science-minded but who love dogs. I would be even more pleased to be of use to those who are genuinely curious about how one can study scientifically the behavior of dogs and who would like to know whether there really exists a canine mind, and if so, how it might work.

I feel very strongly that I owe this work to those whose interest has encouraged our studies. Of course, I owe it to the dogs as well, to Flip, Jerry, Balthasar, and Casper, from whom I have learned a tremendous amount, both about being human and about being a dog.

The book makes frequent reference not only to the scientific literature and the data acquired by my own observations, but also to some of the results of work done jointly with my colleagues. In this respect I am particularly grateful to Antal Dóka, Márta Gácsi, Ádám Miklósi, József Topál, and Péter Pongrácz. Many graduate students work with us, and the ones who have made a particular impact are Zita Fekete, Zsolt Förgeteg, Enikő Kubinyi, Szima Naderi, Réka Polgárdi, Krisztina Soproni, Viktória Szetei, and Zsófia Virányi.

Flip and Jerry could not have enjoyed the pleasures of being ill-mannered family dogs had it not been for the invaluable emotional and practical assistance of my wife, Éva Nádai. I must also thank my friend Tamás Dávid for his help in a critical phase of Jerry's upbringing. Our friends Zsuzsa Kovács and Endre Kovács helped us innumerable times on those occasions when we had to leave our dogs for shorter or longer periods.

Special thanks are due to my friend, the philosopher Bence Nánay, with whom we discussed many questions about the canine mind.

Further thanks are due to the directors of a number of institutions that deal with dogs. Among them, thanks to Col. Frigyes Janza, the director of the Dunakeszi dog training institute of the police, and to Péter

Vasteleki, the director of the Seeing Eye dog training school at Csepel. Both have been very helpful in our research, even when this added considerably to their workload. A few organizations that deal with dogs in other countries also helped us by permitting us to observe their work. In particular, we learned a great deal from the staff of the British Association for Seeing Eye Dogs, The Guide Dogs for the Blind Association, and from the workers at an Austrian training institution for dogs that assist the disabled, the Verein zur Förderung der Partnerhunde für Behinderte.

Many thanks to all of the above, but particularly to the countless dogs and their owners who participated in our experiments.

Vilmos Csányi

Index

Page numbers in *italics* refer to illustrations.